Spaces of the Mind

FRONTIERS OF NARRATIVE

Series Editor

David Herman, North Carolina State University

Spaces *of the* Mind

Narrative and Community in the American West

ELAINE A. JAHNER

UNIVERSITY OF NEBRASKA PRESS
LINCOLN AND LONDON

© 2004 by the University
of Nebraska Press

All rights reserved

Manufactured in the United States of America

Library of Congress Cataloging-in-Publication Data
Jahner, Elaine, 1942–
Spaces of the mind : narrative and community in the
American West / Elaine A. Jahner.
p. cm.—(Frontiers of narrative)
Includes bibliographical references and index.
ISBN-10: 0-8032-2598-9 (cloth : alk. paper)
ISBN-13: 978-0-8032-1833-8 (paper : alk. paper)
1. American literature—West (U.S.)—History and
criticism.   2. Authors, American—Homes and haunts
—West (U.S.)   3. West (U.S.)—Intellectual life.
4. West (U.S.)—In literature.   5. Community in literature.
6. Narration (Rhetoric)   I. Title.   II. Series.
PS271.J34 2004
810.9'3278—dc22   2004007212

Contents

Acknowledgments	vii
Introduction	ix
1. Theoretical Foundations	1
2. The Narrating Community	40
3. Narrative in Transit	82
4. Narrative Redirected	113
5. The Stranger's Language	138
Conclusion	157
Notes	169
Works Cited	179
Index	185

Acknowledgments

Spaces of the Mind is a project that owes much to many people and was long in the making. The work began when Mary College (now the University of Mary) developed an educational grant for Standing Rock Sioux Reservation. I participated in the project, and in conjunction with courses I was taking at Indiana University, I began to develop my work on spatial categories in Siouan folk narrative as indicators of cultural continuity. The linguistic and anthropology departments at Indiana University gave me grants to extend the work into other cultures.

The Vetter and the Wald families were kind enough to tell their stories of immigration to me. Members of my own family also contributed to the immigration materials.

The final stages of this project owe everything to Gary Dunham and his editorial work. Without his efforts and the contributions of the University of Nebraska Press, this project would never have been completed.

Introduction

Narrative and the varied ingenious uses we make of it as we negotiate among different cultures, histories, and locations constitute the primary focus of this book. As anyone realizes, though, that statement implicates much of the theoretical debate and strategic maneuvering that have characterized recent research in several disciplines. All the talk and writing has created a situation in which, as Bill Nichols has said, "narrative's not the thing it used to be. More than standing as one form of artistic expression to be worried over by those attending to the nature of art, narrative has become a central preoccupation in its own right, pushing matters of art and levels of culture to the side. . . . This was always, however, a science with a difference."[1]

If *levels of culture* are set aside when narrative takes center theoretical stage, that move merely emphasizes narrative's central role in any study of culture, a role that takes on some extra and time-honored importance when the critical perspective is cross-cultural. Narrative orchestrates the organizing principles setting up an entire cultural field within which agents improvise on the cultural script.[2] And as for *art*, well, that term is but our way of designating the transformations of experience occurring when virtuosity informs high-intensity improvs; and when the critical spotlight is on cross-cultural narrative, it reveals previously unsuspected artistic moves and countermoves. But this book is by no means an unrelentingly abstract rehearsal of academic theory. It is a book about actual people and places and the stories that these people use to account for who they are in relation to where they are. It is a book about stretching critical boundaries a bit to include more art in social science and to encourage the poetic speculation that can be a happy side effect of detailed empirical analysis.[3] Therefore, each chapter tells a theoretical story that is no more or less than a precisely plotted critical design to allow a few people to have their say on the global stage and to give the worldwide audience some clues about how to find contemporary significance in these historical and local dramas.

The first chapters of this book contextualize narratives that I learned in two strikingly different communities: the Yanktonai Sioux in North Dakota and their German-Russian neighbors. These communities exhibit about as much cultural, historical, and linguistic contrast as can be found anywhere in the world. Both have had a history of colonial rule even though the two colonial experiences encompass as many variations as we can imagine or account for with our academic understandings of what colonialism has meant for different peoples in shifting political relationships to nationalisms. What the contrasts and similarities characterizing each group's historical experience might have to do with the narratives told in each community is one of the controlling questions around which my critical narrative develops. And, of course, today both groups share a landscape and they have both used stories to transform its places into spaces of the mind; therefore that process of transformation can focus our contemporary interest as we give more nuanced attention to what kind of variable place is in the dynamics of human agency.

Colonial and postcolonial studies now come in for enough academic discussion that one no longer need rehearse all the terms of academic efforts to find a legitimate position from which to develop responsible criticism that recognizes how power relations cross-cut just about every other relational category.[4] But the question of how to factor in the countless variables engendered by personal history in definite communities seems more intractable, precisely because it is a task more appropriate to the poet than to any theoretician. The local frames the irreducible splendor of what is unique, even idiosyncratic, and the theoretical generalities of any discipline insist on eclipsing that quality. If, however, we think of theory as a form of translation, perhaps even as a kind of subtitling allowing audiences from diverse positions to follow a performance that takes place in the mind and follows the energies of individual intellect and spirit, then theory is no more or less than a convenient adjunct to help the international crowd keep up with what is happening as the exquisitely detailed and immediate is gathered into some bigger picture, which theory communicates to global participants. That easy observation implies a process of getting quickly to the theoretical perspective and comment that counts, that communicates something that really matters to actual audiences. And that achievement is by no means easy or guaranteed by any method.

In other words, theory does not just have to connect; it really should do so in ways that respond to audiences that we may choose to make more inclusive than just that group of colleagues who share our current predictable methodological moves and assumptions. To do this we have to remember that theory can be narrative too; as metanarrative, hopefully it can gather in some of the momentum by which any really good plot engages readers and listeners of all kinds. As we elaborate our theoretical plots about human knowing, we do well to enrich our critical tales with details that we can gain only by listening to what ordinary people actually say about their own places on the map. Or, to get at the more common twentieth-century condition, we have to listen to what people say about what it has meant for them to move from place to place, about what has given them a necessary security in the midst of transitions of all kinds that take them from place to place. And giving some actual detail to the narrative process that accounts for what has been called "the interpenetration of person and place" is a primary purpose of this book.[5]

Even though there is a growing body of theoretical literature about place as constitutive of subjectivity, I find that much of it still remains aloof from the literal actualities of place, the kind of thing that the western writer Ivan Doig was asking about when he said, "Tell me why it is that details like that, saddle stirrups a notch longer or sunshine dabbed around on the foothills some certain way, seem to be the allowance of memory while the bigger points of life hang back?"[6] I decided to place a lot of my theoretical bets on commonplace details, trusting them to advance me one definite step at a time to some of those bigger points of life and theory. And for me, at least in relation to what I do in this book, the commonplace is empirically exact. It is actual spoken or written language that can be traced back to a real human interactional context that opens out onto others and so on to community after real community. Furthermore, these speakers and writers remain in touch with places where the weather changes and so do other definite factors like real estate taxes and the distance to the best supermarket or school; and all these changes pose yet other questions about narrative that can take us anywhere, even into cyberspace. But the real interactional contexts where it all begins have their histories, and I have listened to how real individuals talk about the histories that give them a definite purchase on the meaning of their present positions in their present communities.

By referring to "listening" instead of reading, I allude to another theoretical and methodological subtext occurring in every chapter of this book. The primary texts I analyze in the first three chapters are oral. The exceptions are memoirs written by amateur historians, usually with family members as the intended audience; therefore one can argue that these texts are, for the most part, transcriptions of the oral traditions or that their function is the same as that of the oral texts. Such texts pose a whole series of questions about context that can be summarized by saying that the critic always has to move back and forth between questions about history as narrative, narrative as history, and narrative in history. As a practical heuristic strategy, concentrating on narrative's meaning-effects also allows for the critical insertion of the analytic incongruities set up by distinctions between oral and written texts. Each perspective implies slightly different critical procedures, different approaches to cognitive style. And that brings me to the most basic critical subtext in this book. It is a book about cognitive style in narrative.

All of my work on cognitive style goes back to my initial efforts to understand the strategic vitality of oral narratives that I was learning among the Yanktonai Sioux. People told me that their stories were an indispensable part of how they managed to live with their past and present experience. I believed them. But at first I had to take it all on faith. I could not really understand why the material I was hearing and recording should be so important. What I was learning was so different from the tales I had found in earlier collections that I had to question whether any continuity connected the older to the more recent narratives. I entertained—and rejected—the idea of a complete cultural break as a consequence of changes imposed first by reservation culture and then by a second relocation as a result of flooding when the Oahe Dam was built on the Missouri River. I chose to try to interpret the texts as evidence of how narrative is an active force at work in all spheres of adaptation. That decision, though, did not quickly lead to any theoretically adequate approach to this material.

As I studied the Sioux language, analyzing text after traditional text, examining all the available manuscript material on Sioux culture, I began to see distinctions at work that revealed a cognitive terrain quite different from any that can be directly translated into European categories. The sheer excitement of that first insight has never diminished; and if linguistic research is admittedly tedious, its results are such rich testimony to the options available to human intelligence that I now believe that comparative linguistic studies should receive as high a priority in research about the nature of human knowing as that which we give to any physical science. The Sapir-Whorf hypothesis deserves further exploration. Only when I began to concentrate on specific features of spatial categories in Siouan languages and their effects on narrative forms did I begin to catch on to the experiences behind narrators' insistence that the life of local narratives was intimately bound up with the community's geographical setting.

The next step was to find ways to move from all that detail to something other than a purely formalistic study of narrative. I had to gather all the detail derived from analysis of specific semantic and pragmatic categories back into the bigger questions that had motivated the search for all that detail in the first place.

We can document historical events. It is far harder to document a history of interpreting those events. I was fortunate enough to go on living for many years in the communities whose narratives focused my work, so I could follow through and test what I was beginning, tentatively, to understand as a comprehensive relationship between cognition and narration that was communicated at the level of style and not just through content. More to the point, that set of factors summed up by the word *style* was a verifiable set of traditional features that supported and guided changing adaptive content. The effort to formulate theory with enough descriptive adequacy and predictive power to generate a critical account of the relevant features of continuity motivated my revision of my developing theories of cognitive style. Clearly the narrative features that I was trying to specify were defined by a communal context. Equally clear was the fact that these features derived from narrative performance conditions rather than from semantic content alone. Simply by taking seriously what people said about their stories, I had wandered into all the questions and problems of relationships between narrative structure and developing ideas about how to address narrative context and pragmatics. Some of these problems admit of exact methodological framing, and what is learned by so doing opens the way to other critical considerations that are more daring, more creative, and, therefore, less easily reined in by precise theoretical models. These less constrained pursuits have proven, at once, closer to the emergent strategies characterizing cultures and more likely to motivate collaborative explorations of a changing matrix of questions. The intensely detailed empirical focus and the more widely ranging speculative critical studies proved to be necessary, balancing perspectives.

Over the years I have published different phases of a developing theory of cognitive style. One basic early analysis gives some of the technical linguistic data supporting critical judgments I make in my chapter on Cannon Ball narrative traditions.[7] That article along with the first chapter in this volume, "Theoretical Foundations," gives evidence of the ethnolinguistic foundations for discourse theory that generate the hypotheses guiding more general chapters. I want the material published here to retain a certain lively readability even though each chapter derives from precisely developed analytic foundations that I address in the theoretical chapter that sets up the rest of the book's organization.

The concept of cognitive style, as I was developing it, seemed to work as a method for marking surprising features of continuity within Sioux narratives. But what about other traditions? Could the critical strategy work for oral materials from altogether different cultures? That question was an important impetus and guide for my research in German-Russian communities. Of course, it was not the only one. Equally basic was a whole set of questions about the role of the researcher. From the beginning I remained vigilant and distrustful of the academic tendency to make observations and data fit the needs of imposed theory. I worried about the ingenuity that lets a researcher find whatever fits the theoretical bill, even as I pursued a range of theoretical means to account for observations about collected narratives. By combining analysis of my own culture with that of another group, I hoped to use each situation as a way to guard against inevitable blind spots, unrecognized presuppositions, and sheer theoretical creativity. I tried to make productive use of the equally inevitable dynamics of insider/outsider. I also tried to let what I was learning in each community assume its own appropriate critical narrative structure, because I believe that many of the implications of the experiment can become manifest only through the actual process of writing as the critical narrative sought and dictated its own form and style. I believe that is what happened, but my critics will necessarily see and understand more than I do. That anticipated exchange is part of the purpose of this book. The Yanktonai Sioux and German-Russian chapters are paired and placed in their Dakota setting. These chapters explore aspects of cognitive style as it operates to establish specific textual communities.

My emphasis on the cognitive implies a knowing that prompts the leap from the individual to the community, from *I* to *we*. Whatever sparks that leap is knowable; it may not have any easy or direct articulation, though, and that is why it motivates so much narrative, especially when cross-cultural contact challenges the boundaries of group identity. I had to make that leap, not just describe it. My own position in relation to each community had to function as part of the theoretical story. Just how to describe that position and what part it might play as a responsible element within the critical narrative remained, for many years, an insurmountable obstacle to publication. I regularly revised and reconsidered the crucial personal distances and tensions that had to be part of the analysis I was making of stories told to me by people whom I could never call "informants" because they are the friends and relatives who give meaning to my own life. Finally, changing critical attitudes throughout academia as well as my own growing conviction that the material I possessed could and should add to the general, international understanding of cultural and narrative dynamics resulted in my writing the critical story—or stories—keeping my sights firmly fixed on the theoretical goal while gathering in as much concrete human detail as the narrative could sustain. I tried to tell responsible historical and theoretical stories about stories that were about history and theory and actual people building modern communities.

My primary academic discipline is literary criticism, not history or anthropology or cognitive linguistics even though I routinely move among all these disciplinary positions. I spend far more time teaching and writing about written literatures than I do oral ones. If cognitive style proved to have heuristic value in relation to oral texts, I therefore assumed that I should be able to make the concept work for novels, even for poetry. I gradually explored those discursive transfers, testing the usefulness of my developing theory of cognitive style as a critical concept for different written discourses. I did so first in relation to novels that were obvious experiments incorporating some of the epistemological assumptions of oral narrative performance into the dynamics of writing and reading. Usually such novels concentrate on a single cultural tradition with its many possible points of intersection with other global traditions. More and more I found that the concept of cognitive style could highlight a range of different literary strategies that different authors employed to explore the cross-cultural negotiations at work in different discursive registers. That led to my writing a whole series of articles and chapters in books that depend on the theory of cognitive style in relation to different discursive formations at work in several different cultural traditions.

One of my earliest articles was on James Welch, the Montana writer.[8] Other critics were publishing fine responses to his early work, but I needed to find my own way among his words. I wanted my own "spaces of the mind," a phrase I borrowed from one of Welch's poems. The writing that followed was particularly satisfying to me. Few of my essays have ever been so quickly completed or accomplished with so much continuing sense of discovery. In the meantime James Welch has written novel after fine novel. I read his new works but never found the time to give myself the satisfaction of finding my own way through them as I had done with *Winter in the Blood*. Never, that is, until now. In thinking about the second half of this volume, I decided to give myself a long-deferred critical satisfaction and, at the same time, give the theory of cognitive style another test, this time in relation to showing how history can be a source for new features of cognitive style. As stated, this goal represents an apparent contradiction, one that only a truly good novelist could possibly resolve. I wanted to pursue my early sense that Welch was intuitively motivated to work this apparent contradiction as just the right source of narrativity to give him a genuinely distinctive take on otherwise ordinary events. And since I am a westerner (North Dakota, Wyoming, Nebraska) living now in New England or in Europe, I wanted to see if working with Welch's novels would help me articulate a more nuanced critical take on what the West means and what the West hides even as it advertises itself as the "last great place." My answer to my own question constitutes the chapters of this book that transfer the question of cognitive style from oral to written literatures.

Writing about Welch pulled me into the context of Montana novels in general, and that made me take another look at the whole issue of regional writing. The timing was right. The shifting critical winds are blowing in a fresh determination to redefine and generally refurbish the notion of *regional* as an adjective qualifying the noun *literature*. In an issue of *American Literary History*, Michael Kowalewski speculated on a new regionalism in American literature, and I find in his statements a complex common sense that I miss whenever the critical debates about regionalism get pulled into debates about power politics:

> *A new attention to place in American literary studies might do more than simply add another molecule to a model of identity now defined in terms of race, class, and gender. It might help alter the model itself, perhaps by way of a few new metaphors, like photosynthesis or an ecology of the self, in place of omnipresent notions of "constructed identity." Yet the force of such a new emphasis will only be successful if the "ecology" turns out to be something challengingly new and not simply a rubric under which to smuggle in thoughtlessly familiar terminology. The new regional studies must be capable of exploring regional identity without reverting to mere local localism. It will need to establish a new critical equilibrium, one as wary of redemptive pseudotheology or appeals to*

environmental determinism as it is of geographical ignorance and representational melodrama. It is hard work but it is already well under way.[9]

Perhaps, with a bit of stretching, cognitive style implies an ecology in that it always implies interaction between personal history and how a person uses the history of a community as placed or replaced. Even without that stretch, I could see that cognitive style has a certain instrumental value for studying regionalism, new or otherwise. With that value in mind, I reread a novel about Montana that I had found in a used bookstore many years ago. That novel was *Winter Wheat* by Mildred Walker. It rang true, somehow, not just to my Montana experiences but also to my childhood experiences in western North Dakota. I started to write about that novel, then I set the work aside because of other urgent agendas and all but forgot about it. Then one day, browsing through a bookstore, I found a Bison Books reprint of it with an introduction by none other than James Welch. Now I have finished my study and made it a companion piece to my reading of Welch's novels. It also happens to work as a companion to the study of the German-Russian immigrant community paired with the Cannon Ball study in the first part of this book. The German-Russian fieldwork emphasizes community, almost to the point of excluding individual experience. Mildred Walker's novel, by contrast, depicts the loss of community on the part of an immigrant woman who comes from Russia and marries a Vermont-born American with whom she then moves to an isolated farm in Montana. What can a novel such as this tell us about the impact of that absent communal dimension in relation to language and cognitive style? That is the subject of my final chapter, which reveals the primary structure of this book. From the theoretical first chapter, I proceed to two chapters about actual communities in North Dakota; then as the region moves westward, I move into novels that allow for a different kind of approach to discursive space. Each chapter, though, advances my approach to cognitive style.

As I responded to various requests for articles and occasionally taught advanced seminars, new dimensions of cognitive style kept falling into place. Soon I was talking and writing about it so often that I could almost anticipate the moment when someone would ask, "But what exactly is cognitive style?" I needed a few direct, clear statements about just what I had been doing in essay after essay, seminar after seminar, for so many years. I now answer that cognitive style is the linguistic evidence of historical processes at work in speech acts that function to define an individual's place in a textual community; I do have definite statements about stages of analysis involved in achieving the critical perspective that guides the essays in this book. That answer is now the purpose of my first chapter, "Theoretical Foundations." I have been evolving a whole series of analytic steps, each taking into account different sources of information, different discursive elements, and, therefore, different subsidiary critical frames. The foundations, though, are definitely dependent on linguistic analysis and the application of discourse theory allowing for attention to specific speech acts and the conditions of their performance.

Cognitive style is always bound up with an aspect of communication that taps the very sources of narrativity. Its elaboration by way of narrative is an inherent aspect of our existence as cognitive beings. It does not lead the analyst to rules governing linguistic or even narrative competence or structure; it leads the analyst to elementary cognitive factors affecting narrative performance. The initial specification of culturally specific cognitive features in relation to the semantic fields controlling narrative themes reveals what I call the "implicit narrative." This is an abstraction that gives explicit critical formulation to related cognitive themes, themselves the hypothesized basis for assertions of continuity between a tradition and the individual narrative in question, which may or may not show direct continuity at the level of content. These cognitive themes, orchestrated by way of narrative, prove adaptable to many different discursive conditions and, in fact, empower different kinds of discourse by instrumentalizing their adaptive function.

My goal, as noted above, has been to keep that initial analytic groundwork in the background, inserting only what is really needed to sustain an argument or validate some surprising move. Since few readers are likely to have the patience for repetitions of the kind of exact demonstration I give in the chapter on theoretical foundations, I have concentrated on maximizing narrative energy while substantiating theoretical claims. Each chapter depends on every other one although each can, if it must, stand on its own. Chapters move from community to community, assuming a process of communal individuation that is directly analogous to the process of individuation shaping each person's psychological integration. My best hope is that individuals from other places and cultures will recognize how the steps that I illustrate could enable them to do something similar for vastly different communities and regions.

The various chapters of this book take a definite position in the present from which to look at some of the details by which the past is constituted as a force in the present; and at every stage of this book's preparation, I have thought about how the people and events that I study can seem extraordinarily distant or remote in a world where the word *space* is immediately associated with *cyberspace* or *outer space*, which conjures an ever-expanding cosmos; and *time* automatically invokes the distinction between real and virtual time. Spaces of the mind are now enabled by faster and faster technology with greater and greater memory capacity. Therefore, it is, I believe, appropriate that a television advertisement finally gave me the image that allows me to set all of the decidedly backward-looking work to which this book calls attention in active conjunction with experiences enabled by new technology. This particular Sprint advertisement begins with a man standing in the street outside one of those featureless skyscrapers that house legions of urban workers. He is shouting to those within that they should come out. It is OK. Weary-looking individuals whose sun-starved skin tones and blinking eyes imply self-imposed incarceration in front of computer screens slowly emerge, shielding their eyes from the intense light. The healthy cheerful herald hands each of them a cellular phone with Internet capacity. They are mobile again. But as every viewer knows, they are also living in parallel universes, moving about in cyberspace and geographical space at the same time. For these exemplars of our contemporary world of work and communication, E. M. Forster's famous admonition "connect only connect" is now a very real survival strategy as they move between cyberspace and whatever requirements a particular parcel (or freeway stretch) of geographical space may be making at any given moment. And there is nothing surprising or accidental about the fact that such a commonsense admonition comes to us as a citation from a novelist with an eye for minute psychological detail and the talent to trace that detail to contexts that often involved more than one culture.

Narrative, in any space, is primary evidence of the human mind's astonishing capacity to connect and to reflect on its own powers. Studying narrative from any place or any time is always a matter of studying human intelligence at work making connections; and those who have been looking at narrative with an acute working awareness of how different cultures have used it to sustain distinctive categories of experience have anticipated the formalisms of the future in the way they have utilized the categories of the past. We may be ready for a new look at formal analysis. But formalism, new or otherwise, is only the elementary beginning. It merely launches us. What matters is what we do with the insights that can come from a careful look at how form gathers significance to a particular focus and application.

Spaces of the Mind

1. *Theoretical Foundations*

Cognitive style, as the term is used in this study, is the linguistic evidence of socio-historical processes at work in speech acts that function to define an individual's place in a community; the primary purpose behind its analysis is to show how history has shaped not just discursive content but also the presuppositions that give that content its pragmatic force. The cognitive dimension of cognitive style derives from the fact that the method traces strategies of knowing that are mediated through semantic and/or pragmatic presuppositions for certain speech acts. The style dimension derives from the fact that the method follows key elements of content through discursive variations and transformations in order to show how basic communal assumptions and narrative conventions shape discernible patterns that retain their structuring force through time. While all speech acts reveal cognitive style, this study emphasizes narrative, personal narrative in particular, because narrative form sets up an analytic stance by framing propositions that are open to explication. Concentration on narrative allows for a multifaceted display of connections between events and the cultural assumptions governing the linguistic expression of event structure. The effects of contrasting cultural positions that are a consequence of radical change within a group or that have to do with radically differing cultural positions among participants in a speech act remain a dominant theme and motive in this study.

As illustrated by the example that concludes this chapter and by the various case studies constituting other chapters, analysis of cognitive style depends on a diversely constructed body of contextual data. The point of all this detailed effort is to develop a fine-tuned critical vocabulary, a kind of tracking device that lets us follow not just the facts but also the central features of the expanding associative significance of those facts as we switch back and forth between text and context, between historical and emergent, between a specific sender and the receiver of a particular text. The whole effort is analogous to the development of scientific instruments that "listen" for sound waves moving through time and space. What we listen for with our critical apparatus, though, is evidence of the dynamic concatenation of significance that we clumsily, but conveniently, label as "cultural continuity," and we start the analytic process with whatever text is at hand, whatever bit of narrative that directs our attention to its suspected possibilities as strong evidence of what may be going on when individual subjectivity connects with the language of a particular time and place and the community that makes the times work for the place.

Initially historical contextualization, narrative comparison, and details of linguistic analysis provide different perspectives on the text. These first stages involve little more than standard, old-fashioned critical spadework, the most ordinary sort of preliminary information gathering mixed with a dash of intuitive alertness to possibilities that may be hidden by the deceptively self-evident. However, even the most comprehensive encyclopedic collection of data can never get beyond telling us what people know, never how they know it. We get a little closer to the how of it all (the cognitive style) at that moment when linguistic evidence suddenly hints at a previously unimagined horizon of textual significance. That moment when our own cultural blinders seem to slip a little, nudged aside by the sharp empiricism of historical or ethnolinguistic data and we begin to see what they may have obscured can also be the juncture where all that sheer information begins to generate definite hypotheses about cognition and narrative. Each stage of work yields generalizations from which to develop the implicit narrative that shows how people imaginatively chart different positions in space and time. What is "implicit" in this critical narrative is the significance associated with pragmatic presuppositions rather than with the explicit referential significance of narrative content. Explicating the implicit narrative is a matter of making critically explicit the relevant cognitive sets (i.e., the primary semantic and pragmatic features relevant to a given narrative event) and showing how these features constitute cognitive themes (i.e., minimal units of the cognitive system; contents that are no longer in a one-to-one relationship with the particular aspects of the linguistic system from which they are inferred).[1]

The elaboration of the implicit narrative should reveal the ideational shape of a probable (culturally typical) narrative context. The relationship between the context and various other narrative elements is fluid and adaptive. The assumed context can shape all features of a narrative. While the implicit narrative has definite constraints (it is not just a matter of reader response), it is, nevertheless, a story in and of itself that goes beyond the listing of semantic or pragmatic features or the decoding of semiotic codes in order to tap into the motivating power of the contextual. It should show how interpreting and decoding always get drawn into some other discursive frame, some other staging of assumptions about what and how we know and what we make as a consequence of that knowing.

What do the rhetorical boundaries shaping the pragmatic dynamics of communication have to do with the geographical ones that mark the places where the historical experiences of distinctive communities shaped interpretive perspectives for language? That question is among the most important ones that shape this work, and the problem of working assumptions for developing strong hypotheses about the relationship between rhetorical strategies and geopolitical or traditional identity constitutes another primary problematic that guides this analysis. That initial question sets up others. Are there communication strategies that serve as linguistic and paralinguistic analogues to the passport or the green card or even citizenship? Are there definable linguistic marks of exile? One of my most fundamental assumptions is that narrative analysis reveals primary processes that, in turn, support second-order processes bound to specific local conditions of language and culture. I give considerable importance to strategies of adaptation that maintain, for a time at least, the enabling features of cultural distinctiveness in multicultural settings.

The term *cognitive style* represents such a likely set of deductions from so much twentieth-century thinking that it has been independently invented and used by various scholars. The usage that bears direct comparison to mine is Dell Hymes's. Although I knew other parts of his work while I was developing my theory of cognitive style, I did not find his writing on cognitive style until late in the development of my own work. Hymes's notion of cognitive style is quite different from mine, although both depend on precise linguistic analysis. His is a projected plan for a language typology that he sees as "a main unfinished business of anthropology." He assumes that different languages can be classified according to their particular cognitive style, and he envisages a survey of languages in terms of four sectors of interest, that between content and form and that between what is more manifest and what is more latent. His example taken from Chinookan languages explores these sectors in terms of grammatical processes and grammatical categories.[2] If the project envisaged by Hymes had, in fact, led to the kind of language typologies that he proposes, my work would have a secure base of empirical data from which to develop hypotheses about how the cognitive style of a language shapes individual narratives. But Hymes's proposed project of developing language typologies has not been pursued to the point where we have the database he called for. Therefore, my work is dependent on observations of particular languages in comparison with English, and I remain limited to what can be deduced from particular narrative examples. Nevertheless, certain contrastive themes such as the dominance of motion or the relational nature of ownership can be deduced from existing grammatical research, and I use such themes in relation to individual narrative to account for my approach to cognitive style as it appears in individual instances.

Methodological Precedents

Each analytic stage explicating cognitive style owes something to the history of narrative and discourse research, as it has gradually led to the current state of relations in narrative study, literary criticism, linguistics and cognitive science, even anthropology. Different stages in the explication of cognitive style call on different disciplinary developments that reach across a range of twentieth-century agendas, with the history of narrative study being obviously the most central of these developments. Twentieth-century narrative study is in itself evidence of the generative force of a combination of diverse intellectual trends that continue to diversify and expand as we seek responsible intellectual positions in the aftermath of postmodern questioning. In an essay published in a watershed 1981 volume titled *On Narrative*, Seymour Chatman situates modern narratology at a juncture between the Anglo-American heritage of Henry James, Percy Lubbock, E. M. Forster, and Wayne Booth and the mingling of Russian formalist (Victor Schlovsky, Boris Eichenbaum, Roman Jacobson, and Vladimir Propp) with the French structuralist approaches (Claude Lévi-Strauss, Roland Barthes, Gerard Genette, and Tzvetvan Todorov).[3] This extremely broad and currently dated mapping still suggests how central the study of narrative has been to setting up some of the most formative critical thinking of the century. For purposes of my own work, such broad survey indirectly indicates the genealogy of the "style" component of my cognitive style. Initially, I attempted formalistic analyses for the texts I was collecting on Standing Rock Reservation and for Sioux texts collected before me by Ella Deloria, Martha Warren Beckwith, and Clark Wissler. A work like Propp's *Morphology of the Folktale* stands in direct relationship to Alan Dundes's *Morphology of North American Indian Folktales*.[4] Since I worked with North American Indian materials, I also attempted Lévi-Straussian structuralist studies. My efforts to use these and other formalistic works, like those of Algirdas Greimas, in relation to archived texts and in relation to actual materials from living communities proved that the scaffolding of abstracted meaning that is the residue of formalist or structuralist analysis really did seem to highlight important elements of relative stability that allowed me to demonstrate a basis on which to postulate continuity from earlier, more structured oral folktales to more recent, more natural narrative genres.[5] However, all that formalistic work also highlighted everything that has to be excluded from such analysis. And that excluded material encompassed most of what I later came to gather under the rubric of "style." The methodologically excluded material was also the data that struck me as most important for my own purposes, namely to show how narrative shapes the details of historical continuity at work in relation to definite communities in all their sociopolitical complexity.

The work of the French structuralists, all of them faithfully operating from phenomenological premises, certainly incorporated much more of what I call style than did the Russian formalists, but the structuralist assumption that their objects of study were mental structures that excluded the historical and transcended the geographical meant that what are basically pragmatic categories with traceable historical trajectories were conflated with unchanging semantic structures, and the temporally paced contingent critique that history accomplishes was excluded from structuralist analytic focus. Then too individual agency and artistry have no place in the interpretive scheme. Furthermore, the universalist emphasis that denied the significance of what might be purely local features and the power that such local features have in maintaining the integrity of distinctive communities, even as other aspects of communal life participate in the surface trappings of a global culture, were central to my goals.

In *On Narrative*, Barbara Herrnstein Smith proves herself the contributor who looked ahead to what became the major emphasis in narrative studies in the latter part of the twentieth century when narrative study freed itself from old constraints, took on new directions, and became an important element in analyses of issues of class and race, feminism, youth and old age, film, even cyberspace—a burgeoning situation of narrative studies that motivated David Herman to call his 1997 book on narrative *Narratologies* in recognition of the current increasing heterogeneity of narrative research methods as they have appropriated more and more insights from related fields of study. First Herrnstein Smith reviews the history of the field from the standpoint of dualisms (such as story versus discourse, version versus versions) that have been basic premises in narrative study. She stresses the limitations of dualistic thinking on grounds that it works to eliminate agency from narrative study. Herrnstein Smith, though, goes well beyond perceived constraints on research as she attempts to formulate an alternative account of narrative variability from that which derives from formalist or even structuralist models. Her account points to use of whatever is best from the structuralist and prestructuralist analyses without getting trapped by dead-end methodological requirements. She advocates conceptualizing narrative in terms of social transactions and speech act theory in order to explore the "structure of motivation" that prompts individuals to participate in narrative occasions and that motivates changes in the narrative itself.[6] In this she was preceded by William Labov's groundbreaking work on the structure of personal narrative and by Mary Louise Pratt, who made comparable arguments as she advanced her hypothesis that "a descriptive apparatus which can adequately account for the uses of language made outside literature will be able to give a satisfactory account of literary discourse as well."[7]

Herrnstein Smith's structure of motivation "directs attention to the *particular* motives and interests of narrators and audiences."[8] With this emphasis on particularities of the interactional and interpretive context, we move closer to the place of the "cognitive" in my approach to cognitive style. The individual, caught up in the needs, desires, and ambitions of the moment, activates a relationship to language through the narrative experience that subjects the inchoate to the rules and constraints that constitute the terms of narrativity. Individual desires and needs become the basis for a particular kind of testing of communal resources as a way to name and direct individual awareness and thereby to construct a diverse array of cognitive thresholds. As individuals activate the latent significance of narrative's associational networks made up of images and events, all given coherence through discourse conventions, they implicitly or explicitly extend the significance of these same networks, adding new features of signification, showing how old and new connect to particular sites.

Narrative depends on and constantly revises and updates linguistic polysemy. Each narrative genre arises from and implies a particular set of relationships to cognition; in fact, one can argue that these differing relationships provide the strongest justification and basis for genre distinctions. Myth with its imagistic focus on founding moments and the differences that constitute the social body signs the boundaries of any society. It does not, however, leave those boundaries undisputed, as any pluralistic society demonstrates. The interactional dynamic whereby individual interpretation can turn into a radical critique of the fundamental energies of any narrative form and thereby completely undermine its original impetus has, in our secular age, speeded up to the point where we can mark the power of myth best through the fallout from its having reached limits that transformed it without, however, its losing all its defining features and particular cognitive potential. One powerful and well-known example can make this point. As older myths were losing their power to marshal belief, the twentieth century gave us a parallel development (a transmutation?) to mythic performance through psychoanalytic theory, which transformed the cognitive and interactional dynamics rooted in myth into a story and theory of human development, which, in turn, altered our entire relationship to language and cognition. Mythic dynamics were transferred from a socially predominant to an individual level, but the psychoanalytic example also includes evidence of attempts to shape social theory according to its paradigm of human development. At the other extreme of contemporary mythic dynamics, we see movements like the various and growing religious fundamentalisms or the New Age phenomenon, all of which reveal the human quest for myth as straightforward referent for belief, for narrative stripped of its critical potential and endowed with unmediated cognitive reference.

Other genres have their own cognitive permutations. Legend enjoys undiminished vitality as a means of endowing places and people with the aura of celebrity, and the legendary interactional context allows for a whole spectrum of ways of participating in or playing on this aura. Personal narrative and knowing (narrative knowing) constructs itself out of the entire field of relationships to other narratives and speech acts, and through those intersecting connections it picks up the cognitive signatures of those genres, allowing for a fundamentally relational knowing. Among the individual motives for the performance of personal narrative, the act of placing oneself within the field of possible relationships established through narrative has to be primary, and it certainly represents the major cognitive payoff.

This overview of cognitive potential as motivational matrix circles back to the question of analytic procedures for demonstrating such potential. The first step in the analytic game plan as I develop it is to make explicit the relevant cognitive features guiding motivations of speaker and audience for a specific narrative. Some of these are determined by text (here is where formalistic analysis of the text proves its value). That leaves us with an endlessly proliferating set of variables to be gathered under the label of context. We can isolate one important subset within the vastness of the contextual through historical research that gives some initial sense of what brought a group into existence, allows it to retain its distinctiveness, and motivates individuals to perform significant aspects of that distinctiveness. While that is clearly a conceptually reasonable step, it is practically out of reach because it implies an entire historical archive. We can catch sight of some more practical steps, though, by referring to the way cultures demonstrate certain key ideas with insistent redundancy because this reiterative ideological compulsion within any culture allows for some definite limits to the historical contextualizing of any narrative whose participation in this reiterative project is limited and limiting, a fact that gives narrative its particular value for the study of cognitive style. Articulating this aspect of the historical context provides the set of narrative presuppositions that sculpt the event structure of the narrative at hand. This analytic stage accounts for the greater part of what I claim to articulate in the implicit narrative, but like any story this one requires some question, some lack, some compulsion to animate its elements and make it a story, not just a collection of information. In this study that animating force comes from speculation about what the narrative elements might show about the narrator's and the narratee's relationship to language and cognition, and the ways our cultures form and reform both.

It is precisely the line of disciplinary development that includes concepts such as Herrnstein Smith's structure of motivation and leads to ever-more-insistent calls to context that accounts for my particular point of contact with other contemporary approaches to narrative, including those using ethnolinguistic and sociolinguistic insights and those that build on various advances in pragmatic theory. The May 2001 special issue of *Narrative* devoted to current questions in narratology concludes with Gerald Prince's recognition of the difficulties of "devising protocols for a sound assessment of interpretive strategies and affective responses." Yet, he claims, the development of such protocols is "an important undertaking for narratologists today."[9] The analysis of cognitive style might be seen as one partial approach to the assessment of interpretive strategies because the pragmatic presuppositions that are made explicit in the process account for one kind of socially grounded interpretation. In the same issue of *Narrative*, David Herman argues that we should pay attention to "the logic that stories *have* and the logic that stories *are*." Stories, as he points out, constitute a logic, "providing human beings with one of their primary resources for organizing and comprehending experience."[10] My implicit narrative concentrates on explicating the logic that stories are by showing how narrative organizes cultural assumptions about the logic that stories have.

The implicit narrative traces the cultural history of key figurations in any narrative and presents this historical dimension as a primary source for presuppositions guiding the formation of event structure in narrative. Individual motives may be fascinating, eminently worth pursuing, but it is the collective motive operating behind the individual one that reveals most about continuity and social coherence; therefore my work in cognitive style always moves between the individual motive and the collective assumptions that allow for individual communication. Since the collective also depends on particular spatial conditions, it points directly to questions of social space and collective identity in the process of a group's memory formation.

Events and Event Structure

Event is one of those key terms whose technical meaning changes from context to context. Generally in narrative theory, it applies to elements that are put into sequence by the plot and whose relations to each other (such as hierarchy or equivalence) affect the cognitive processing of any narrative.[11] As such it seems relatively nonproblematic, a simple matter of taxonomy and logical analysis. If, however, one starts to ask how decisions are made about the beginnings and endings of a particular event or if one questions how the boundaries of event might change from culture to culture or if one wonders how events might interpenetrate each other and be embedded one within the other, then questions proliferate and they become critically decisive, especially in relation to historical narrative. Once these questions are set in play, event is revealed in all its arbitrariness that threatens to relegate it to the dustbin of futile formalistic distinctions. But formalism highlighted the fact that narrative form carries its own meaning, quite apart from content; documenting that claim requires showing how units within narrative advance the narrative process, make their own demands, and deliver their own cognitive rewards. That basic claim has survived the downfall of specific approaches to characterizing event, and it may be the foundation for current moves toward any new formalism, serving new ends, which will require a revised notion of how to address the question of basic units of narrative. However far postmodernism may have taken us from various philosophical premises and literary methods, we will still always work with language as a structured and structuring tool, and that will require ways to get at units that we can analyze. The example par excellence of event structure at work is today's television serial which is, no doubt, shaping our contemporary expectations about how much one event should deliver before being overtaken by another one.

Whatever its drawbacks may be, event is the unit designation with the most distinguished, if heterogeneous, history of usage. In studying event structure, sociolinguists have followed the lead of William Labov and Joshua Waletsky, whose 1967 paper on personal experience narrative set up a six-stage sequence for organizing events in narrative, thereby establishing the agreed-on terms for comparative research in that field of narrative study and an agreed-on concept of event as reported experience captured by sequences of clauses in narrative.[12] As Labov discusses such issues as displacement sets (clauses that can be displaced without altering the temporal sequence of the narrative) he is exploring what I call "event structure," namely the linguistic and thematic shape of a particular event.

In the area of ethnolinguistic studies, the term *event* has been reserved for the actual occasion of speech act performance.[13] However, Dell Hymes implies a concept of event that is directly comparable to the way I use the term. He demonstrates intratextual units for presentational form and he identifies linguistic markers that isolate units within that form. Therefore, one can say that he identifies event structure for narratives of the northwestern Native peoples, and, as such, his work marks an important comparative moment in the study of event structure.[14] History, though, is the discipline wherein the emphasis on form and event can be construed as posing a threat to the cognitive claims made by historians. For this reason historians and philosophers of history have produced much of the critical work on event and event structure that proves most valuable to my study of cognitive style.

In this study I maintain a concept of event that is in line with the story/discourse distinction of traditional narrative theory, and I keep to the dynamic sense of event that motivates contemporary philosophers of history. Like Paul Ricoeur, I distinguish between "historical explanation and configuration by emplotment," and I see event as the textual effect of configuration by emplotment, as an effect of a shaping consciousness that is necessarily, often intuitively, isolating units of narrative.[15] I am assuming cultural tradition to be a major factor in determining what constitutes an individual's sense of how to shape an event, and I am assuming that historical research provides a basis for understanding themes and conventions that contextualize elements of narrative. I am tracing the significance of spatial categories. Therefore I characterize events as thematically constituted units describing the completion of a significant pattern of movement from one spatial domain to another. Sometimes several actions are required to complete an event. Sometimes the action is merely implied. Convention can dictate how much and what kind of detail is deemed appropriate to the linguistic expression of event. Every event has its own high point and its own resolution, but how that climax or resolution is emphasized or deemphasized is another way in which convention affects individual choice. Therefore, I follow whatever cultural clues I can find in establishing those textual units that I call events or macrostructures. I do not deny the element of arbitrariness in all this. My choice of a spatial thematic emphasis derives from the importance of this theme to the cultures I study, so it is not a random choice. Spatial and temporal categories are basic to any narrative structure, and this is another argument against sheer arbitrariness. Nevertheless, another thematic emphasis might lead to another approach to event structure. Event realizes a cultural thematics, and that statement admits of various kinds of testing. Event structure represents a hypothesis, not a fully tested conclusion.

Event structure in historical narrative has been most carefully considered by historians and philosophers of history like Paul Ricoeur, Louis O. Mink, Hayden White, and Hans Kellner to name a few of those concerned about the issues arising from event as a narrative unit. Mink states what has been a fundamental assumption for this group of philosophers of history. He has written that "both historians and writers of imaginative fiction know well the problems of constructing a coherent narrative account with or without the constraint of arguing from evidence, but even so they may not recognize the extent to which narrative as such is not just a technical problem for writers and critics but *a primary and irreducible form of human comprehension, an article in the constitution of common sense*" (emphasis mine).[16] Demonstrating how narrative itself is a factor in human comprehension requires analysis of event structure. In each of my four very different case studies, I isolate events (or follow the lead of narrators as they intuitively isolate them) that I then analyze with enough detail so that the presuppositions actively structuring them become evident.

Work like Paul Ricoeur's definitely plays into a project such as this because it takes a dynamic approach to the question of event. I am assuming along with Ricoeur that the act of performance (and writing is a mode of performance) is also the act that shapes event according to the structures of historical temporality; it brings event into being as the circumstances of performance structure it. For Ricoeur, the dialectic between structure and event is constitutive of tradition itself, and that dialectic shows the whole question of event structure to be more than mere formalistic quibbling. It shows that concentration on event can be one way to trace the inner dynamics of a tradition as it functions in a given speech act. Ricoeur addresses questions of event in all his writing, but one of his more sustained analyses is the essay "Structure, Word, Event" published in the United States in *The Conflict of Interpretation* (1974). The task he addresses is that of reclaiming "for the understanding of language what the structural model excluded and what perhaps is language itself as act of speech, as saying." To avoid the naive assumptions of psychologism or mentalism, Ricoeur claims that the task at hand requires that we "produce the act of speech in the very midst of language, in the fashion of a setting-forth of meaning, of a dialectical production which makes the system occur as an act and the structure as an event." The unit that he designates as the site of this intimate look at the emergence of event is the discursive utterance. It is itself an event that always exhibits new choices, new combinations, all for the sake of achieving reference, a goal that Ricoeur has presented as always endangered, always in need of its safeguards. Each utterance implies its own manner of designating the subject of discourse. The task at hand requires a specific focus, an exact means for tracing what is happening to the system and to the event, and Ricoeur calls on the word with its particular problematic to do this task. Only within discourse does the word leave behind its value as mere sign of difference and acquire referential meaning that can be explicated. He gives us a memorable image that helps us grasp what is at stake in any analysis of event when he says that within discourse, the word becomes "a trader between the system and the act, between the structure and the event." For him the word is a "point of crystallization," it is a "tying together of all the exchanges between structure and function." In the event that discourse is, the word acquires new use-value that it then returns to the system. This movement between the old and the new, the system and what is emergent, is the life of tradition, the gift of history as shaped tradition. The word mediates between event and structure because event is not a given but an effect of dynamic structuration. He writes, "In rising from system to event, in the instance of discourse, [the word] brings structure to the act of speech. In returning from the event to the system, it brings to the system the contingency and disequilibrium without which it could neither change nor endure; in short it gives a 'tradition' to the structure which, in itself, is outside of time."[17]

In his monumental three-volume study of time and narrative, Ricoeur sees temporality as setting up event structure.[18] The ways in which we structure our access to the past and set up the future all lead to narrative movement between structure and event, exactly the dynamics that activate tradition. A sense of event mediates between universal time (cosmic time) and lived time in order to configure historical time.

Within the Native cultures that I study here, spatial categories take precedence over temporal ones; but that does not mean that Ricoeur's thinking lacks validity for my work. In cultures like those of the Sioux, time is conceptualized as realized movement through space; therefore spatial terms allow for the explication of temporal structure, a point that I seek to demonstrate and document first of all in terms of the brief event the analysis of which ends this chapter. Then, in my chapter on the narrating community, I demonstrate the same points in relation to an expanded repertoire of narratives, all of which retain their continuity with older tales on the basis of similar uses of spatial categories. Event structure hinges on the way these categories accommodate new materials.

My work tries to trace cultural evidence that would enable us to identify event structure for different cultures, and it seeks to show both the stabilizing features of event (formal comparability) and the dynamic features of event (features that come into being by way of performance). That process has to begin with simple recognition of how event structure can vary culturally. As Dell Hymes and others have so consistently pointed out for Native cultures, that process is facilitated in these cultures by the fact that features of performance regularly mark the beginning and ending of events in folktales and other speech genres as well. Oral storytellers sometimes use definite linguistic markers such as the Lakota *ske*, roughly translated as "so they tell," to mark event segments. My translations in the book *Lakota Myth* (1983) are designed to highlight those event markers so that comparison is possible between a nineteenth-century Lakota sense of event and our mainstream contemporary sense of event. I find a tendency in late-nineteenth-century Lakota storytelling to have extremely brief truncated events in those instances in which cultural information is highly condensed. I am assuming that the brevity of the event places responsibility on the listeners to respond on the basis of shared presuppositions about the event.[19]

Traditional storytelling conventions often dictated brief pauses at the point of transition from one event to the other, which would have allowed an audience time to access the implied cultural knowledge. I am also assuming that in oral performances, event structure changes according to performance variables so that it is generally reflective of features of the teller/listener relationship.

Finding the units of event structure provides likely clues to several pragmatic presuppositions that are bound to narrative structure and not just to content. Most of my work on comparisons between oral and written literatures assumes that much of the experimentation that follows from the decision to make an oral text into an infrastructure for the written is, in fact, a series of attempts to make one kind of event structure reflective of another.[20] Tracing event structure in highly structured genres like folktales also sets up strong hypotheses about event structure in ordinary speech acts. In fact, much of my Standing Rock material shows just this point. Ordinary speech reveals its closeness to the arts of tradition as it approaches the event structure of those highly structured traditions. There is a continuum rather than a radical break between natural narrative and formal, traditional narrative genres.

In terms of this book, the short text, the analysis of which ends this chapter, is an example of a single macroevent with its structure of movements among definite significance-saturated points in space. An interplay between historically shaped presuppositions and textual structure is demonstrated in great detail. That analysis demonstrates and, I believe, proves the historical nature of the sense of event out of which the text in question arises.

Pragmatics

The implicit narrative that I construct for the various narratives in this study is distinguished from ordinary straightforward, historically based textual commentary by my reliance on pragmatic presuppositions (both prepositional and textual) for information that I then integrate with semantic data in order to construct the implicit narrative. In other words, the interpretive point of view is established primarily by way of context cues that I then use to show a narrativizing process at work in my examples. My research attempts to reconstruct elementary principles of communicative competence needed to have a local understanding of the text and to use these principles as cues for interpreting the functions of events. The significance that I want to highlight shapes narrative form by guiding event structure and a whole series of rhetorical features that follow directly from the speaker's or writer's relationship to the community addressed. Although I do not deal with any such texts in this book, it is entirely possible to imagine a speaker who is trying to transcend the constraints of local communicative competence. In that case the rhetorical signs of such an effort would constitute the implicit narrative. What I do have in this study, though, are texts that appeal to a community even when the community is no longer certain of which elements of its competence apply to the communication in question. I also have texts that show the speaker or writer using language to rediscover some of the principles of competence that were feared lost, and I address the immigrant's question of how to function in an environment where the social context is too new to give much communicative guidance. What is it like to speak or write into the winds of unknowing? How does that necessity shape a text? These are the questions that make the implicit narrative into a rich cultural resource and a means of negotiating between past and present as well as between different cultures. It is these common situations of near loss that make the implicit narrative worth the explicative effort and that shift so much of the explicative burden to pragmatic inferences.

To talk about pragmatic inferences is to raise the question of the relationship between semantic and pragmatic features. To state simply (and accurately) that pragmatics is the study of contexts in which speech acts are performed does not say very much about the situation Robert C. Stalnaker addresses when he says that "in most cases, however, the context of utterance affects not only the force with which the proposition is expressed, but also the proposition itself." Pragmatic presuppositions differ from semantic ones in that the pragmatic ones are propositional attitudes, not semantic relations. As Stalnaker states, "People, rather than sentences or propositions, are said to have or make presuppositions in this sense." Stalnaker's summary of the relationship between semantic and pragmatic presuppositions accounts for the fact that in practice, we are always moving back and forth between semantics and pragmatics: "In general any semantic presupposition of a proposition expressed in a given context will be a pragmatic presupposition of the people in that context, but the converse clearly does not hold."[21] The implicit narrative has to get at pragmatic presuppositions that are not part of the set of semantic presuppositions in a given context; but most of what gives coherence to the implicit narrative will be presuppositions that are shared by the semantics and pragmatics.

When the presuppositions in questions are discursive rather than prepositional, the question of what is properly assigned to the pragmatics rather than semantics represents disputed territory, a matter I leave to specialists in discourse theory. My concern is with inclusiveness of experiential constraints in narrative processing and interpretation. Like Dennis Jonnes, I see the pragmatic criteria for a description of story as a set of constraints conditioning the autonomy of the narrative system.[22] Furthermore, it is a verifiable set of constraints that shows narrative's institutional efficacy.

My reliance on pragmatic presuppositions for an interpretive perspective is a departure from much of the past's standard narrative research, but it is in line with current directions. For all their differences, current theorists seem united in their turn toward greater emphasis on pragmatics. In a 1997 issue of the *Journal of Narrative and Life History* devoted to the consequences of William Labov and Joshua Waletsky's important 1967 paper, "Narrative Analysis: Oral Versions of Personal Experience," most of the papers note that continuing the work of William Labov depends on honoring his original but largely unfulfilled agenda of using more of the contextual data supporting personal experience narratives. Gerald Prince proposes several components to a model that might advance work on narrativity and the factors affecting it. He calls for a structural component, a narrating component, a semantic component, and a pragmatic component, which would specify the degree of narrativity of presented structures and "perhaps more generally, specifying the basic cognitive and communicative factors, affecting their production and processing."[23]

A recent book that follows comparable lines of narratological refinement is Monika Fludernik's experiential approach to narrativity. For her, narrativity is constituted by what she calls "experientiality," that is, by the "quasi-mimetic evocation of 'real-life experience.'" Experientiality depends on the way cognitive parameters narrativize language sequences, and this function defines narrative itself. I am assuming that her cognitive parameters would include the cultural presuppositions that I privilege in this study and that these presuppositions allow for a relatively controlled take on that broad field she calls experientiality. According to Fludernik, "Experientiality, as everything else in narrative, reflects a cognitive schema of embodiedness that relates to human existence and human concerns."[24]

Fludernik proposes a four-tiered model analyzing narrative according to the way the cognitive enters the narrative experience in order to "naturalize" it. Her third and fourth levels correspond closely to the kind of narrative analysis engaged here. For levels one and two, cognitive parameters are transcultural, basic-level experiential frames. In this study I give only passing attention to such frames. Level three categories are "culture specific, and to a large extent, acquired, even taught, as abstract categories." Her level four "concerns the interpretive abilities by which people link unknown and unfamiliar material with what they are already familiar with, thereby rendering the unfamiliar interpretable and 'readable.'" My implicit narrative renders explicit the cognitive assumptions and stylistic transformations that cover much of the same analytic territory as Fludernik's levels three and four. Her concern, like mine, is for explicating the cognitive assumptions that are triggered through the *interpretation* of narrative. Furthermore, she too wants to find means to give a legitimate diachronic description to the cognitive parameters that guide such interpretation. My persistent emphasis on verifiable pragmatic presuppositions means that my methodology is much narrower in its focus than hers is. Mine is not a theory of narrative in general. Mine is a method for tracing particular forms of communal continuity through narrative. Therefore, the conjunctions between theory of narrative and what I do are important, but I am in no way competing with or supplanting any particular theory of narrative. Another way in which Fludernik's study complements this work is in her argument that oral and written literary texts should be viewed as a continuum of functions rather than positing radical distinctions between the two. She attempts to document how "written narrative refunctionalized features of the oral tale for their own purposes."[25]

As with so much else in this study, the turn to pragmatic presuppositions was necessitated by my questions about how to deal with historical contexts as they shaped narrative form. The questions I seek to address all depend on what I can learn about the history of communicative competence that characterizes a typical speech act context for the statements in question. The assertion of "typical" suggests a significant problem area. Whether I was dealing with Native or immigrant data, I had to confront situations in which historical data are inadequate and critical studies of history virtually nonexistent. With so much lost, what could I do? I had to use whatever historical data I could get—ceremonial, ethnographic, political—in order to reconstruct what might constitute a typical context of reception in the past. My work paralleled that of an archeologist. Many of my initial clues came from the analysis of ceremonial data or statements about beliefs. From those clues, as the example ending this chapter shows, I could build hypotheses about more generally based principles of interpretation. Local statements about the meaning of ceremonial action or beliefs brought me into a local hermeneutic process. As Dennis Tedlock has observed with his Zuni materials, a teller of a traditional tale or belief is not just repeating, he or she is also giving a criticism at the same time.[26] The way the text links old with new, possibility with realization of that possibility, reveals a constant process of interpretation. Each such example provides another set of clues for a local critical tradition. Language offered one important source of contextual data, but to use it, I had to make certain leaps between the semantic and the pragmatic.

Pragmatic analysis always sets up the need for careful methodological refinements. While this study does not follow the step-by-step procedures of any other theoretician, it is guided by the primary assumptions and definitions of two major methodological studies that provided me with essential data as well as methodological insights. These models are Madeleine Mathiot's study of Papago ethnolinguistics, *An Approach to the Cognitive Study of Language* (1968), and Teun van Dijk's *Macrostructures: An Interdisciplinary Study of Global Structures in Discourse, Interaction, and Cognition* (1980).

If one thinks in terms of narrative as representing "primary and irreducible forms of human cognition,"[27] those forms include what van Dijk and associates would label "macrostructures." In a chapter titled "The Cognitive Basis of Macrostructures," van Dijk states, "It is argued repeatedly in this book that macrostructures have a cognitive basis." His statement of the scope of discourse pragmatics is one I follow in this study. He claims that the aim of pragmatics is to state the appropriateness of discourse units. "We say that a speech act is appropriate or inappropriate in a given context.... This context, then, is specified in terms of certain properties of the communicative situation: speaker, hearer, their social relations (e.g., dominance), and a number of their cognitive properties: knowledge/beliefs, wishes/wants, preferences/evaluations." Later he states, "So *how* language users really interpret utterances as certain speech acts or which grammatical categories are applied to convey a certain action concept are problems for the cognitive basis of pragmatics."[28]

In my attempts to present a critical narrative that is built around the close relationship between semantic and pragmatic elements of the narrative, I do not present all the detailed formal analyses for all the texts I analyze. That would compete with my goal of maximum readability; but I do include enough detail and enough different contextual elements so that the question of how individuals use that detail to interpret changing microstructural features according to historically defined macrostructures achieves as full an answer as can be achieved in a book like this.

Methodologically, I am most indebted to Madeleine Mathiot. Her study of the Papago language from a cognitive perspective gave me indispensable comparative data for any other Native language that I might use in this study. No one has attempted a similar study since hers.

Mathiot's method is so detailed in terms of Papago categories—semantic, syntactic, and pragmatic—that it opens the way for understanding what might otherwise be incomprehensible aspects of other Native languages. For example, she notes that with the phrase "several chairs" the Papago language makes a lexical distinction between several chairs from the same household and several chairs from several households."[29] Much of what Mathiot discovered in Papago turns out to have parallels in Lakota that can be traced once the analyst is alerted to their possibility. I adopt Mathiot's distinctions among the semantic, cognitive, and conceptual, and I am assuming that pragmatic presuppositions arise from the cognitive component. This allows me to control my arguments about separate methodological stages involved in literary analysis.

Mathiot's basic distinctions are as follows: "The semantic domain of a language is the relation between the signs of that language and the reality they stand for, i.e., denote and connote. The cognitive domain of a language is the relation between the speakers of that language and reality as mediated by the language." The cognitive is further elaborated in relation to the conceptual:

> *As understood here, a cognitive system refers to the unformalized conception of reality—or aspects of reality—held by a people. A conceptual system, on the other hand, refers to the formalized conception of reality— or aspects of reality—held by an analyst. Instances of conceptual systems are philosophical systems, mathematical systems, the systematic description of language or of culture. The importance of the distinction proposed here is as follows: it allows for varying degrees of awareness on the part of members of a culture of their own cognitive patterns. The analyst, on the other hand, strives for a high degree of awareness of the cognitive patterns which he aims to describe.*[30]

The implicit narrative that I extract from all the gathered historical data is designed to show the signs of awareness that get gathered into the narrative momentum.

Sapir-Whorf Hypothesis

Although I work almost exclusively with English language texts, I try to make the point that some of the texts are evidence of a form of English that still bears the marks of semantic distinctions made in an older state of the Sioux language. I believe that I have examples of texts in which English is fundamentally shaped by its relationship to some other language. In the case of the example analyzed in this chapter, I go further and claim that distinctions that exist in Sioux and translate only indirectly into English are the primary ones that shape the presuppositions giving specific historical significance to the text. The worldview reflected in the governing interpretive presuppositions is most directly reflected in the Sioux language and expressed in English only by way of indirection.

Moving back and forth between language and worldview is hardly a new approach to anything; the entire analytic activity immediately recalls the well-known Sapir-Whorf hypothesis that asserts that language determines cognition.[31] While subsequent research has generally judged that position to be too deterministic, a weaker version of it continues to influence research. In its weakest form, the assertion is simply that language affects cognition. The question continues, though, about how to pose problems that would allow us to test the Whorfian hypothesis in any of its forms, strong or weak. In the most recent research, the hypothesis is invoked in relation to questions about whether language itself has a dominating role in cognition, and research along these lines is still at the level of developing appropriate methodology.[32]

Mathiot's position is both productive and, as yet, inadequately tested. In her introduction to her monograph, Mathiot explains the relationship of her research to that of her eminent predecessors, and she breaks away from some of the limitations of those earlier language and culture studies. Hers is the position I follow in this book, and therefore, in spite of its length, I choose to quote her position in full because paraphrase cannot do it justice:

> *The hypothesis underlying the present approach is that the theme structure of the language is related to the theme structure of the culture. The degree to which the two structures are related constitutes the degree of integratedness of the language into the total culture. Such a hypothesis, therefore, allows for varying degrees of integratedness of a language into a culture, as may become apparent both in the synchronic comparison of different language-and-culture situational contexts and in the diachronic comparison of the same language-and-culture situational context.*
>
> *The assumption implicit in the usual interpretation of the Sapir-Whorf hypothesis is that the cognitive domain of language is directly related to culture thus influencing cultural behavior. In the present approach, this assumption is replaced by the postulation of two separate theme structures related to each other in varying degrees. Thus instead of direct correlations, an intermediate level is proposed. This means that language and culture relations are expected to emerge on a higher level of abstraction.*[33]

By refining the Sapir-Whorf hypothesis, Mathiot enhances the descriptive adequacy of scholarship that can take into account a much greater range of variables. The intermediate level of relationship between language and culture is one in which individual as well as cultural cognitive sets can come into play. In an exceptionally useful footnote Mathiot further elucidates her position on the Sapir-Whorf hypothesis, and we can see how she achieves a complete turnabout in the usual interpretations of language and culture relations: "the aim is limited to gathering the information regarded as a prerequisite to the testing not only of the Sapir-Whorf hypothesis—i.e., the extent to which language determines cultural behavior—but also that of its opposite—i.e., the extent to which cultural behavior determines the world view that is manifested in language."[34]

Reading in order to discern the traces of cognitive style is a matter of attending to a struggle that dramatizes the inadequacies of the original Sapir-Whorf hypothesis while recognizing its necessity and power. By starting with behavior and hence with individuals, scholarship can note emerging conventions and interpretations. The history of American Indian languages suggests that the linguistic features most closely bound to prereservation worldview quickly slip into disuse as people adopt a worldview more directly influenced by Euro-American conceptual categories and the English language, wherein these categories dominate. Interpretations of worldview, though, or the conceptualization of cognitive assumptions, seem to have a different historical contingency, one among the many hypotheses that this study sets up without, however, resolving. Mathiot's methodology suggests the scholarly positioning needed to relate the history of interpretation to the history of worldview and of language so that the radical historical disjunctions and discontinuities retain motivational force in the critical and/or creative narratives seeking to bridge the disruptions at the very heart of language.

In her book Mathiot sets in place some fundamental working principles for each analytic stage. Her technical, minimalist descriptions of cognitive features found among the Papago people in Arizona are the scaffolding for structures of perception and attention that allow us to take a few secure steps toward empathetic response to a tradition other than our own. The reader who brings imaginative agility to Mathiot's analysis of cognitive themes can find in her work the creative excitement of discovering a previously unimagined orchestration of signifiers.

Once basic historical and/or linguistic research has uncovered a body of data that holds interpretive promise, and that data has been historically linked to texts and shown to shape the implicit narrative of a text, we are launched into the study of how a few basic pragmatic presuppositions shape a text's capacity to designate its users as members of a given textual community.

The Spaces of Narrative

As stated above, this study concentrates on how cognitive style reveals historical continuity within textual communities. The term *textual community* came into the literature of various disciplines through medieval studies. Brian Stock defines the textual community as "a group in which there is both a script and a spoken enactment and in which social cohesion and meaning result from the interaction of the two."[35] Anthropologists have appropriated the term for their own uses. Joanne Rappaport uses the notion of textual community to refer to the dynamics of a Columbian Andean community "in flux," using both oral and written texts to define their identity and making no crucial distinctions between the two.[36] She, in line with Stock's original characterization, makes the important point that it is not the texts that define the textual community but the activity of the local historians engaged in constantly interpreting these texts, oral or written, along lines that define the community's distinctiveness. The act of continuing communal interpretation defines and maintains the textual community. That is my point too, and I have used the idea here and elsewhere to refer to the process whereby individual interpreters use defining ideas for the group and create narratives about the process. The degree and kind of recognition that a community gives to such texts reveals much about the cognitive themes that maintain a community's distinctiveness.

My emphasis on a communal process places this study in the context of work that is being done to describe the power of culture to transform places into spaces of belonging. Recent anthropological debates on how to conceptualize relations between self and other have also problematized relations between home and the space of the other. Study of travel writing, of migration, and of postcolonial critiques have further complicated the "location of culture," to use the title of Homi Bhaba's influential book. A global economy disperses people and ideas. If we think of the "other" as at home among us, then we have to ask about differences in how that sense of home is produced and enacted. As Akhil Gupta and James Ferguson claim, "Instead of stopping with the notion of deterritorialization, the pulverization of the space of high modernity, we need to theorize how space is being reterritorialized in the contemporary world."[37]

The essays in this book look at relatively coherent communities. Nevertheless, each of my case studies gives a different take on how space is being reterritorialized. The Yanktonai Sioux were moved twice from what they considered as the spaces of home; first they lost territory when the reservation boundaries were established in the 1890s, and then they had to move away from their villages when those villages were flooded in the 1950s. The German-Russians also had to adapt to two drastic moves, first from southern Germany to the Ukraine, then a century later from the Ukraine to the United States. Each of my two literary studies examines how reading novels from the perspective of a precisely realized and historically contextualized sense of place reveals the impact of space or its loss on individual subject formation. Each of these chapters makes the point that the questions arising from reterritorialization or respatialization have to be addressed on a regional basis that takes into account a range of environmental factors, not just the social environment.

One way to make regional studies of literature into a more vital endeavor is to insert more information about how region affects basic presuppositions and motives into the criticism of the literature. In a genuinely innovative approach to regional criticism, the details of regional identity would take precedence over other features of novelistic significance, not in some naive, obvious way that merely mentions a few regional facts, but in a manner that assumes region to be a central factor in human cognition and hence in the process whereby the events of the novel can be experienced. Any novel, with the possible exception of science fiction, can be read and criticized as a regional novel. *Regional criticism*, as I use the term here, applies to a mode of reading and interpreting, not to any inherent qualities in the novel.

Nadia Lovell, in her introduction to *Locality and Belonging* (1998), gives some sense of how to escape from wooden, naive linkages between person and place and to ask the questions that show a continuing dynamic interaction. She makes the important point that we need to look at how the natural environment guides and paces other kinds of perception: "The inscription of nature onto bodies and of bodies within nature, transforms the relationship that humans entertain with nature into a dialectical process embedded in memory. Its transformative properties also become embedded in phenomenological terms, as synchronicity of time and space allow for movement through history. The landscape itself becomes historicized."[38] The historicized landscape is what I seek to mine for presuppositions that allow for a truly regional criticism. It also shows cognitive style at work in establishing the boundaries of textual communities and in achieving cognitive mapping.

Cognitive Boundaries

The analysis of cognitive style can be an adjunct to the study of *cognitive mapping*, a term that has two fundamentally different meanings depending on whether one is speaking from a geographer's perspective or from that of a literary theorist. Both the geographical and the literary theoretical meanings can come into play in relation to the present study. The geographers Roger M. Downs and David Shea define cognitive mapping as "an abstraction covering those cognitive or mental abilities that enable us to collect, organize, store, recall and manipulate information about the spatial environment."[39] Cognitive maps give frames of reference and analogue models for organizing our spatial knowledge and they reflect basic, possibly innate human skills. On a broad scale they reveal how literal spaces operate as spaces of the mind. In analyzing cognitive style in narrative, I uncover some of the history of cognitive maps as well as some central features of their role in structuring narrative.

What kinds of analogical functions do mental maps take on? How do older and newer mental maps coexist? How do people change their mental maps? These questions take on ever-greater significance in a context of global movement of people and ideas. The Native materials are particularly rich resources for showing how places take on analogical functions so that they can map a worldview at the same time as they map actual places. The example analyzed at the end of this chapter makes that point with stunning clarity. The immigrant data reveal cognitive maps in the making as older maps are recruited for new kinds of service until such time as the new environment can serve the psychological as well as the practical purposes of cognitive maps.

Cognitive mapping also happens to be a phrase made briefly famous among literary theorists by Frederic Jameson in the 1980s and early 1990s. Jameson's usage of the term can be compared only with geographers' usage if one remembers that all cognitive maps are frames for managing experience. Jameson assumes a language of forms by which we map our intellectual lives, and the way we manage these forms constitutes the act of cognitive mapping. There is less difference that one might at first suppose between theorists like Jameson and novelists like Leslie Silko, who asserts that "the stories are all we have to stay alive."[40] Narrative is the basis for Jameson's cognitive mapping. His persistent postmodern worries about a global context in which we will no longer be able to insert ourselves as individual subjects into "an ever more massive and impersonal or transpersonal reality outside ourselves" are as apocalyptic and as extravagantly productive as anything a novelist might imagine about a world in which artificial intelligence dominates language. For Jameson the study of cognitive mapping is no "mere intellectual curiosity." It is a search for "signs of some new, so far only dimly conceivable, collective forms which may be expected to replace the older individualistic ones."[41] Jameson's approach to cognitive mapping is a way of referring to structural coordinates for a play of figuration that is generated by some unifying and totalizing force, in his instance capital. At the end of *Postmodernism*, Jameson states directly: "'cognitive mapping' was in reality nothing but a code word for 'class consciousness'—only it proposed the need for class consciousness of a new and hitherto undreamed of kind, while it also inflected the account in the direction of that new spatiality implicit in the postmodern."[42]

Boundary contexts seem to prove that Jameson's fears might be alleviated somewhat by concentrating on the adaptability of forms. Productive collective forms have existed in all cultures and continue to achieve new contexts of action amid their constant modern or postmodern transformations. And they remain evidence of communal accomplishment that, if highlighted, can weaken the specter of massive impersonalism. The question is recognizing these transformations in relation to constantly changing social entities. Ours is a global condition of rapid, often frightening changes in the relations between groups. Questions of social instability are among the most important we face. Analysis of cognitive style does little to reduce intergroup tensions, but it can help us value the past of groups whose contributions to the present play of ideas are often either minimized or written off altogether, and it might help us to recognize emerging collective forms that may yet be an important part of the solution for a globalism that depends on new forms of communication.

Operationalizing Cognitive Style

To illustrate the move from textual analysis to the formulation of hypotheses about cognitive style as it operates across a range of different texts, I want to present a detailed commentary on a single incident of textual production in which I myself participated, because this text can serve as an elegantly simple and direct dramatization of how cultural presuppositions support basic narrative conditions that, in turn, shape textual style in and through a broad range of secondary textual features.[43]

While I was living in Solen, North Dakota, on the Standing Rock Sioux Reservation, a chance occasion gave me the opportunity to watch an array of linguistic and cognitive distinctions come to vivid and practical narrative life. That incident resulted in two brief texts (more accurately, perhaps, one text in two languages), which provide a window onto the linguistic and historical processes giving rise to a narrative that was written as gift and as explanation for an impromptu dinner gathering.

Although the context in question was no more than an incidental occasion, the fact that it was immediately and spontaneously transformed into a narrative illustrating a proverb makes the resultant text an exemplar of traditional discourse strategies. Conclusions reached through microanalysis of this text stand as the necessary demonstration to ground the more general assertions on which this entire study is based. A single text can do no more than reveal what is possible when a person with traditional textual competence responds to a situation with a narrative; but that revelation can serve to heighten alertness as to what might be happening in other texts. At each stage of this study I am trying to illustrate my point that cognitive style is the linguistic evidence of historical processes at work in speech acts that function to define an individual's place in a textual community. Close analysis of a single incident is only one step in the study of cognitive style. It is the means for showing what kinds of facts generate hypotheses about how cognitive style operates. Testing the various hypotheses that emerge from this kind of analysis requires comparison with other texts from the same and from other speakers. When other texts from other speakers reveal similar processes at work, then we can assume that we are dealing with more than an idiosyncratic cognitive style. It is my belief that adequate testing is possible only through collaborative work that would bring together representative samples of community members. It all has to start, though, with close analysis along lines illustrated here.

Now back to the incident in question. At the time, the unpredictability of my work schedule made mealtime into a matter of chance. Late one afternoon when I had been too busy to stop for lunch, I decided to combine lunch and dinner, so I made a complete three-course meal just for myself, and I took plenty of time to enjoy it. When I was nearly finished, I heard a knock at the door. Lillian and Harry Fast Horse had come unexpectedly for an evening of visiting and teaching. Of course, that included dinner. I was learning the Dakota language from them, and I depended on their mentoring to guide me through the intricacies of local politics. I was genuinely delighted to see them, but the sight of my almost-finished dinner triggered Lillian's embarrassed realization that I would have to prepare yet another meal. Graciously negotiating the unexpected with her typical ease and pedagogical concern, she told me that the Dakota people had a traditional saying that they used in similar circumstances, and she repeated it first in Dakota and then in English. Her English version of the proverb is "The ghosts loved us and so they pushed us here," and the general intent behind the proverb is to suggest that somehow individual responsibility had been usurped by higher forces whose intervention proved to be their evening gift to us all. Ella Deloria included a similar proverb in an unpublished collection of Dakota idioms. She gave as its significance: "ghosts take him along, giving him a push now and again, causing him to stagger as he goes; to happen upon something nice, to stumble upon good fortune."[44] Both Deloria's reference from the 1930s and Lillian Fast Horse's from the 1970s are definite in their implications that those whom spirits push along some path toward good fortune are not acting solely on their own volition. There is an implied dynamic of determination and freedom, volition and submission. Given the emphasis on volition in traditional Dakota thought, an emphasis that can be traced through ceremonial practice as well as in linguistic structure, this point is exactly where the force of the proverb lies.[45] It is also the point at which the socially convenient significance of Lillian's short text opens out into broader issues of how cognitive style negotiates the consequences of beliefs even within settings where all do not necessarily understand those beliefs or where a history of beliefs may be invoked merely to explain possible attitudes toward a social situation.[46]

In keeping with my position as someone learning from her, I asked Lillian if she would write down that one short proverb while I began another dinner; I handed her one of those yellow writing pads that seem always at hand in academic households. Some time later, the meal well begun and cooking, I joined my guests in the living room. Lillian gave the writing pad back to me. Instead of the one

Dakota line that I had expected, there were two short paragraphs, one in Dakota and one in English. Both texts expand the single line proverb into a narrative of actual events leading up to her use of the proverb. The narrative is based on what she and her husband had done during that day, but their specific activities are implied by references to *where* they had been during the day. The significance of what they did is bound up with the implied conditions characterizing the places where that action occurred, and these same conditions are shown as affecting decisions Harry and Lillian make about what to do and where to go next. In other words, volitional options are imagistically bound to habitational conditions (i.e., those cultural presuppositions assigning significance to distinctions within space). Lillian gave us a cognitive map (I use that term in all its several possible ways). Her brief texts clearly illustrate a style in which nominalized spatial references function as highly condensed semantic indexes encompassing a range of references to basic Dakota beliefs about how specific spaces can affect human freedom.

While the Dakota language version is far more complex than the English one, both texts are so intensely condensed that at first reading they appear to be quite the opposite of stylized. It is important, therefore, to note that Lillian spoke and wrote excellent idiomatic English and that her knowledge of Dakota was of the highest order. Neither the English nor the Dakota version was typical of any writing or speaking style I had noted previously (and here I use the word "style" in its weakest, idiosyncratic sense). The texts she wrote for me seemed to require a range of cultural and historical references, and the pressure of that need led to the creation of nominal phrases that sum up a virtual historical archive. In the Dakota version these referentially compact and dense nominals anchor a complex verbal play of cognitively powerful distinctions within verbs of movement that English simply cannot accommodate. Therefore, the English text (in which the same verbs of coming and going can only be repeated again and again) seems to be an extremely simple construction based on those ponderous and disconcerting nouns, while the slightly longer Dakota text with its varied verbs, each implying differing degrees of conscious control, presents the culturally nuanced reference that allows the whole narrative to move toward the implication that the convivial evening at my house was no more or less than a matter of being in the right places at the right times and knowing how to respond when the spirits moved them in the right directions. With that as introduction, I quote the texts first in English, then in Dakota.

> *Today at the Beadwork House at Our Father's House, I did beadwork. When the hour came to stop, my man came after me so we came. And so I said, "At Solen all will gather." So we came; and we came to Solen, but they didn't do it. So I said, "We will go to see Elaine. So we came to the place. She was sitting near a Holy Man's House. So she cooked for us and*

fed us. So I said, "The ghosts loved us and so they pushed us here." We ate well.

Anpetu kin le el Ateyapi Oti kin heciya Waksupi Tipi kin hel waapi-waye, na wana oape ayustanpi kta iye hantu; canke wicasa mitawa kin mahiyohe canke ungliyayapi. Unkan hepe "Solen ekta lehanl omniciya kta ske," canke unkupi na Solen ekta unhipi; keyas econpisni canke hepi, "Elaine ekta unyankin'kte." Canke ekta unhipi. Wicasa Wakan Oti wan el yanke ca hel unhipi. Unkan lolunkin hanpi na wounkupi. Canke hepe, "Wanagi teunhlilapi ca pajekje unakaupi." Yupiya waun-yutapi.

Lillian Fast Horse's expansion of her proverb outlines the implicit narrative in its emergent state. Her narrative points to the cultural factors that link the proverb to a narrative. She advances from cause to effect, from an incident to the conditioning factors linking the incident to cognitive sets that relate what is happening here to other aspects of the tradition. The brief narrative achieves all this by mapping the pattern of movement that Lillian and her husband had followed that day before arriving at my home; it also shows how their placement achieves a progressively realized association between them and the spirits who led them onward; but most of this is implied and works by way of cultural assumptions that work as narrative presuppositions.

The single macroevent can be broken into a series of exceptionally brief events, each representing a single action with specific cultural resonances. Because this narrative is so explicitly about the cognitive themes of place in relation to movement, my definition of event as a thematically constituted unit describing the completion of a significant pattern of movement from one spatial category to another allows for a breakdown of the narrative into elements that link place to history and history to motivation. As I stated earlier, I find that intensely condensed cultural information leads to extremely brief events, using action that advances the narrative line as the basis for determining when an event begins and ends.

1) Today at the Beadwork House at Our Father's House, I did beadwork. When the hour came to stop, my man came after me.
2) So we came.
3) And so I said, "At Solen all will gather." So we came.
4) We came to Solen but they didn't do it.
5) So I said, "We will go to see Elaine."
6) So we came to the place.
7) She was sitting near a Holy Man's House. So she cooked for us and fed us.

8) So I said, "The ghosts loved us and so they pushed us here." We ate well.

The first event is in every way an event of placement, and through the way it highlights those ponderous stylized nominals Beadwork House and Our Father's House, it reveals an entire aesthetic at work. Lillian Fast Horse's nominals are cryptic structures conjuring historical ideas about the power and nature of design within Sioux culture. At their most obvious level, the nominals triangulate the action of the narrative between the two places mentioned in the first event and the third point in the triangle, my house in Solen, also stylized as a Holy Man's House. Thus they establish the spatial pattern whose correspondence to narrative temporality remains in question in the first event, where the action of beading simply designates Lillian as agent, achieving one kind of art and initiating another—the verbal design that makes the primary significance of her day transferable to another person. If we remember that the point of the narrative is to tell how the Fast Horses fell under the influence of spirits, then we start to question the motive behind those stylized nominals that call such attention to themselves. The history of nineteenth-century Sioux ideas about art and design gives us the information we need to shape a series of presuppositions about how design relates to habitation and placement, to volitional options and to temporality. Because they relate to basic notions of form and structure, these presuppositions animate a whole range of narratives. They prove Lillian's narrative to be exemplary evidence of what is involved in making something that connects people, places, and the spiritual forces that are part of the network of relations in which all making participates.

The first nominal, Beadwork House, is definitely the operative one for the entire narrative because it focuses a range of ideas about art, women's art in particular. Lillian was a superbly accomplished beadworker. While her husband took care of tribal business or indulged in informal political speculation with other tribal leaders, she worked at art that, as she knew well, had once symbolized the way the life of the group required form and placement. Lillian was inclined to speculate on this older significance for women's art as consistently as her husband entertained ideas about political options for the community.

The historical assumptions that support all that is implied by the term Beadwork House provide the background from which I abstract the pragmatic presuppositions for a whole range of other references in this particular text and in other texts in which similar issues of gender, art, and dwelling are at stake. The first clue that distinctions that do not translate into English are at work here is hidden in the contrasts between Beadwork House and the other nouns. In English the term Beadwork House is exactly parallel to and aligned with the other two nominalized locatives. However, in Dakota Beadwork House is in definite and direct contrast to Our Father's House and Holy Man's House. With the latter two nouns, the locative marker *o* is prefixed to a verbal in order to indicate that the activity of that verb occurs in a restricted area (*ateyapi oti* and *wicasa wakan oti*).[47] The semantic emphasis is squarely on the *place* of the narrated action. Beadwork House (*waksupi tipi*) is a verbal noun. The noun *tipi* refers to any structure, thus the emphasis is less on the act of inhabiting than on the beadwork and all that it implies. Historical research proves a range of connections between beadworking and human volition or choice. In the working out of their designs, women were seen as mediators between originary powers and humans whose lives require that power always be part of a design.

We can get the first clues about this far-reaching idea from Clark Wissler's famous study of the decorative arts among the Sioux. He gets to the central issue when he mentions ancient beliefs regarding certain women who dreamed complex abstract designs. Wissler is right on the mark when he notes that all such designs "are believed to emanate from the same sacred source." He sums up his brief description of this important facet of Sioux thought by adding, "It seems that a dream design is, after all, not so much a distinct type of design as an illustration of the manner in which Dakota philosophy accounts for the origin of the present styles of decorative art."[48] I add that more than just decorative art is at stake here. We are touching on the core principles guiding the Sioux philosophical understanding of form itself, of all that structures cosmic primal options.

Designs that "emanate from the same sacred source" do not come without a price. According to Sioux belief, women who dreamed new designs were Double Women dreamers; this fact takes us directly to the mythic foundations for a rich array of cultural distinctions and for the operations that establish those distinctions along the lines of gender complementarity.[49] Lillian Fast Horse knew these traditions and on another occasion told about her own knowledge of the Double Women or Twin Women (see chapter 2). The Double Women were two women, different from each other, sometimes presented as opposites but always acting in consort and always bound one to the other. References clearly affirm that they control the assignment of gender roles and sometimes even change what they have assigned.[50] They also control spatial orientation and can cause people to gain heightened spatial perception or to lose it altogether.[51] When all this is brought in relation to the fact that they are the stated source of the traditional designs for women's art, we can begin to see a few of the connections between design, the whole idea of localized powers and feminine agency. Women who introduce certain designs (localizations of power) act in conjunction with spiritual beings who initiate the designs and the actions of the women who cooperate with them. But, as I stated earlier, there was a price to be paid. The portrait of the Sioux artist does not include seeking dreams of the Double Women who would grant the powers of innovative design.

No one sought dreams from the Double Women, who were actively feared, partly because they destabilized sexual identities and partly because they usurped individual volition. Men who encountered them became berdaches. Women experienced an intensification of their sexuality and were often accused of promiscuity. But no one ever denied the excellence and importance of the designs that came about through the intervention of the Double Women. These beings who were seen as the originators of designs were also among the most feared spirits.[52] Only the very strongest possessed the willpower to resist what they suggested. They usurped human willpower; yet those who were strong enough could sustain their influence and retain the artistic gifts they bestowed. Most women repeated the designs of others, but even these workers, engaged in the safe side of their craft, must have thought of all that was associated with the origins of the designs.

Women, through what they make (children or food—especially meat that has been cut and piled up on drying racks that "decorate" a camp—or tepees or abstract quill or beadwork designs), always bring into being the basic phenomenological forms in relation to which men can achieve their particular roles of giving immediate, named hence individualized, social significance to these forms. Fundamental to these considerations is the realization that it was a woman, the White Buffalo Cow Woman, who brought the Sacred Pipe to the Sioux and thereby established the forms of all the major ceremonies.[53] All these interconnected domains prove that we are not engaging in fanciful attribution when we assert that for the traditional Sioux, certain forms or designs possessed a dynamic vitality that was in every way tied to ideas of human agency in relation to spiritual powers.

We find further proof that nineteenth-century Sioux women were consciously aware of these ideas through an all but accidental allusion found in the James R. Walker papers. Walker observed, "Another peculiarity of the Sioux women's technique for beadwork of any kind is that they first mix the beads of all colors and then pick out each bead as it is to be used. This is because glass beads are made by white men who do not know how to control their potencies and by mixing the beads their potencies are equalized so that no bead may have the power to overcome other beads and the potency of the design will not be disturbed."[54]

Other ethnographers have recorded concrete evidence that certain designs were understood by the Sioux as localizations of powers. Royal B. Hassrick notes that the spider web and the dragonfly designs "implied kinship with Thunder and hence became protective in character."[55] Bit by bit, the evidence reveals how the form of culture and the form of women's art were analogies, one for the other; this seems to have been as true in the verbal arts as in the visual ones. Women tend to shape their autobiographical narratives to show this dynamic at work.[56] Ella Deloria is getting close to the wellspring of these practices when she introduces ideas about art into her discussion of culture change, moving quickly from considerations of change to references to women who dream new designs. She notes that culture change was continuous; then, without obvious transition and as her most important example, she notes that "new ideas of art, especially in the matter of design, were always appearing 'dreamed' by certain women whom the tribe regarded as being supernaturally endowed."[57]

While writing the text under discussion here, Lillian was calmly and thoughtfully describing an event that flowed from her many hours of meditating on the significance of her craft as a beadworker. Therefore, we have the argument of that concentrated attention as reason to look at how she instinctively followed the guidance of the tradition as she set her first noun apart from the other two by a deft stylistic distinction. But having spent her time working with powerful designs, she becomes part of another design, one being enacted as she lives out the effects of having spent time in the beadwork house.

Lillian's next nominal phrase, Our Father's House (literally the first noun in the Dakota version where that preliminary sentential position subordinates it to Beadwork House), is a quite precise historical designation, probably used in this instance without irony or cynicism. It refers to the entire complex of tribal government offices at the agency. The term *father* is a reference to the tribal agent. The ascription of kinship recalls a history of the use of performatives. Kinship provided a repertoire of behavioral styles, and anyone or any being who became a functioning part of Sioux life assumed that role by way of a designated kinship term. The ascription of kin terms was performative because the assignment of the term was supposed to mean that the person so designated would act in ways appropriate to the role. This performative dimension of kin terms was not understood by most non-Indians, who both explicitly accepted and betrayed such reference without any understanding of the wide-ranging kinship implications of the term. While Lillian was quite aware of how successive agents had failed in living up to what the term *father* implied to the Sioux, she nevertheless retained respect for the role itself. Therefore, the actual location where political power of all kinds was enacted remained, in her estimation, a site deserving of respect and a place imbued with power. Furthermore, political action was a role generally associated with masculine prerogatives, a historical aside that, in this case, accords with the actual position of Lillian's husband, whose arrival is the action of the second event.

The first event also introduces a temporal dimension to the narrative. The narrative conjunction between spatial and temporal categories begins at this point. In Dakota the temporal dimension is introduced with the words *na wana* (and now). The action from this point on gives narrative place to all that is implied through the nouns. Historical and individual action are conjoined. In a literal and figurative sense, Lillian Fast Horse's use of the phrase "and now" can appropriately be aligned with Paul Ricoeur's reference to the same phrase. He says that it marks the present of preoccupation and it is a "making-present" of that which has been awaited and will be retained by the memory.[58] Lillian instinctively recognizes the importance of this placement in time.

The second and third events are closely linked, but each implies a different set of decisions having to do with place and time and hence a different kind of participation in the thematics of time and place. All of the action in these two events is expressed in English through the verb *come*, but the Dakota has a much more nuanced series of verbs with which to refer to distinctions that give the entire episode its peculiar significance. The distinctions implied by the Dakota verbs are, in my opinion, significant enough to justify dividing the separate elements into discrete events, each with its own implied structure of significance. Features of significance connected with movement constitute a basic cognitive theme in Dakota culture. The complexity of this theme and its marking in the Dakota language set up this event distinction.

Since Lillian's text is so explicitly based on a day's travels, we can easily move from that fact to noting that for the Sioux, conscious movement is the basic trope for the energy of life. One can easily quote beliefs and myths about abstract movement in relation to the concrete differentiation of form. According to all the oldest known beliefs, origins are a matter of energy amid living form, which is itself habitation, creating the model for other forms of habitation. This belief, in its general outlines, is not unique to the Sioux, and I refer to a frequently quoted, well-known nineteenth-century articulation of the idea taken from Alice Fletcher and Francis La Flesche's study of the Omaha people. Because it expresses connections between Native ideas of form and concepts of human consciousness, this statement sets up considerations about categories of volition and sanction in relation to cognitive themes of movement among different spatial domains, the forms within which humans live and move: "An invisible and continuous life was believed to permeate all things, seen and unseen. This life manifests itself in two ways. First, by causing to move—all motion, all actions of mind or body are because of this invisible life; second, by causing permanency of structure and form, as in the rock, the physical features of the landscape, mountains, plains, streams, rivers, lakes, the animals and man. This invisible life was also conceived of as being similar to the will power of which man is conscious within himself—a power by which things are brought to pass."[59]

The primal life force manifests itself in movement and in whatever causes permanency in form. The Fletcher quotation adds an interesting and cognitively decisive correlative with its reference to the belief that human willpower as a cause of movement is also understood as evidence of how the primal life force functions.

Permanent form establishes a conceptual matrix that structures whole sectors of knowledge in terms of movement to and from centers or matrices, the most basic of which is the human mind itself, which, according to Sioux belief, extends outward from the human being and not just inward toward contained consciousness.

Although I doubt that Lillian Fast Horse had ever read Fletcher's statement or heard anything quite so conceptually inclusive, her narrative still illustrates its points with the sort of detail that lets us see how these concepts translated into modes of seeing, evaluating, and thinking. Lillian shows how "the invisible life" and the life of consciousness are both bound up with real experiences in definite places and times. Her narrative so directly dramatizes these basic beliefs because she most certainly possessed a pragmatic understanding of ways in which social thinking among her own Dakota people invoked a complex play between environmental qualities, the belief system, and the linguistic system. The dynamic interaction among these systems is revealed through the way the verbs show Lillian and Harry Fast Horse moving among the different spheres referentially established by the nouns. These same spheres imply how Lillian and Harry experience the volitional effects that are structured by each habitational domain.

The Dakota semantic domain that was intricately marked by these features of the belief system is constituted by the verbs of movement. Three sets of semantic distinctive features are evident from the linguistic data and exhibit sharp contrasts to comparable fields based on English. The relevant semantic features have been labeled as *direction*, *stage of completion*, and *location*. The resulting variables permit a highly condensed precision of reference that sustains cognitive coherence within the traditional worldview.

The origin and goal of human movement affect the significance of that movement through the way they entail human volition and freedom. Direct quotation from Boas and Deloria's "Dakota Grammar" can indicate how consciousness itself played into the formal dramas implied by culturally established spatial categories. Boas was struggling to use grammatical categories that derived from the Indo-European language family and could not, therefore, account very well for his data. Nevertheless, his examples let us glimpse how syntactic features of possession and sanction worked in relation to the semantic field constituted by verbs of movement. Ownership and belonging are closely related ideas in this worldview, and together they affect human freedom. A highly nuanced set of relationships between consciousness and place was part of the traditional worldview, and it undoubtedly leads to syntactic contrasts with English that strain the resources of grammatical description in English. Boas and Deloria explain, "Verbs of going and coming have peculiar forms expressing going and coming to a place where one belongs permanently or temporarily, clearly related to possessive forms, although differing from the more common forms. . . . The simple forms as well as the possessives (expressing going or coming back) have second datives."[60]

Deloria's English translations are actually descriptive glosses meant to illustrate how the datives include cognitive features that mark sanction (conscious, volitional agreement). She gives examples like *ikiciyaya*, which she glosses as "he has gone in his stead with his sanction." In addition to sanction, verbs of coming and going were marked for purpose. Again, the examples point toward distinctions most of us rarely, if ever, have occasion to take into account. The prefix *hiyu*, used for going away from where one belonged with a particular purpose in mind, could be further modified with possession so that going somewhere to get something that belonged to oneself could be distinguished from going somewhere to get something that belonged to someone else.

All of these referential permutations involve cognitive values that link them to a range of cultural phenomena and therefore establish them as a cognitive theme; but at this point in my analysis, I am still attempting a simple explication of Lillian's text, and all the references to grammar are brought into this essay as a way to illustrate how a traditional belief about movement as evidence of life translated into the cognitive and grammatical features that together form the cognitive theme. Lillian Fast Horse's verbs establish the permutations defining the significance of the movement among those spatial domains that her complex nominals sum up.

All of this lengthy survey stands behind my choice to let the English phrase "so we came" stand as an entire event with an implied internal structure. The Dakota is *canke ungliyayapi*, which, through the morpheme *gl*, is definitely and clearly marked for possession. It is glossed "to start to go to the place where one belongs." The fact that they planned to go directly home when their journey started is stated only in the nature of the verb. Something else has to happen on the trip to reveal that under the guidance of the spirits they will go elsewhere. Through its verbs, the narrative sets up a consistent moving back and forth between the perspectives of home, where conditions require conscious responsiveness, and those conditions existing in other spaces, conditions that make Lillian and Harry vulnerable to what "pushes" them somewhere other than what they had consciously chosen.

Like the previous two events, the fourth and fifth could be combined, but I argue that Lillian's active intervention has its thematic own structure. Up to this point, she has revealed herself as a beadworker but she has been following her husband's initiative. That changes when her active intervention alters their literal direction as well as the direction of subsequent events. She shows herself as the one who shapes the action. In every possible respect, her words design this narrative, this gentle series of events constructed entirely with language that gathers in the significance of the day's literal actions. Lillian notes that she is the one who thinks of a meeting at Solen, the town in which I lived. The active insertion of her spoken decision is definite and formal: *Canke hepe*, meaning "And so I said." This is the narrative move that shows Lillian to be the subject acting on behalf of the spirits to give direction to the whole event. Everything implied before in the narrative lies behind that "and so."

As soon as the trip to Solen begins, the English version of the event immediately gets repetitive. I designate the second use of "came" as a separate event, the fourth event, because the Dakota version uses two different verbs, which advance the action by showing changes in goal orientation. In the Dakota version the first verb (the third event) is *ku*, which shows a continuity of action with the previous verb. It refers to the fact that they just continued to come on back to where they belonged. But they don't arrive where they belong. They "come" to Solen, and that verbal action in Dakota (*hi*) (event four) is differently marked for possession. The verb *hi* designates arrival at a place not one's own. Between the two verbs, both the same in English, attention has been deflected away from home. They arrive in Solen but to no apparent purpose. There is no meeting. Lillian's assumption was misleading.

The action requires another agential intervention, and so we return to the plot level of this minidrama between the good spirits, presumably connected with the beadwork house and their gift to the Fast Horses, who find themselves at loose ends in Solen instead of at the home they had so definitely set out to reach when they left the tribal offices. With the fifth event the narrative shows Lillian redirecting events again. She speaks "canke hepe" (and so I said). She announces that they will go to my house. The verb designating movement to my house is simple undirected movement, *ya*. The fact that the next verb is *hi*, signaling yet another arrival at a place other than their home, is my reason for designating each movement as a separate event.

I designate the clause "so we came to the place" as the sixth event because it completes the triangulation of places and sets up the importance of the third one of those nouns that anchor the action. Because she has so definitely stylized the first two nouns, we expect that she will do the same with the third one just to maintain the symmetry of the composition. She does so but not immediately. First she simply highlights the fact of arrival. Then she situates me in relation to the Catholic Church and its rectory that she designates as a Holy Man's House.

The seventh event involves the reference to eating. With the final eighth event, we can note a slight but nevertheless interesting narrative change from what actually happened. Lillian's last assumed narrative position, her last "and so I said," occurs after eating and pronounces the meal to be good even though it was written while the meal was in early stages of preparation. That element of the narrative, while obviously consistent with basic courtesy, is also an evaluation of the entire sequence of events. Her pronouncement creates the work of art that this narrative is. She has made something memorable out of the fact that they have been pushed, perhaps as the Deloria translation of the proverb notes, they have "stumbled" to my place as part of a benevolent process that rewards them. Lillian's narrative gives quite literal domestic significance to the idea of being in the right place at the right time.

Within this verbal event, action has been communicated through a constant referential interplay between Dakota verbs and those stylized nouns. The verbs of the proverb prove to have their own value. We can begin to follow that verbal action by focusing on the verb in the quoted proverb, *pajekje unakaupi*. The dominant verb *unakaupi* is the first person plural of *akau*, which Deloria translates as "bringing something to someone."[61] It is a first form dative with the feature of sanction unmarked, whereas the second and third forms of the dative are distinguished through addition of semantic features of sanction. For example, *kicau* is glossed as "I bring his with his sanction." The fact that the verb refers to the way Lillian and her husband are being "pushed" or "brought" to my house without any particular sanction is exactly the point of her entire exercise. She shows how and why agency and control have shifted away from the human actors to the spirits doing the pushing (*pajekje*) along the road from Fort Yates to Solen. The operation of the entire narrative permits us, at the very least, to entertain the likelihood that Lillian is asserting that her beadwork repair was a process that put her into a relationship with spirits who did not want the partnership to end. So they stayed with her. She and her husband did not arrive alone; they came in company with the very spirits who pushed them and were with them every step of the way.

That stylistic turn is further emphasized by another feature of her particular wording of the proverb. Her English usage states that the spirits "loved us," and I further note that Deloria's transcription of the same proverb does not refer to spirits loving those they push along. It merely says that the spirits take them. Lillian's Dakota lexical choice for "love" is one that emphasizes neither benevolence nor companionship—both these forms of love are regularly expressed by other verbs; her usage emphasizes value. The root verb is *tehila*, which includes the notion of high value (another gloss is "expensive") and an unwillingness to part with something. So the Lakota version implies that because the spirits valued their relationship with her, they were unwilling to part with her company; therefore, they came along and pushed her to a feast. An entire day's activities had been the immediate pretext of that beneficent partnership and the entire scenario began "at the Beadwork House."

Where does all this extremely detailed analysis of Lillian's spontaneously produced bilingual texts lead us? First of all, it should demonstrate how the implicit narrative, the thematic cognitive structure, is deduced from a particular instance of narrative production. The implicit narrative depends on historical reconstruction of primary cultural presuppositions. That process gradually allows for the emergence of themes (in this case, themes related to the significance of place and movement between places). Together the themes shape a macrostructure that accounts for microstructural elements and stylistic choices. Because the themes are so fundamental to the culture itself, they consistently recur in various cultural practices from ordinary conversation to ceremonial practice; therefore, at the macrostructural level, they provide a basis for comparison among various speech acts. The whole process demonstrates, I believe, the necessity of using narrative rather than simple elicited assertions as the source for cognitive themes and sets. Lillian intuitively responded to the need for narrative when she expanded her single-sentence proverb into an imagistically condensed narrative, which points to the implicit narrative of cultural framing involving all the links between art and particular spatial dynamics. That relationship between the narrative surface structure and the implicit dynamics shaping that structure is itself a force, a kind of internal narrative energy, that directs style as well as content. My most general hypothesis about cognitive style follows from the way this simple text participates in and points toward other culturally distinctive narrative dynamics. That primary hypothesis postulates a linguistic process of transference controlled by the linguistic categories that are most directly expressive of the means whereby the culture has enacted the terms of its distinctiveness. This process occurs across the entire range of a culture's expressive resources. The dynamic of transference generates evidence of cognitive adaptation in ongoing interactive relationship to linguistic categories. The implicit narrative, the story behind the story, has the stability of determined historical reference and the dynamism of a constantly changing field of application. Lillian's spontaneously produced text gains its particular value from the way it demonstrates the continuity of certain semantic and pragmatic presuppositions persisting into the 1970s. My division of the episode into events, each of which implies its own relationship to a spatial domain, allows for comparison between Lillian's narrative and other Sioux narratives, most particularly her husband's (see chapter 2 for comparison with her husband's narratives).

My division into events also suggests some terms of cross-cultural comparison. For example, if I chose to move from this division to Labov and Waletsky's scheme, I would claim that the first event constitutes the orientation, events two to seven are the complication, and event eight is the evaluation. This kind of overview highlights the fact that virtually all the complicating elements are achieved by way of implications stated by those complex Dakota verbs that do not quite find any good English translation. The complication is language specific. Such comparison also draws attention to the fact that two out of the three stylized nouns whose particular realization practically demands attention to history occur as part of the orientation. We have an elegant formal realization of something we already knew, namely that history forms the threshold to understanding the complicating factors of human action.

Although the event structure may be arbitrary, the effort, in and of itself, dramatizes a series of relationships between different kinds of habitational conditions and the action that brings people into these conditions. To choose another example from the history of narrative study, if I were to set up a semiotic square for Lillian Fast Horse's narrative in the manner of Algirdas Greimas, I would set up the spaces of home and the spaces of a host as one set of contradictions; the other set would be volitional action and determined action. Volitional action and the space of a host thus appear as contraries, as do determined action and the spaces of home. Relations of implication are the most interesting aspect of what emerges from the semiotic square. In this instance, volitional action implies action toward home and determined action implies action toward the spaces of a host. It all works out exactly according to the terms of Lillian's original intention, but the formal structure is far less interesting than the precise stylistic details that make it live in a definite place and time.

If there is always a degree of arbitrariness in any formalistic exercise, it nevertheless reveals a frame for the implicit narrative that can make meaningful connections and explore the important dimensions of what constitutes the motive and energy of form. The historical basis gets at a cognitive set that grounds the exercise in an epistemologically sound manner. The rest is a matter of inference and interpretation. To use the words of the poet Eavan Boland, history gives us "the outlines underneath / the surface," with the surface, in this case, being the narrative. We start with "singing innuendos" and end, hopefully, with the resonance of truth.[62] As we observe how narrative is structured so as to return us to the same themes again and again, amid entirely new narrative territory, we are seeing what I call a cognitive style in action; we are seeing how different kinds of narrative show diverse and sometimes elusive evidence of the same cognitive themes. That is my task in the next chapter, in which I examine more narratives from Lillian and her husband.

In a very real sense, Lillian's narrative expansion is itself a supplemental commentary for the proverb that summarizes the implicit narrative. In analyzing the traditional Lakota *ohunkakan* (folktales), I consistently find that marking the cognitive valencies of major semantic fields reveals a culturally specific thematic structure (or implicit narrative) that is directly comparable to the way in which Lillian constructed her narrative. References to habitation and dwelling set up event structure just as they control the selection features that give cognitive force to the way verbs refer to interactional dynamics and to movement among different places of habitation, each of which places different demands on the individual. In the next chapter, I move away from the relatively mechanistic aspects of linguistic analysis as I present Harry and Lillian Fast Horse's repertoire of tales within their local context, and I present these narratives in terms of how they represent adaptations to the early reservation years. At this stage I move beyond the precise detailing of this chapter to a more inclusive consideration of what narrative conveys about the community at large.

The initial stages of analysis, as presented in this chapter, constitute a rather specialized task. Ongoing collaborative efforts to produce comparable case studies based on detailed linguistic analysis of texts would provide a significant base for other kinds of cultural studies. Few people will be prepared to engage in analysis for more than one culture, but that fact only argues for team efforts. Even within a single culture, gathering a sufficiently large database to make judgments about an entire community argues for team efforts. Together teams can establish the rich factual foundations that grant credibility to cultural studies.

From linguistic analysis to narrative performance to novelistic recasting of oral narrative, we can follow a trajectory of signification and a pattern of cognitive transformations that together constitute a cognitive style. The resulting implicit narrative summarizes themes of *indigenous cognition*, a technical term guaranteed to confuse people outside the fields of cognitive sciences because indigenous is a term carrying altogether different meaning in different political contexts, with the political contexts that most concern me here being the very ones most concerned with preserving strict definitions of indigenous. John W. Berry's definition immediately addresses the potential for confusion: "while not yet precisely defined, indigenous cognition is what people do cognitively in their daily lives, *whether in our own or in some other culture*. . . . In addition to emphasizing the mundane aspects of cognitive life, indigenous cognition involves the cognitive study of cognitive life, in the sense that it takes into account not only cognitive performances by individuals, data is also concerned with how people understand what they are doing and how they interpret it. Implicit also is the view that these subjective interpretations require investigation guided by the emic tradition in cognitive anthropology."[63]

Berry then gives his scientific definition of cognitive style. Cultures emphasize different cognitive goals and different ways of achieving those goals so that the tension between the local and universal leads to the position that there are "likely to be variable patterns of developed abilities that are functional in and adaptive to local contexts: these generically are cognitive styles."[64]

The *variable patterns*, the functional local adaptations of what may be universal abilities, are manifestations of the pragmatic specifications imposed by what is local; they reveal the culture-making dynamic across a broad spectrum of intellectual activities. Psychologists like Berry who study the entire range of human cognitive abilities as they test assumptions about relationships between universals and local and/or individual adaptations are still a long way from exploring how the cognitive styles they note through behavioral research, generally bound to discrete learning tasks and clearly specifiable cognitive schema, might work in relation to literary narratives where multiple schema interact and allow complex reactions on the part of all participants in the event of performing/reading/hearing. The workings of literary language with its expanded capacity to modulate and calibrate differences between the universal and the local constitute a narrative focus that involves different kinds of specialization.

For the literary critic, empirical analysis gives only the necessary informational foundation on which to build further hypotheses about what is emergent and therefore in the process of assuming a functional relationship to those basic cultural features that enable and support perceptions of continuity. Narrative, not only by virtue of its content but also by virtue of its structure and its style, dramatizes this interplay between established features of signification and whatever destabilizes meaning in the process of mediating new references. Information uncovered through empirical analysis of narrative significance launches the critic's descriptive trajectory, specifying the beginning stages, keeping them firmly grounded in cultural data and establishing the thresholds between the internal (and/or aesthetic) and the external (and/or social) determinants of the text.

All the necessary theoretical language should not obscure the fact that we all intuitively respond to cognitive style. We know when something different is going on; we know the breakdowns in communication that occur when styles clash. Historians, literary critics, psychologists, legal scholars, and diplomats are all addressing facets of this communicative context, this process of translation that goes beyond semantics into the conditioning impact of culture on daily linguistic usage.

The analysis of cognitive style does not give us any new critical theories, but it can recruit a lot of the tried and workable ones operating within different disciplinary fields, and the particular configuration of analytic methods is definitely new. Furthermore, it has finally brought me closer to the local power of narrative as it shapes communal coming-into-being; it has taught me more about spaces of the mind in relation to those quite literal geographical places. While I do not claim to be working in entirely new theoretical territory, I definitely do claim to have taken a new look at how storytellers have smuggled the secrets of local spaces into their tales and their lives.

In postcolonial cultures no one can resist the insistent interrogations that history imposes. Sometimes consciously, more often unconsciously, people feel the tug of many interpretive possibilities bound to different locales and different histories. Images, beliefs, and customs that derive from those beliefs all insinuate their way into awareness to become part of the "feeling" that reminds people another way of experiencing is possible. Moving across cultural boundaries, eyes wide open to the divisions, betrayals, and gifts of history, people go on seeking words to claim and account for their steady obsession with others.

2. The Narrating Community

In a poem titled "We Must Call a Meeting," the Native poet Joy Harjo demands her language to be given back and "build a house / Inside it." Her poem draws attention to the way in which language, as social practice, functions in a manner that is often poetically expressed by analogies to shelter. All the intricate nuances of local linguistic usages and associated bodily gestures subtend a sense of home and belonging; or, conversely, they can drive an individual who is out of touch with that local significance to an experience of radical homelessness. There is a rich experiential basis behind the claim that a community's formalized language "houses" the individual. Correspondingly, there is a communal history of individuation that informs the personal history of those who find their language in and through that communal process as the idiolect and the dialect move between the language of a place and the placement of language within the spaces of individual memory and psyche. Formal history tells the consequences of all this, and legend holds history to its popular local task. Or, to use the language of Michel de Certeau, historiography "recounts in the past tense the strategies of instituted powers" while "the 'fabulous' stories offer their audience a repertory of tactics for future use."[1]

But even as we give quick, casual assent to these basic and thoroughly functional metaphoric statements, scholars remain theoretically undecided about how to make the transitions from actual local narratives to the theoretical commentary that situates them. Therefore, studying the narrating community is a task that is routinely honored as a desirable agenda but seldom pursued in any but the most selective fashion.[2] Obviously, selectivity at the level of data is necessary; but if we keep in mind that our goal is one of documenting how narrative updates, renews, and refashions a community's self-identity, then that extremely general goal can give a critical frame for the analysis of any activity that prompts people to reflect on and articulate their relationship to local language by analogy to the shelter that is home. Our goal is to show how the idiom "mother tongue" echoes through knowing, feeling, and the rhetorical conventions expressing both.

Many years ago now, I came to understand life in one Native community through the way its narratives allowed me to see its losses in relation to evidence of what has sustained belief in local initiative and creativity. In retrospect I realize how I viewed most of the ordinary events of daily life through the lenses provided by different kinds of narrative because the very people who had the most influence on the way I thought about my experiences there were also initiating me into the village's narrative traditions—all sorts of traditions, from stories of personal experiences to oral history and even the more formal legends and myths. That community was Cannon Ball, North Dakota, on the Standing Rock Sioux Reservation. It is the home of the Yanktonai Sioux people. The two individuals who taught me local tales were Harry and Lillian Fast Horse. Many others also told me stories, and the entire community taught me how to contextualize that learning; but the main part, the heart and soul of what I learned, came from the Fast Horses. As the years pass, my obligation to respond to these two extraordinary people with my own considered and informed tribute to their ability to transmit a vision of communal hope remains with me, and it continues to challenge me to ask new and ever harder questions about the role of narrative in maintaining communal identity.

Their lives, their tales, and the narratives that maintain identity in Cannon Ball deserve a book-length study. But some thoughts about Harry and Lillian Fast Horse's stories and their function within the community can anticipate that longer and truer project. To write that book I would need to live in Cannon Ball again to learn the details of how people have changed. I would also have to assess that other distance, the temporal one that has taken me to many other parts of the world, inevitably giving me new perspectives from which to chart how my early views may have been cluttered by private hopes and ignorances. Perhaps that more complete study should be done by someone else. Ideally it would be someone from Standing Rock Reservation, thereby setting up a productive discursive distance and debate between my view and theirs. It is with that hope that I begin the project at last. My belief that ordinary, commonly told narratives reveal traces of cognitive features moving through a universe of meaning that is every bit as dynamic and complex as the physical cosmos is supported by the way that people in Cannon Ball found narrative rejoinders to the play of forces that threatened to decenter and disrupt their individual and communal identity.

During part of the time that I lived in Cannon Ball, I taught adult education classes. I also experimented with various ways to help people use government commodity foods. A phrase like "help people use" is absurdly inadequate and potentially misleading. Most of the food in question came in white paper bags marked with black lines and letters. The bags were labeled "USDA" (United States Department of Agriculture). They looked like prototypical packaging for what later became a short-lived phase of American generic marketing. We presumed that the USDA thought the foods so ordinary everyone would recognize them. That was definitely the case for the butter, cheese, and even the powdered eggs; but for several other products it was a false presumption. Every time I opened one of those mystery containers, I proceeded through a series of questions. What is it? How can we possibly prepare it so that anyone will want to eat it? Does it have enough nutritional value to make the whole process worthwhile? Working out daily answers to those questions and sharing the results with anyone willing to taste-test them led to a lot of good conversation, laughter, and many a ridiculous anecdote, even one song, none of which has any but the most indirect academic significance.

Yet the experiments did draw attention and indirectly they led to my learning what really does have significance well beyond the confines of one district on Standing Rock Reservation. Harry and Lillian Fast Horse heard about the goings-on at the house where I was living, and they began to visit and to tell their stories about the community. Then one day, sitting in the kitchen, coffee cup in hand, Harry announced that he wanted me to tape-record some of his tales for use in the schools because the children were not learning what they needed to know about "how things are for us Indians here." At the time he did not have a tape recorder. I did. That simple fact led to a joint enterprise that lasted well beyond my summer job of identifying mysterious government commodity foodstuffs. Harry understood that legal proceedings depended on records of local understanding, and he wanted to be sure that his perspective became part of the larger record. He was also well aware that his status within the community involved responsibilities to local children, and that made him eager to cooperate with reform initiatives in the local school system. For the next two years Harry and I did workshops for the area's teachers, and we tried to help them see the possibilities of local history and culture in relation to other things they were teaching. But those subsequent days of trying to work with school authorities were hard to predict during that first summer, when Harry decided that the time had come to record his repertoire of narratives and I began to use those narratives to understand other aspects of what I was experiencing at Standing Rock.

My Cannon Ball education had actually begun during my very first nearly sleepless night there. Dogs, coyotes, and other wild animals set up such an insistent nightlong howling that, by comparison, city sounds and sirens seemed mere white noise. The next day when I wanted to know whether the wild nocturnal concert had been the exception or the rule, I was told that the area was generally noisy because the dogs and coyotes echoed the ghosts and spirits who were lamenting the loss of the former village site. The village that all the older people recalled with great and fond detail is now covered by floodwaters from the Oahe Dam, constructed in the 1950s. My neighbors went on to tell me that my first few nights there would almost certainly be the loudest while the spirits got used to me, but I could not really expect very much quiet in a place where so much had been lost that even the coyotes continued to protest. And so, in a dizzy, hot haze of fatigue, I began to examine my surroundings from the perspective of losses that the people, the animals, even the trees had sustained.

It was an appropriate visual and intellectual angle from which to examine things, even as I gradually learned about other features of community life that involved celebration, laughter, and a determined search for an economically improved future. At that time most of the dwellings were still the one- or two-room "six fifty houses," so called because the government gave every family six hundred and fifty dollars to build new houses when the ones they had had near the river were covered with floodwaters. At least that was the story that everyone repeated with assurance. Whatever the monetary facts of that settlement, the story was entirely credible. The houses were minimal, one- and two-room log and adobe shelters scattered to the north and west of where I lived. To the east I could see only the Missouri River dammed to extraordinary width by the Oahe Dam so that all of the agriculturally rich bottomland was flooded. The tops of trees that had once given shelter from summer sun and year-round driving winds were still evident as leafless skeletons standing slightly above the waters. The sight of those tall, reaching, dead branches would not have connoted such insistent howling grief if there had been more trees on the remaining land, but vegetation of any kind was rare on those semiarid bluffs, and trees were a seldom-cultivated exception. Even historians like Elwyn Robinson fell into anthropomorphic poetic language when they wrote about the many species of trees that came into the state from eastern regions but quickly "retreated to the riverbank because the thin, light soil of the Missouri Plateau rarely supports anything but shrubs."[3]

To the southeast of where I lived, I could glimpse the Community Center, at the very edge of the waters. That simple, barnlike, medium-sized building was the social and symbolic but by no means the geographic center of the community. Coming to know its interlocking practical and imaginative significances meant taking one's first step toward comprehending other community dynamics, a step I learned about as soon as I tried to find people who would tell me what I needed and wanted to know. Almost everyone told me, in one way or another, that before I could expect to accomplish much of anything, I should take time just to look around and to listen to what people said about the day-by-day events that were behind the ordinary and enduring feel of the village. They added that the place for the best listening was definitely the Community Center.

My notes include a series of quoted comments about that building, erected in 1892 to serve as a sub–issue station for the food rations that were so crucial during those first reservation years when the buffalo were gone and the beef herds had not yet been developed. It was the oldest surviving building in Cannon Ball. The social role of the Community Center had changed little since it was first built. Government commodity foods were still distributed there, and it remained the place for meetings and gatherings of all kinds. Only by considering it as a symbol of communal continuity could I sense the significance that people attached to that entirely functional, aesthetically unappealing building. Thomas Black Hoop's comments were typical of the way that reference to the center could and often did encompass all of Cannon Ball's history. He managed to cram references to the entire history of the community into a few short, conversational sentences that recalled the "old days before the flood." "We came to Cannon Ball with Chief Two Bears. Have you been to the Community Center yet? That's the oldest building here in Cannon Ball. It was built in the old days before the flood. We used to have big root cellars there where we stored food. They were in the side of the hill and are all flooded now. On ration days everyone gets together and talks there. That's our oldest building."

As I soon learned, such casually condensed history lessons were no exception. An entire generation seemed to rehearse a segment of history every time they spoke about landmarks like the Community Center. Ambrose Eagle Boy made telling leaps from history to architectural reference to patterns of community interaction as he introduced himself to me, and, like Thomas Black Hoop, he urged me to spend time at the community center. "I am one of the old-timers. My father was the catechist for the first priest here. See that building over there? That's the Community Center. That's about all we've got left from the old days. We had good times there. Everybody got together. We had district council meetings there once a month. Still do. That's where you got to go to get to know Cannon Ball."

The history of the community may be symbolized by the Community Center, but like any other symbol, this one requires considerable specification if it is to be understood by outsiders or even by younger members of the community, and the Sioux at Cannon Ball were by no means indifferent to the importance of exact, written historical documentation to support their oral historical data. That is partly because the primary motive behind their current preoccupation with historical documentation derives from their legal claim to land and water rights. As soon as Thomas Black Hoop learned of my interest in the community's history, he brought me his copy of the report that Harry H. Anderson had prepared for the Indian Claims Commission.[4] Several copies of this report were circulating in the community. Thomas Black Hoop's was a water-stained, well-thumbed document that he quoted whenever he needed official authorization for his statements about local history and land claims. The purposes of Anderson's forty-five-page historical study corresponded exactly with the reasons that Cannon Ball people have for treasuring it as the written basis for legal claims, some of which have been officially filed while some, perhaps, will never be filed. But juridical processes have definitely established a set of assumptions about the function of historical narrative that are an inescapable part of the reservation political environment. History, as a word and as an idea, has taken on iconic significance that exists quite apart from any particular content even as it motivates the Cannon Ball people to gather facts related to land use and water rights, facts that they hold in trust for their children.

Anderson expressed his own purposes in his foreword, and that brief statement with its precise surveyor's references can explain in and of itself why his official report competed with the Sioux translation of the Bible as the most valued written document in the community. He was stating facts related to land use and occupation, data exact enough for any legal setting. That very precision takes on the quality of a promise to the community because no one can argue with it. "My assignment in this case was to determine, as of the time of the Treaty of April 29, 1868 and back to the time of the Louisiana Purchase of 1803 and as long before that as documents permit, who used and occupied the country whose exterior boundaries are defined by Stations 1 through 23 as shown on the wall map. . . . Later, I was directed to limit my written report to that portion of the area lying east of the Missouri River and this report is so limited."[5]

The Yanktonai Sioux living on the west side of the Missouri River, at the edges of the territory flooded in 1961, carefully studied the scientifically surveyed and authoritatively documented history of their claims. Anderson's pamphlet, written for the Indian Claims Commission, took on added value when the Oahe Dam resulted in even further land loss. At least it did for Thomas Black Hoop, Harry and Lillian Fast Horse, and others of their generation. Therefore, some of that historical documentation should preface any examination of the narrative traditions whose regular conversational telling linked history to daily life as people speculated on what would happen next in their economically underdeveloped community. Such speculation was inevitable because the unemployment rate for the village was usually well above 50 percent. To find work, people had to go elsewhere, and the permanent resettlement of the best young people threatened the very survival of the village and the cultural identity that village life sustains even for those who live elsewhere. People genuinely feared the loss of that identity, just as they recognized the need for good jobs, better education, and all the benefits of economic security. Talk of convincing some corporation to build a factory in the area was common, and such talk is an index to belief in renewing general communal vitality. In Cannon Ball, history is recalled across the warp of economic depression, and those facts remaining in oral tradition are repeated because they support belief in economic self-determination.

In his report Anderson competently and quickly summarized the assignments of lands to different Sioux bands, thus noting the rudiments of today's political district organization within different reservation boundaries. These facts are, of course, well known to Cannon Ball residents, but reciting them and even reading them serves as a way of framing the grand sweep of events that bit by inexorable bit whittled Sioux lands to their current size. "The Sioux Indians whose history is to be examined in this report are the Pine Ridge, Rosebud, Lower Brule, Crow Creek, Cheyenne River, Standing Rock, Santee, and Fort Peck Sioux tribes. At the present time nearly all of the descendants of the Teton and Yanktonai Sioux who live on reservations may be identified as follows: the Oglalas on Pine Ridge; the Brules on Rosebud; the Lower Yanktonais on Crow Creek; the Lower Brules on Lower Brule; the Miniconjous, Sans Arcs, Two Kettles and Blackfeet on Cheyenne River; and the Hunkpapapa, Blackfeet and Upper Yanktonais on Standing Rock."[6]

When I lived there, the Upper Yanktonai at Cannon Ball still possessed a cultural distinctiveness that set them apart from other bands on the Standing Rock Reservation. One community leader, Charles Shell Track, emphasized this distinctiveness in his summary of community history, asserting that "the Yanktonai never lived with the western Sioux together in one camp. They lived close together but they didn't mix."

The 1823 report of William H. Keating and Stephen H. Long,[7] as quoted by Anderson, includes a short description of early-nineteenth-century Yanktonai life, and from this one can deduce aspects of their continuing and regular contact with other northern tribes like the Ojibwes, the Mandan-Hidatsas, and the Arikaras: "This is one of the most important tribes, as its population amounts to one-fifth of the whole nation. They have no fixed residence, but dwell in fine skin lodges, well dressed and decorated. Their hunting grounds are very extensive, spreading from the Red River to the Missouri. They frequent for purposes of trade, Lake Travers, Big Stone Lake, and the Shienne River. Their principal chief is Wanotan, (the Charger)."[8]

Their trade definitely included that most important of all commodities, information, especially political information and strategies for dealing with the encroaching dominance of the United States federal government. In 1867, after the Fetterman Battle, the United States sent a commission made up of military officers and prominent civilians to confer with the Sioux. At Crow Creek on June 5, 1867, members of this commission met with the Yanktonai. Records of that meeting include a comment by Two Bears, the leader of the Cannon Ball community. His statement, recorded by the commission and quoted by Anderson, also lived on as an often-repeated part of the oral tradition of the Cannon Ball community. Two Bears stated unequivocally, "My tribe live upon both sides of the Missouri River." Another of Two Bears's recorded statements echoes in Standing Rock politics today: "Now I will tell you one thing that I don't like: you are going to put all the tribes together and I do not approve of it. I speak for my own band; our country is on the other side of the river—we are the Yanktonai. The trouble was begun by the whites rushing into our country. There is one thing that I must tell you: though I want to make peace, yet I don't want to sell my land to the whites. It is the whites who will break the treaty, not us. I don't give permission to any white man to chop wood and get hay in our country."[9]

To the Cannon Ball residents who read these statements of their founder and leader in the circulating copies of the Anderson report, the sight of the drowned trees showing above the waters stands as proof that Two Bears had not even imagined the worst. No one can chop wood or get hay on the best lands now, and no one who stays in the community can forget that fact. Michael Lawson in *Dammed Indians* has summarized the effects of the Oahe Reservoir on the Indian lands:

> *The ecological balance of the entire region, and that of the Dakotas, in particular, has been permanently upset by the destruction of flora and fauna. The inundation of precious forests and bottomlands not only eliminated the natural wildlife habitat but also created serious erosion problems. . . . The marine environment has also been subjected to increased attacks from chemical and bacteriological agents introduced by the runoff or discharge of organic and solid waste from commercial feedlots and by residues from agricultural chemicals. . . . Long praised for the harmony that they traditionally established with their environment, the Sioux are agonizingly aware of these problems.*

Lawson concludes one chapter with a quotation from a local leader, who says, "We look back now to see that we lost everything . . . we had the best part of our life in that area."[10] In Cannon Ball, Charles Shell Track echoed that sentiment: "Then the Oahe Dam water backwatered and there's nothing left. No railroad, no depot, no trees, nothing."

The history of double displacement in less than a century affects every aspect of life in the community, and narrative as an index of community dynamics indicates shifts in most of the obvious structures and themes aligning prereservation narratives to the stable features of local social dynamics. The old themes could have only the relevance of remembered culture once the people had settled on the bluffs above the floodwaters. While such memory has its irrefutable importance, it can only indirectly motivate hope for a future under drastically changed conditions. In a sense, after the flood, the old narrative forms were orphaned, using the concept of orphan as it applied in prereservation culture to anyone cut off from the developmental conditions that kinship established and signified. Following through with the metaphor, we can say that the modern narratives have had to be adopted. Just as the ceremonial adoption of individuals simultaneously creates a transversal realignment of a whole series of other kinship relationships, so too the local adoption of western historiographic forms realigns the entire system of narrative functions within the narrating community. As Michel de Certeau states, "*A way of using imposed systems constitutes the resistance to the historical law of the state* of affairs and its dogmatic legitimations. A practice of the order constructed by others redistributes its space; it creates at least a certain play in that order, a space for maneuvers of unequal forces and for utopian points of reference."[11]

In Cannon Ball oral history is the ordinary continuing narrative practice that best accounts for the way people use other narrative genres, whether imposed from outside or developed from within. As the generative force behind virtually all current political thinking, oral history has had to take on many of the roles that formal myth once performed, most notably the task of addressing why the people inhabit certain lands and of explaining how basic cultural resources correspond to daily behavior. Oral history is closely aligned with personal history so that one leads naturally to the other. The cognitive structures of history serve a definite pragmatic and political function in that they set up a dynamic interplay among the presuppositions informing the performance of all narrative genres. We can make the move from theory to practice by noting how Charles Shell Track gives two contrasting historical explanations for the name of the town. Shell Track recalls that on the Parkins ranch "there were natural rocks about three feet around . . . Parkins got them from the hillside and strung them along a chain. They called it Cannon Ball Ranch." But this historical reference is accompanied by another relying on religious rather than colonial reference. When the older Yanktonai thought about stones in connection to the village name, they recalled rocks that were somewhat farther west, stones on which they believed the spirits once wrote, constantly updating their hieroglyphically coded advice and proving that a kind of arche-writing lies at the foundation of the tradition and the town. Or, at least that was what Charles Shell Track stated: "There is a stone way out west about seventy miles. It was standing up and it had Indian markings on it—sign language. People going through made that a first stop. They said, 'God (no, not God, the Holy Spirit) is here.' And it's really something that's written on there. . . . The next day the writing changes. . . . The stone is still there."

The style in which the Cannon Ball people think about and transmit history is one that borrows from and relies on the performance conditions and the semantic and pragmatic presuppositions that supported mythic narrative through time. This process of transference of presuppositions from myth to history no doubt happens in other communities, both Indian and non-Indian. What I am trying to show through this narrative analysis is a method that allows us to recognize and document the process. And, in relation to legal claims, the collective historical memory returns to mythic notions of origins for some of the epistemic force that explains why the people fight so hard for the ongoing claims.[12]

For someone like me, once professionally inclined to value the more formal structures of myth and legend above the almost conversational structure of Cannon Ball's oral history, it took a long time to realize how important the redistribution of narrative functions in favor of history was for the health of the community. Local leaders like Harry Fast Horse had progressively updated a whole system of narrative dynamics in order to gather the memories of a proud communal past into a thoroughly pragmatic vision of a workable future. Harry had made communal and personal history into a means for calibrating the significance of political history and adjusting it to local need and individual critique. Of course, people like Harry did not think in these theoretical terms. They simply responded intelligently to their understanding of what narrative is supposed to do in a traditional Sioux community. Referring to the existential circumstances of one's own life as a way to give concrete reference to a process of adaptation for the entire group has always been a hallmark of Sioux narrative traditions.

In his report Anderson was quite rigidly bound by the precise historiographic conventions of bureaucratic rhetoric. Other documents give us a more humanly focused view of life in Cannon Ball during the early years of the century. Aaron McGaffey Beede, first an Episcopal priest, then a district judge, took copious, if random, notes about life there. Only some of this material is available and among this only some is legible. One brief passage recalls life at its best in the village before the Oahe floodwaters. He notes that the Indians of the Cannon Ball district "have fairly comfortable homes with food and clothing sufficient for health and many of them have remarkably good homes with many luxuries. They labor at agriculture and stock raising similarly as whitemen do in the vicinity. Nearly all of them speak the English language, many of them read newspapers and books and are as well posted as white people in the vicinity. As a group, they are better posted than some groups of white people that may be found in the state."[13]

The unpublished Beede manuscripts present a documented view of the community that comes as close as any we can find to giving an insider's view of the first reservation years, the time of Harry and Lillian's youth, when the people were putting the war years behind them and reassessing all their options. The economic outlook was questionable, but the ranching and farming possibilities offered a coherent economic vision for the future, one that allowed the Sioux to maintain some features of their lifestyle as they anticipated new cultural developments. Leaders like Beede were optimistic. But the Pick-Sloan Plan establishing the Oahe Reservoir would severely test everyone's optimism.

When I read the preface to Elizabeth Cook-Lynn's novel *From the River's Edge* (1991), I recognized a haunting evocation of feelings that I had known as I looked out at the waters east of Cannon Ball covering the farmlands and the "remarkably good homes" that the Cannon Ball Sioux had built during the early reservation years. Cook-Lynn, a Santee Sioux, was writing about the same floodwaters that I saw from my bedroom window. She was writing from the perspective of other communities farther down the river, but the same emotions echo all along the river, from north to south, along with the cries of the coyotes and the birds, as river, animals, and people all move through Sioux country. Her language flows directly from the bonds between history and myth that one always senses in a place like Cannon Ball. These bonds are as basic to the mental atmosphere of the place as oxygen is to the physical one. She expresses so well how the web woven of myth, history, politics, and human desire imposes its contemporary responsibilities. Cook-Lynn knows that however one thinks about the spirits of the people who inhabited the old villages, they are remembered by descendants who live on the arid bluffs. These children and grandchildren still hold to their own sense of history, and they still believe that it is just as important to build with language as with wood in order to shelter the community's children.

Cook-Lynn is an accomplished journalist, scholar, and creative writer, and her work translates local ideas and images into forms that communicate globally. She can evoke the feel of a place saturated by communal history in paragraphs that could have been written only by someone who has lived in that country during every season and has watched birth and death along the banks of a river no longer left to shape its own floodplains. Harry and Lillian Fast Horse communicated comparable images and awareness of responsibilities, but they did so in a quite different manner. Their messages came coded according to the narrative requirements of the very community whose history they were transmitting, and so there is in even the simplest fragment the traces of older and endangered narrative sources.

Cannon Ball's Narrative Traditions

As I anticipated the recording project with Harry and Lillian Fast Horse, I imagined myself collecting artistic treasures that would equal the fine tales that scholars like Ella Deloria and Martha Warren Beckwith had recorded approximately fifty years before me.[14] To my initial disappointment and my later appreciation, the narratives that I actually did record were nothing like the richly elaborated ones my predecessors had found and preserved. But then, neither was the community anything like the old village where Two Bears had been the leader. His youngest wife was still there to remind me of that fact. She was more than a hundred years old when I was in Cannon Ball, so I heard acute assessments of social changes from someone who had seen them all and judged them with the firm determination of a woman who is so sure of her own values that she can refer to Sitting Bull not as a heroic figure known throughout the world, but as someone who was her husband's political opponent and about whom the young women had gossiped because no attractive woman ever missed his attention.

The tales that I learned from Harry and Lillian Fast Horse were in every possible way keyed to the task of explaining "how life is in this place," and that pragmatic endeavor rightly drafted all features of style and content to a task of cunning narrative economy. None of this should be surprising; yet in community after community whenever someone sets out to record traditional narrative, the question arises anew about how to discern traces of an older style and structure amid drastic alterations. Discernible and defensible continuity matters. This is due, in part, to individual desires and needs to identify with a community, its history and symbolic resources. But, as noted above, American Indian communities have additional legal reasons for seeking defensible evidence of cultural continuity deriving from treaty rights. Once I began to grasp how the narratives that I was hearing could be understood against the background of the very tradition from which these fragments seemed such sharp departures, I could also see that I was collecting evidence of how the people had bridged the historical gaps between what they remembered of prereservation life and the reservation era, which was itself divided into a period before the Oahe Dam had flooded the bottomlands and the period after it. These sharp historical divisions span so short a time period that Harry and Lillian had personally lived through most of the radical changes in the lifeways of the Yanktonai and Blackfeet bands of Sioux.

Born in 1900, Harry was the son of Paul Fast Horse. The family had come to Cannon Ball with Chief Two Bears's band in 1878, so the Fast Horses are one of the town's founding families. Harry's personal sense of having a clear right to power and authority within the community derived from his knowledge that he was in a direct line of descent from men who had for generations assumed leadership responsibility within the band. This family history was the source of much of his authority and pride, so Harry wanted no confusion about his ancestry. He drew a genealogical diagram for me showing how Two Bears had had three wives with the descendants of each, who assumed distinct surnames. That history gave a sociohistorical foundation to the emotional emphasis within Harry's statement that "the Yanktonai are my people; Cannon Ball is my place."

The fundamental importance of Harry's exact reference to place is such that almost all narrative elements can be traced back to it. The first time that Harry and Lillian Fast Horse and I met to record stories, we stayed outdoors and recorded the initial comments in full view of the Missouri River. It was one of those rare days when the wind had diminished to a breeze and the summer sun gave just the right warmth and light so that the bend of the river where the Fast Horses had their home seemed the perfect place to begin the project. Lillian brought chairs out from their log cabin. We all talked randomly while she made some lemonade. Then, sitting in a circle, we began to record. Clearly both Harry and Lillian considered it an occasion of importance. Harry held the microphone, treating it as though it were an instrument with ritual significance. He began the event with an unvarying statement that he consistently used to initiate a storytelling session. Even his vocal intonation stayed the same as he faithfully repeated this formula, evoking the image of the village now beneath the floodwaters. As he did so, he also linked his exact geographical position in that lost village to his current authority as a local historian and storyteller. "I'm Harry Fast Horse. I was born May 31, 1900. The Cannon Ball post office used to be across the river. Our depot when the first railroad came in 1906 was there. I was born there."

That solemn linkage between geography and historiographic authority is fundamental, not just as a conventionalized way of beginning a session but as a key to the cognitive and stylistic principles guiding the development of all the subsequent tales. It is not merely the statement of an individual; it is also evidence of a historical process that gives legitimate significance to the idea that where one is implies basic features of who one is; cultural placement summarizes identity. The subjective positioning in Harry's autobiographical statements depended on a listener's capacity to grasp that the narrating subject represents a communal position. It is a traditionally authorized position; the future of the narrating subject is assumed to be directly bound to the collective future. When the narrator assumes that stance, he also assumes responsibility for carrying out a traditional act. However, at first I understood none of that implicit cognitive and figurative energy. It took me a long time to learn how much cultural history went into the sparse wording of this opening phrase. The epistemic foundational force implied by its status as historical summation is what makes it a cornerstone for all the narratives built on it.

As it happened, my most crucial clue about its pragmatic significance came to me entirely by accident. One afternoon, while Harry and I were giving a workshop for local teachers, we gave them a coffee break and the two of us went outside. We were quietly gathering our ideas about the next phase of our work. Harry broke the companionable silence by pointing to a hill and saying that just beyond that hill was the place where he had grown up. That location was a good ten miles from the old village. Why then does the stylized reference to his dwelling in the old village have such recurring significance as a way of introducing his stories when he had lived elsewhere for most of his life? I had to talk to Harry and study many other aspects of the prereservation culture and history before I could get at some of the important significance implied by his always-solemn recurrent introductory statement.

After I had analyzed all the previously recorded Sioux tales that I could find, I began to find various connections between Harry's apparently straightforward autobiographical motif and basic features of Sioux narrative dynamics. Event by event analysis of prereservation tales in the original languages reveals distinctive event and thematic structures, all of which depend on the way Sioux spatial categories establish metaphoric significance. (See chapter 1 for further details about event structure in traditional tales.) One of the most easily discernible patterns of variation occurring among some of the best known and most frequently narrated tales depends on references to dwelling places that act as metaphors of prestige and authority. In tale after tale a hero's leadership status is signified by a brief reference to where he lives in the village. A common motif asserts that the hero who has successfully accomplished some sequence of traditionally prescribed grand adventures concludes it all by going back home, where he quietly "lived at the center of the village." Sioux listeners, of course, would understand the motif as quite other than calm retreat from hazardous duty. The center of the village—where, in fact, no one really lived—represented local tribal authority. Traditional Sioux listeners would interpret it all to mean that mythic heroes had to manage the vagaries of local politics as well as the zestful options of distant conquests.

Bringing all this back to Harry's introductory motif, we can see some of the most obvious connections. He always began a session with his solemn formal reminder that he belonged at the center of the village; that actual site is now buried under floodwaters. He voices the memory of what remains from those prereservoir days. His language must evoke a visually precise but emblematic and metonymic reconstruction of what authorizes his current status; reference to his exact position in the flooded village fills the bill admirably. In this respect, his way of emblematically setting forth the rudimentary surviving traces of historical knowledge is exactly in accord with the traditional way in which Sioux men linked art (verbal and visual) and historical memory.

In the prereservation environment, men's art was clearly understood as a way of inscribing and thereby transmitting the memory of emblematic events whose function was to remind people how abstract possibility translated into concrete accomplishment. The concrete, not the abstract, was privileged in men's art whereas the reverse was true for women. The masculine role was one of proving the value of the culture's store of abstractions by presenting the evidence of concrete realizations. Whether the men drew evidence of their accomplishments on tepee covers or in winter counts, the basic message was the same. The individual or the group exists at the point of conjunction between abstract and concrete, between possibility and realization, and men are the agents achieving that epistemological and social conjunction.[15] The ethnographic details supporting this assertion emerge in relation to all those different occasions when men used the representational designs that they had drawn to commemorate specific achievements. Men drew evidence of their exploits on tepee covers. Men also used representational drawings as autobiographical accounting. In his classic study of Sioux visual arts, Clark Wissler noted that the Sioux artist "singled out those qualities and situations that are not only wonderful from his point of view, but greatly to be desired as means to his own ends. He then proceeds on the assumption that these originate in and are due to some hidden agency, from which it follows that, if he can put himself in the place of one of the favored living creatures, he will, in turn, be the object on which this hidden agency will act."[16]

Considerable other evidence can support Wissler's perceptions about how closely verbal presentation and graphic representation were bound up with local understandings about the continuity of cultural life. The formally structured representations of men's *achievements* had irreplaceable instrumental value as the means for transmitting the implied cultural significance of their actions to their descendants. This mode of transmission was consistently and redundantly articulated in a range of different customs and ceremonies in the prereservation culture. The disjunctions imposed by reservation history intensified the need for careful teaching about how men realized their particular role in transmitting cultural life. At the same time it radically changed the conditions under which this role could be realized. Perceiving the continuities between the traditional warrior/hunter role and the reservation farmer or rancher required precise imaginative reconstruction and intervention. Harry Fast Horse's tales can be read as a set of strategies providing that intervention. He gives an emblematic character to carefully chosen events in the lives of ordinary people. In the way that he structures that choice of event, though, there is always a background against which individual action, even when it leads to defeat, acquires strategic interpretation that shows how the Cannon Ball community can go beyond any narrated defeat. Through the way that he brought stories into relationship with each other and divided his repertoire into sessions, he was making the most of a montage technique, so that the meaning of each element in a session reflected on every other one. The perfect visual image for this technique is found in the pictorial arts where men drew autobiographical accounts in which visual elements were mnemonic devices.[17] Although each of Harry's tales had a formal identity of its own, the overarching structure that bound each session established a significance that went beyond the content of any one tale. By the time we actually tape-recorded the tales, I had heard most of them at least once before as we had all sat around my kitchen table, drinking strong coffee and eating whatever I had managed to cook during the day.

As I heard sessions repeated I realized that all the tales were part of some still larger pattern that was, in turn, bound up with other village patterns. To use one of Dell Hymes's comments, Harry's stories were definitely "a breakthrough into performance," and that breakthrough was, to continue in Hymes's terms, bound to Harry's authority to interpret, report, and repeat traditional understandings deriving from the traditional forms.[18] What emerges through Harry's performance is the continuing force of those cognitive features that fall under the heading of "habitational conditionality," as these can be shown to work within various genres of traditional Sioux narrative (see chapter 1 for a more detailed elaboration). These features have the status of cognitive themes. They set up the presuppositions for narratives throughout the community. Individual speakers simply realize them in distinctive fashion.

That first day in the sun, all of the items that Harry and I recorded were autobiographical fragments. Later, as I came to understand better the way these fragments worked, I also came to appreciate how rich an intersection between social history and narrative structure they reveal and how powerfully they focus the constitutive tasks of subjective agency within the various and rapidly changing economies of early reservation culture. As discursive structures, they represent inversions and transformations of older heroic tales, thereby keeping alive the remembered motivational energies linked to the older tales. Even as they evoke and provoke memories, these truncated fragments redirect the affective energy connected with the memories. The discursive strategy of explanatory juxtaposition reveals itself as a code for other reconsiderations and revaluations that could occur in actual social contexts if the dynamic implied by the tales were only understood. In the way that Harry's narrated autobiographical fragments bind personal and social history, we can see that his rhetorical perspective releases him from a passive position. It gives him interpretive agency. His telling is a mode of action, one that is in clear and direct descent from the traditional men's role as that role dictated the style of men's visual and verbal arts.

In true traditional form, he uses his own experiences to give actuality to the events that he chooses as emblematic of a way of life. Therefore, some further biographical information should preface the fragments presented during that first session. The first six years of Harry's life were spent on his father's farm. Then he had to leave home to attend a boarding school at Fort Yates, North Dakota. His first few weeks at school were traumatic because he spoke no English and understood nothing about Anglo-American culture. In this respect Harry's experiences represent individual happenings that, with slight variations, almost anyone with childhood memories of boarding school life might narrate. From the very first years of reservation life, people from various tribes have interpreted the school experience as paradigmatic evidence of how more broadly based power relations functioned in the reservation environment. The first school was opened at Fort Yates in 1876, the same year that the last of the resistant Sioux bands recognized that they had to accept reservation status.[19] Therefore, the foundational significance attached to education aligns individual experience with communal divisions between insiders and invaders. But for all the insensitivity and sometimes even overt cruelty that were part of boarding school life, the schools also created a fund of shared experiences among people of different bands and tribes. And, of course, they introduced literacy, a skill and a weapon that some, if not many, Sioux recognized from the very beginning as their greatest need and source of hope in the new reservation circumstances. Certainly Harry and Lillian both valued learning, and, even in old age, they retained a politically astute understanding of the necessity for critical thinking.

Two events make up this first narrative, one set in the past, one exploring the present. The word "now" gives symmetry to the events and shows his basic purpose, which is to show how the present stands in relation to the past. In keeping with the traditional discursive precedents, Harry structures each segment so that the event turns on that moment where the personal opens out into social significance. The resulting formal arrangement involves almost verselike variation between personal and social content as Harry weaves both of them around his clear unarguable thematic emphasis: "they would try to change us to a new way of living." That theme is given emphatic spatial reference by the regular repetition of the deictic "there," which gives a verselike quality to sections of this narrative, which open the series of tales designed to show "how it is for us Indians here." This simple rhetorical device reminds us that Sioux tradition has consistently bound volitional options to habitational conditionality; in practice, this has meant that the link between places and ranges of choices is conceptualized in a manner that gives pragmatic detail to the whole problematic of what it means "to be" according to the terms of one or another culture. Or, as Harry Fast Horse stated it, "that's the way we started out, there, trying to be in the white man's way."

> *When I was ready to go to school in 1906, I didn't know a bit of English. I didn't know how to say "yes" or "no." They took me down to Fort Yates to the school there.*
>
> *A bunch of little boys and girls, we didn't know a bit of English. Our folks left us there and they went home in a team and a wagon.*
>
> *I myself didn't know how to say "yes" or "no." Finally they teach us how to wash our hands and they make us comb our hair and then we went to school.*
>
> *They're nice to us, but we kinda don't like it 'cause it is the first time we are away from home.*
>
> *Some of them children came in leggings, some with braids down their backs and some faces were painted. They come in there and that's what I seen and these boys had to cut their hair and they give them shirts and pants and socks and underwear.*
>
> *It's uncomfortable for us but we had to take it because we were there and they would try to change us to a new way of living.*
>
> *We don't know how, but anyway we wore the shoes with laces, the underwear, the belts, whatever.*
>
> *We were uncomfortable, but that's the way we started out there, trying to be in the white man's way.*

> Now our children and this third generation of our family, they don't understand the Indian way. They don't know how to talk Indian. They are ashamed to talk Indian. We should teach our children to talk Indian.
>
> I myself am not well educated. I wanted to go to Carlisle or Haskell or Chemawa, Oregon. Nineteen seventeen or 1916—somewhere around in there—they abolished the Carlisle School and all the pupils there came out and filled all the other schools so I couldn't go to school.
>
> Chemawa, Oregon, was the first one to give me a chance to go to school, but I was too old. I was twenty-two and too old to go to school, but even grandmothers go to school now. It's kinda nice. But at that time, it's twenty or thirty miles to school and it's hard for a country man to go to school.

As we study this autobiographical statement we can see that Harry's alternating emphasis from specific to general is a formal principle that also carries the weight of his beliefs about how his narratives should work in the community. He contrasted the negative impact of statements about racist cruelty with alternating comments about the attitude of determination that drove him to try to get more and more education in order to make the most of the new way of living. School itself was a test, an initiation as demanding as any journey into dangerous terrain undertaken by the hero of a folktale. The old folktale world of moving cliffs that could trap a hero between them or pesky trees sprouting branches of living snakes gives way in Harry's tales to an ordinary elementary school setting. Nevertheless, just as in the old tales, phenomenal chaos generates details of culture and language; strange beings make outrageous demands and out of it all comes a new way of life. Harry repeatedly stresses that he knew no English when he arrived at school. He was just "there," in a place where all the rules of life, as they had been previously understood, were changed and new ones had to be learned step by careful step. The narrative explicitly links this developmental trajectory to "learning to be in the white man's way."

The narrative about school describes breaks in a way of life, and those breaks are linguistically inscribed through an abrupt series of switches from past to present, from narrated event to present consequence. Then the second part of the tale is initiated with the word "now," and all that follows stands in direct contrast to what is described in those narrative segments beginning with repetitions of "there." The "now" sets the visually realized spatial qualities of the historical section against the more abstract temporality of the present. The narrative switch from "there" to "now" also emphasizes how the continuity of heritage is explicitly linked to continuity of the Dakota language. That pervasive narrative theme introduces still another related break, one within the educational process itself. Education requires knowledge of two languages, two discursive systems, two different kinds of teachers. Harry says, "*We* should teach our children to talk Indian." He was highly skeptical of efforts to retain the language through classroom teaching. In his estimation only parents could teach what language sums up and perpetuates.

The ending of the first autobiographical episode anticipates the structural moves of Harry's subsequent tales in that it shows how he kept alive his aspirations even though he was prevented from realizing them by forces beyond his own or his culture's control. The line "We were uncomfortable, but that's the way we started out there, trying to be in the white man's way" is echoed and recalled in the next narrative when Harry repeats the theme that leads me to direct comparisons with the old heroic structure implicit in prereservation folktales: "That's the way the Indian Bureau kept the Indian from doing anything for himself."

Although these lines can be read as defeatist, the broader performance contexts of the narratives oppose that reading. Harry was most definitely and defiantly angry about the way that bureaucratized cruelty had eroded the initiative of vulnerable and talented young people. But the narratives are not just expressions of outrage— or at least that is not part of the traditional purposes of narrative. What is gathered into narrative form should be evidence of a productive pattern for life. Signs that Harry was adhering to this traditional sense of the positive purpose of narrative are evident through close analysis of the narrative logic, especially in his second tale, which shows a series of twists and double takes. Tales like Harry's second one may tell about how a young man was destroyed, but people like Harry are able to grasp the strategy at work and turn it into a narrated warning about what to watch for, how to defend oneself. The narrative form itself operates against defeatism because it establishes a perspective that situates a critical and knowing witness, it reveals an observer quite capable of telling and analyzing. And that knowing is power. There is nothing defeatist about it.

This crucial second narrative of the session was Harry's most frequently told tale. He often brought it up in conversation, where it seemed to work as a kind of test for his listener. The story presents the sort of straightforward depiction of injustice that anyone who knows anything about reservation history could almost certainly match. In any large gathering people could just keep on responding with similar examples, and this easily imagined string of incidents is a possibility that almost certainly has structural consequences for this one narrated example. It launches; it does not sum up. But to see this event and others like it as mere protest statements would be to miss what can be achieved through actual performances, or even test launches of such performances.

What came through in Harry's tone of voice and even in his posture was his enormous pride at how he and others had overcome what could have destroyed lesser people. His anger, of course, was sharp and real, but its quality has to be weighed against that immense pride in all who had held on against such terrible odds. His message to the next generation had every bit as much to do with that defiant pride as it did with the explanation for those who were defeated. His shrewd ability to observe and speculate about and finally to continue to tell about the dangerous manipulations he saw all around him establishes the force of intelligent analysis as a crucial political energy:

> And I am gonna tell you another one. Maybe I told you this before, but I'm gonna repeat it again. At that time when Standing Rock Sioux had a claim or something coming in there, boys and girls who became of age at eighteen years of age, would get something.
>
> We'd get cattle, horses if we say or if we'd say "horses and cattle," we'd get a team and harness and saddle, everything that goes with it, and a couple of milk cows; but if we'd say "cattle," then we'd have to buy cattle with the money—well, maybe a couple horses.
>
> And here, I went after some of my money to buy some harness or saddle or a horse. I went to the superintendent and here a boy was sitting there with his dad. He wanted to be doctor or a lawyer. (I think that "doctor" sometimes means a lawyer too.) He wanted to go to school someplace. South Dakota or Iowa or Indiana someplace.
>
> His dad told him he was gonna give him fifty head of cattle to sell. They also had a lot of horses, about fifty head, and cattle, about two or three hundred head.
>
> And here the superintendent says, "You better get a good examination from the doctor." He named the doctor, I forgot who, in Mobridge, and before they left he gave them an envelope to take to the doctor.
>
> I came back home, and about a couple of weeks later, I came back there for something again to see the superintendent.
>
> And here the same boy was there. His dad was there again too and they brought back the envelope. There was a bunch of us sitting there and it was quite a room there—fourteen by sixteen feet—and around the wall there were benches and people waiting.
>
> Here now, this man and the superintendent, they meet.
>
> And here now, they're next.
>
> The superintendent says, "What you want, Mr. So and So?"
>
> The man says, "Well, you told me to take my son to the doctor and so I did and there's a word in there we couldn't understand. We couldn't translate it."
>
> "Oh, maybe I could tell you," he says, and so he opened the envelope and said (I don't know how he knew it. Maybe he told the doctor to put

a word in there at least a foot long. Maybe he told the doctor what to say) "This means your head and heart aren't right so if you tried to be a doctor or a lawyer, you'd go crazy."

Now then this boy felt bad and the rest of us, we didn't like it.
    That's the way the Indian Bureau kept the Indian from doing anything for himself.
    Here this boy went on drinking. I think he's still drinking. This really happened.

Harry Fast Horse's second narrative item stakes definite knowledge claims. In doing so it maps the themes of an entire narrative terrain. The young man in the tale is claiming no more than what the government has promised him. His quest for professional competence brings him up against the very bureaucracy that his sought-after legal knowledge would have allowed him to control. And we should not go too quickly over the fact that the young man is disenfranchised through linguistic manipulation. Written English, to be precise. He even has to hand deliver the letter that inscribes the instructions about how to prevent him from getting his entitlements. Government promises are subverted by government agents, and written language deciphered proves to be a life sentence: "Your head and heart aren't right." But the story itself gets told, again and again. Someone was there to witness the whole series of events. The telling is the victory. "And here" is a stylistic marker that conjoins past and present, then and there, abstract and concrete, defeat and victory.

Reporting and interpretation are bound together in this story as the mechanisms of oppression take on figural clarity. Harry Fast Horse's often-repeated episode reads the colonizer's false writing and calls the system to account before the Cannon Ball community, who lost someone who wanted to fight for them in the legal arena. It is, I believe, important to note that this story, like the previous one, does not speak to Sioux rejection of the knowledge, especially literacy, which upholds the new culture. The opposite is true. Harry is on the side of those who willingly fought to claim the knowledge they had been promised.

The same theme is picked up in Harry's third narrative, which regularly followed the story of the betraying letter. The third tale extends the symbolic range from the isolated, personalized incident to the more broadly referenced historical order. As he expands his narrative scope, Harry links the story of linguistic betrayal to social history. Once again, an easily ignored reference to place carries much of the thematic emphasis of the tale. Harry shows the placement of events to be speculative before he introduces the reference to the town of Winona, which happens to be the site of events leading to a vigilante-style execution of three young

Sioux men suspected of murdering a white man. These events remained so vivid in local memory that even today reference to a town now under the waters of the Oahe Dam is synonymous with reference to lynch mobs.

In this third narrative Harry also introduces that most painfully difficult of all his themes, namely the distrust between mixed-bloods and full-bloods, a distrust that can grow like a cancer within the developing social order. Significantly and tellingly, Harry alludes to that problem less as an issue of race than as one of access to and appropriate use of the symbolic order that he has earlier identified as the apparatus of bureaucratic control. He shows how the new political regime managed to maintain its grip by creating division and by multiplying forms of exclusion as a way to subvert the possibilities of productive adaptation to the reservation environment. And all this is consistently bound to the cognitive significance of spatial references.

> *I'll tell you what happened to the Yanktonai Sioux on the east side of the Missouri River.*
>
> *They were camping there. I think it was east of Fort Yates there. It was near a little town with a little store that they called Winona.*
>
> *Here soldiers came and took everything they owned in this encampment. They put the belongings in the center of the circle of tepees. They burned them and they told the Yanktonai they were going to bring them across the river to the Fort Yates side where the Sioux band—they call them the Blackfeet—had their territory. The Blackfeet were already there. They were given the land six miles north of the state line. They put us north of Fort Yates then.*
>
> *That was not part of the reservation. That was just a fort. The reservation should have been south of the state line.*
>
> *They took all the horses away from the people.*
>
> *My grandfather on my mother's side was a medicine man. He doctored people—young and old. They paid him with horses and war bonnets. He had thirty horses. The government took all that.*
>
> *In my time now when I try to collect all that, they claim there's only three horses there. So the half-breeds must have been jealous so maybe they interpreted the language wrong. The half-breed got everything he wanted to start on the reservation. He got ten horses. A full-blood like my grandfather got only one horse.*
>
> *That's what they did to keep us down.*

The first session included two other incidental tales of repression in which a single representative of the bureaucracy became emblematic of the entire apparatus of social repression. Harry definitely knew how to use metonymy effectively; it was, after all, the determining trope of traditional narratives. After his metonymically concentrated and fragmentary initial tales, Harry announced that he would tell different kinds of stories the next time we met. He was quite definite, though, about his beliefs that what we had just recorded set up indispensable preliminary considerations.

The significance of the aesthetically minimal narratives that Harry Fast Horse told in the first session began to reveal itself to me only after I had studied all the available collections of prereservation tales. When I began that research, structuralism was affecting global theory and method. Reference to the tenets of high structuralism was a required scholarly gesture in any writing about American Indian narrative traditions. I assiduously read Claude Lévi-Strauss and Alan Dundes's formalist analyses, along with any number of lesser figures who were trying to show how structuralism would let us move with intelligent, systematic evidence and detail from culture to culture, discipline to discipline. I have since realized the intellectual and practical difficulties of that dream without ever really abandoning it. But now I begin to understand how many years of work even the simplest narratives require if we are to advance research toward our earlier goals. However, in those first years after I had recorded what Harry Fast Horse gave me, I had to confront some immediate practical problems. The structural analyses that I did for older collected texts seemed only to increase the analytic distance between the old and new. My first breakthrough came when I discovered intermediate analytic levels at which old and new could be compared. These levels constitute the analytic grounds for cognitive style.

When I used the old tales as the background and the source of models for event structures in the ones Harry was telling me, I realized that I really had been hearing much-updated, transformed, and often truncated variations on the same themes. As I have already indicated, the fragments of the first section recall a range of conventions related to prereservation men's autobiographical art. But no one advertised failures. In prereservation times the idea of making failure emblematic would have been ridiculous. I believe it to have been equally unthinkable for Harry Fast Horse. Analysis of older heroic tales, though, reveals a pattern of movement that includes a period of liminality; and while the tale itself narrates passage from that status to the achievement that finally lands the hero in that coveted position "at the center of the camp circle," an interrupted telling would leave most of the traditional heroes immobilized in one way or another. And, in a very real sense, Harry is performing the interrupted heroic pattern. Any traditional hero could say "we had to take it because . . ." but the traditional tale moves beyond just taking it to action that initiates a new phase of cultural existence. With their pattern of movement away from a home base outward to a world of shifting phenomenal laws and dangers as well as great potential for new cultural options,

Harry's fragments are like the first third of the very traditional tales they seem to replace. Seen this way, the tales recall and promote the old heroic structure that can still reach its appropriate contemporary conclusion if only young people take the tale to a successful next stage. From this perspective we can see that the session is about the conditions that lead to hope; it is not about despair.

The postulated relationship between these personal experience stories and the older narratives puts these tales into a distinct category of personal experience narrative. If, as my own research and intuitive judgment tell me, this is a fairly common phenomenon in contexts where a living, highly formalized oral narrative tradition is part of the narrator's experience, it has not been generally studied. Personal experience narrative is usually studied in separation from analysis of formal folktales. Analyzing personal experience narratives in conjunction with other dominant narrative types in a given culture's narrative history could yield new insights about the structure and style of personal narratives as they operate diachronically.

By the next recording session, Harry was ready to switch to a different mood and set of themes. The weather was hot and windy. Violent storms were threatening and we watched the sky as we recorded. His tales, though, did not reflect the weather; they were positive evocations of what had happened in the past to bring honor to the Fast Horse family. He launched the session by telling about the hunting trip during which his grandfather had earned the right to use the names that he had passed on to descendants. This narrative is superb evidence of a cognitive style that is bound to a specific range of cultural practices and beliefs that affirm naming as a culturally generative act. In the customary (institutional) process by which nomination becomes conventionalized nominalization, this range of cultural practices and beliefs achieves stylistic focus and pragmatic detail.

The range of customs lying behind Harry's narrative all derive from the traditional belief in names as evidence of how a continuing cultural potentiality can be given specific human reference. This belief points directly to cognitive elements that link a particular fragment of family history to those older Dakota styles of projecting naming beyond processes of commemoration to processes that are understood as generative. This projection implicitly summarizes an entire philosophy of language. Within this way of thinking, nomination is analogous to physical procreation, and the enabling cultural conditions and customs upholding this belief are directly bound to the historically adaptive mechanisms and institutions of the culture. Naming is the cultural performance that establishes the body of language as vital, because by way of the performance of naming ceremonies, language descends through the bodies of individual community members who address each other and through each other address cosmic powers.

Alice Fletcher has recorded ethnological data that allow us to assert the force of naming as a generative act perpetuating a continuity other than biological, a continuity that "turns" from ancestor to descendant by way of the named child, who marks a point in an ongoing cultural spiraling movement through time and space, birth and death. The man who names the child explicitly addresses the power of movement, that which is as old as life itself and which animates the body of the child. Through the child the power of movement achieves continuing return to the community. Fletcher describes how the namer, who would normally address the spirits in terms of ascending generation (i.e., "grandfather"), assumes a different position in relation to the spirit world when he names a child. He addresses the spirit within the child as "child," and the fundamental power, the power of movement, addresses him as "father." This act makes him a father on a spiritual as well as a biological level. Fletcher states:

> *A name implies relationship and consequently protection; favor and influence are claimed from the source of the name, whether this be the gens or the vision. A name, therefore, shows the affiliation of the individual; it grades him so to speak, and he is apt to lean upon its implied power; consequently a man does not like a bad nickname, it handicaps him in his own esteem. The sacred import of a name in the mind of the Indian is indicated in that part of the ceremony where "the Something that moves" seems to overshadow and enclose the child and addresses the "wakan" man as "father." The "wakan" man replies calling the god "child" at the same time invoking the supernatural protection and care for the boy, as he lays at the feet of the messenger of the Unseen Power, the offerings of gifts and the honor of the feast.*[20]

As Harry's personal story unfolds, we get consistent stylistic evidence of how intimately he has achieved an imaginative reconstruction of the events that culminated in his grandfather's gaining the rights to confer certain names. Harry's story personalizes and individualizes one of the central occasions in any Sioux camp—the buffalo hunt. The hunt, along with war, was a test dividing the strong and skilled young men from the mediocre performers.

Harry's dramatization of his grandfather's memorable and memorialized hunt depends on beliefs (presuppositions) regarding leadership. According to traditional belief, a leader had a primary obligation to the poor, and orphans exemplified the poorest of the poor; therefore Harry's first significant narrative moves show his grandfather interacting with orphans. Then, our attention is drawn to his eminently practical foresight and good sense: "He must have had good mittens or something." The structure of the entire event is set up so that only after these ordinary daily virtues are established narrative facts do we get reference to powers that exceed the ordinary. "He had something in him." His actions prove his exceptional powers, and this "something" leads to the general questioning and speculation that in the end results in a holy man's pronouncement about their social significance. And that, in turn, resulted in the Fast Horse patronymic that commemorates the entire historical event. Physical procreation and generation are directly bound to narrative perpetuation. From questioning to speculating to interpreting to commemorating, the episodes of daily life evolve into tradition and continuity.

> My name is Harry Fast Horse and my great, great-grandfather's name is Growling Bear. He had, oh I don't know how many wives, but he had so many children. One of them is my grandfather named Sea Walker, and he was a great hunter and right south of Bismarck, north of Linton, on that creek called Bear Creek, they camped.
>
> They looked for buffalo, scouting along for buffalo because they were starving. They also trapped beaver and muskrat and sold them to the whites. They tried to get whatever they could.
>
> And here one boy scout came back and said, "Up this way about ten to fifteen or twenty miles, there's buffalo. There's a bunch of buffalo lying there."
>
> The snow is deep so orphans living with their grandmothers or grandfathers or the old ladies, their sons had been killed, they took their arrows and came to Sea Walker's tepee and say "how."
>
> And then another one comes and says "how."
>
> They brought all kinds of arrows. There was over ten of them that came to Sea Walker's tepee.
>
> Right away Sea Walker, my grandfather, got on his deer- and buffalo-hunting pony and he went to the hunt.
>
> When they came to the buffalo, they took after them, and he must have had some good mittens or something or his skin must have been tough. I don't know. He must have had something in him because he shot over eleven or fifteen buffalo while the others shot only one or mostly two.
>
> Some of them couldn't shoot their arrows. There were about ten or twenty who couldn't get one.
>
> Then they had a meeting, a council meeting and they talked about Sea Walker and his horses. One of the chiefs in the council told my grandfather why it looked like his horses were holy. They don't fall in holes or stumble. "Why are they so swift?" they had asked.
>
> "When you have a son, his name is going to be Holy Horse and the second son, his name is going to be Swift Horse." So that's the way we got the name.

> *That's what they called the oldest son, "Holy Horse." He died around 1934, I think. His name was Moses Holy Horse, my dad's brother. My dad's name was Paul Fast Horse. The bureau enrolled my father Paul Fast Horse. Instead of Swift Horse, they put Fast Horse on the role.*

After narrating the story of the family name, Harry moved on to explaining his personal Indian name. This event gives us a slightly different take on the working of tradition. Harry does not tell what he himself did to earn his name. Instead he gives us the credentials of the man who had earned the right to give a name to another person. This event structure is further evidence of how the transmission of names is in every way bound to relational dynamics and the accompanying systematic authorizations of cultural acts that occur within a living community. One important set of authenticating marks for Harry's narratives is his regular narrative gesturing toward the people from whom he had learned what he was passing on. He carefully incorporates the genealogy of knowledge and authority into his narrative structure. This genealogy adds a set of signifying features that affords a pragmatic parallel to the semantic content of any other narrative being told during a particular occasion. The community is a network of rights and relationships, and a story told by someone who does not have the right to speak has no place in the community.

In the story of the naming ceremony we also note that the occasion of name giving involves giving away goods that a family has been able to amass as a consequence of their own efforts and of having received gifts from others. Both of these ways of gathering goods attest to a family's importance in a community. In the days of the traditional economy, people possessing courage and initiative could acquire goods that were the tangible proof of moral virtues. Occasions like naming ceremonies that included generous giving away of goods were performances of individual realizations of an abstract pattern of communal values. In this respect it reflects the cognitive themes underlying men's and women's arts. Localized potential has to be concretely enacted.

> *My Indian name is Red Spotted Weasel. I was given this by a well-noted chief's son named Mark Red Fish. He is one of the Cut Head Band.*
>
> *When they were going to give me this Indian name, my mother and dad and my relatives gave things away, for instance, a war bonnet or a buckskin shirt or beaded moccasins or pipe or beef or some horses.*
>
> *This fella that was gonna name me, he gives away a bunch of stuff like a war bonnet, a buckskin shirt or leggings, or a horse and saddle to name me. He was a noted name so he could speak to give me a name.*
>
> *This man was in the White Riders' Lodge. They were noted men. Anytime there was a celebration or a congress, a Catholic congress or an*

> *Episcopal convocation or a congregational get-together. There was a big camp and they all helped. They help those who have bad luck coming in with horses so they can't make it. Some of the horses get diarrhea, or the horses lose a shoe. They help all those people.*
>
> *That's why this White Riders' Lodge picked him to name me.*

Recording the tales that made up his part of the Cannon Ball story was apparently Harry's idea. At any rate, he was the one who proposed the plan to me. Yet I would not be at all surprised to learn that Lillian first thought of it. She was always present while we worked and visited. She always put on a freshly ironed apron when I arrived, and the change of aprons became as much a part of the ritual of recording as anything else. When we began to work, she sat straight, tall, and energetically attentive. Generally she did not speak very much, but she was by no means a passive presence. Her active listening enabled Harry's performance. Her presence made the narrative occasions something other than encounters between an outsider (me) and an insider (Harry). Lillian was the understanding participant whose knowledge matched her husband's. In more theoretical terms we can say that she enabled the dialogism on which discursive integrity depends. Going even further, we can see that all aspects of her role, from her demeanor to the content of her tales, demonstrated the traditional women's gender roles, showing how their narrative styles worked in contrast to those of men.

She had tales of her own, and during the session that performed the narrative tradition giving significance to the Fast Horse names, she narrated that part of the tradition that belonged to her side of the family. Her performance style can be characterized with the same adjective she used to describe her father's personality and the medicine that was his visionary gift. That adjective is "soothing." Her story shows how the human qualities here summed up as soothing are both gift and consequence of disciplined grace whether we refer to Lillian herself or to her father.

When Lillian speaks, the quality of her voice and the pacing of her narrative all seem to derive from a meditative distance in which she has discovered an extraordinary gift of reflexive comprehension. A listener can sense her meditative approach to the events she is narrating. She began by narrating incidents that are part of her father's life history, but she presents them in a manner that shows how she lifts a more general significance from the specific events. Her style first frames an event, then achieves a speculative step away from that action in order to describe some abstract pattern that the event suggests:

> *I want to tell a story about my father, Herbert Welsch, who became an Episcopal minister. When he was just a young man he got land from the government. Oh, the government issued him some cattle for the first time.*

THE NARRATING COMMUNITY

So he was taking care of the cattle on the hillside and he unsaddled his horse and put the saddle on the ground. He laid down and he went off to sleep.

And then he saw a man coming toward him. He had a black cape. To him it looked like a black cape. And his hair was straight down and he was singing a very beautiful song. My father, when he was living, used to sing that song and it really sounded good. And when this man came dancing toward him, he almost stepped on him, so my father woke up and here it was an eagle that woke him up.

The words of the eagle's song were, "My robe is holy."

And afterward the way my father understood it is that he should use an eagle for his medicine or for some kind of holy act.

And then at one time, he went up the hill again to watch the cattle and while he was waiting, he fell asleep again. He lay flat on his stomach again and he had his arms for a pillow on the saddle and then he saw a man coming towards him.

This time the man was all naked and he had his hair all tied up on top of his head and the only thing he had on was a breech-cloth, and he too sang a song and the words were, "This ground is holy."

And again this man almost stepped on my father, so my father awoke and here it was a root.

This plant had a thick flower and a brown top. The root is something like Vicks. When you put it in your mouth, it is soothing and it always cures toothache because I use it myself.

I suppose in our way, our Indian way, my father would be a medicine man and he would use those things he saw in his dream. But he thought about it and well, he had a cousin then in the Episcopal ministry. His name was Philip Deloria and he told him he shouldn't use those things. He told him to be a minister and preach the gospel of Jesus Christ. So he didn't go according to his dream, but he studied ministry according to the Episcopal Church.

To my thinking, the symbols were to use in the Christian world, to tell the gospel of Jesus Christ so that he would heal by these dreams he had using symbols of his medicine.

This medicine is so soothing to the skin and even in the mouth and that's the way my father turned out to be.

This was told to me by my father.

"To my thinking." These words of Lillian epitomize her fundamental style. They show how she steps back from the concrete events of her father's life and concentrates on their potential meaning for a later time. Lillian and Harry were both members of the Episcopal Church. At the time both the priest and deacon at that church were Sioux, the priest an Oglala from Pine Ridge while the deacon was a member of the Cannon Ball community. Both were known for their loyalty to and knowledge of traditional religious beliefs as well as Christian ones. The little Cannon Ball parish had an impressive tradition of permitting syncretistic beliefs and practices. The first pastor who came to Cannon Ball in the 1870s, Aaron McGaffey Beede, had seen the obvious good sense of combining religious practices, but the more orthodox bishop did not approve of syncretisms, and Beede soon lost his parish.[21] Nevertheless, the precedent was set, and Beede continued to have considerable influence at Standing Rock, where he eventually became the judge in the district court. The theme of the session, though, was names, not relations between traditional beliefs and Christianity; and in accordance with that theme, Lillian told about her own Indian name, Call-upon-Woman.

To all who knew her, the name was entirely appropriate. She had a rare gift of being able to help people and make them feel privileged to have participated in the interaction. As she begins her tale, we note another of those carefully articulated links in the traditional chain that Harry and Lillian were both revealing through their tales. She mentions that her father gave her the name, and we are reminded how the person who confers a name also remains a part of all that is encompassed by the nominal reference:

> *My father gave me my Sioux name. It means "Call-upon-Woman" because my father's grandmother, in the camp, women came to her for help. Like if their baby's sick or anything, they need help in, they'd come to my father's grandmother and call upon her. That's the way they named her Call-upon-Woman.*
>
> *My father gave me the name when I was a small girl. And it seems like today especially my family calls upon me. I guess my father gave me the right name.*

After telling about her name, Lillian told a story about the Twin Women (or Double Women or Double Woman) that is an exceptionally intriguing addition to our knowledge about a set of beliefs that links gender roles and artistic practices in ways that outsiders can only clumsily imagine from information given in ethnographic sources. As we give ethnographic expansion to beliefs only alluded to in Lillian's story, we can also see why and how Lillian's presentation evokes the whole structure of beliefs related to women's cultural role and the styles connected with that role.

The Twin Women were credited with teaching quillwork to Sioux women and with inspiring the abstract designs that women produced. Where men's art represented a movement from abstract potential to concrete realization, women's art represented the reverse, the movement from concrete realization to abstract form. In various domains of expressive culture, women concentrated on the conditions for the coming into being of the fundamental cultural forms or designs. Women's quillwork or beadwork designs represented cultural potential. We have some evidence allowing us to assert that an analogous style characterized women's narrative arts. In those rare texts in which we can follow a woman's characteristic narrative moves, we can note that women tend to stress narrative patterns that show how fundamental cultural forms can foster new realizations.[22] If assertions about women's narrative styles remain tentative for lack of information, we are much more certain about the visual arts (see chapter 1). All of these basic observations about art, women's gender roles, and the mythic figure of the Double Women or the Twin Women require considerable ethnographic specification. In his study of Oglala societies, Clark Wissler summarizes the ethnographic data related to these beliefs, and his entire summary is necessary contextualization for Lillian and Harry's modern tales:

> *A mythical being sometimes called the double-woman plays an important role in the supernatural affairs of the Oglala. . . . Allied to this, but in a way not clearly understood by us, is the quillworkers' cult. Quill work seems to have been especially wakan. It is said that once a young woman dreamed of the double-woman who taught her the use of quills. Before this no one imagined porcupine quills of any practical value. So the young woman asked for a porcupine and a separate tipi. When these were ready she went into the tipi alone and warned everyone to keep away. There she plucked out the quills and assorted them according to lengths. Then she went into the brush looking for dyes; she selected red, blue, yellow and black. Also, she asked for white gull (called the woman's bird). The feathers of this she dyed blue. Now she asked one to dress a skin for a buffalo robe.*
>
> *She worked alone in the tipi. No one saw her save at meal time or when she came out to make her toilette. The quills of feathers she split and with them laid on the colors.*
>
> *Now, she invited a girl friend and instructed her. They took the dressed robe and decorated it with quill work. Then she made a feast and invited many women. She sang songs and explained that all came from the double-woman. . . . In this way the making of quill work was celebrated ever afterward. It was very wakan.*
>
> *Dreams of the double-woman take many interesting conventional forms. Thus she may appear inviting a woman to go with her, conducting*

her to a lone tipi before which stands a skin dressing frame of curious pattern. As the woman comes up to the door and looks in she beholds the two deer-women sitting at the rear. By them she is directed to choose which side she shall enter. Along the wall of one side is a row of skin dressing tools, on the other, a row of parfleche headdress bags. If the former is chosen, they will say, "You have chosen wrong, but you will become very rich." If she choose the other side, they will say, "You are on the right track, all you shall have shall be an empty bag." This means that she will be a prostitute and otherwise an evil woman. In the future she may wear a miniature headdress pouch as a symbol of her experience. Such women are wakan, but not regarded as exactly normal; they are always running after men and have unusual powers to seduce them.

At the close of the dream the two women run away as black-tail doe.

A man may have a dream in which a male messenger calls for him. For him the tipi has skin dressing tools on one side as before, but bows and arrows on the other. If he should choose the former, he will live as a hermaphrodite or a berdache.[23]

Lillian's story is about a berdache, and this makes it exceptional among available texts about Double Woman experiences. Other features of Lillian's text also set it apart as extraordinary. There is, first of all, the calm, commonsense tone of her narrative. She accepts and passes over the fierce doubling that is prelude to a berdache's visionary acceptance of his lifestyle, and she considers only the cool, practical aspects of the beliefs about Twin Women. As we listen to her, we learn about someone consistently overburdened with housework. Unlike other housekeepers, this one knows that he can count on the Twin Women for help in getting the work done. There is nothing the least bit mysterious or overwrought about that motivation or any other feature of this understated narrative. The most startling aspect of the tale comes quietly at the very end. Lillian mentions that when she was a child, she herself once followed and watched a berdache as he left his quillwork for the Twin Women to finish while he gathered his day's supply of wood.

Finally, we need to set this narrative with its many subtle connections to women's cultural role in contrast to the way that Harry's narratives both enact and represent masculine gender prerogatives. Harry and Lillian each followed through with a performance style that can be traced back to the traditional complementarity of gender roles. Harry used personal experience to establish the concrete actuality of what he wanted to have in place as part of Cannon Ball tradition, while Lillian presented only the broadest outlines of a pattern of beliefs that together constitute the mythic paradigm that derives from the way Sioux culture made sexual difference the foundation for a way of knowing.

> *I'm going to tell a story. This is not a fairy tale. It really happened. In our band we camped here and there. We talked with nature.*
>
> *They called it the Twin Women. You don't see the other one. The one that is visible will start to make a moccasin; in those days they used porcupine quill. She'd start to make a moccasin, then she'd put it down and cover it up and be gone for quite a while.*
>
> *Then she comes back and uncovers the article which she was working on, and it is already finished by the invisible woman.*
>
> *This is told by older women and it really happened. When I was about ten years old, that was in 1930, there was a (I don't know what you call those men, they act like women. He does all that a woman would do) [berdache]. He'd start on it, leave it, and cover it up and go after water or wood, and when he'd come back, the article would be already finished. This is a true story among the Sioux Indian women.*
>
> *I know about that because I followed a man.*
>
> *This is what I wanted to tell.*

Lillian Fast Horse's text is cultural testimony to the way the doubling signified by the Twin Women and by the berdache (a man performing a woman's cultural role) is an image of a reciprocity that subtends woman's gender role. The Twin Women, who must remain always outside the frontiers of the culture, nevertheless slip across sometimes to bring to completion what has been begun. As Lillian tells this single incident, she touches on fundamental, powerful, and frightening beliefs in such a manner that their uncanny power is gathered into a style that also binds that power to calm images of domesticity. Her story is "soothing" even as the beliefs that she touches on retain all the fierce energy that is evidence of what is originary.

After Lillian had told about the berdache and the Twin Women, Harry decided to follow with his stories about comparable figures. His repertoire included two tales about deer or elk who take the form of humans and seduce people. But what makes Harry's stories exceptional is the way a belief most commonly linked to women is instead ascribed to a male figure. In *Dakota Texts*, Ella Deloria has summarized beliefs about elk and deer beings. She writes, "Just as the elk spirit stands for masculine charm, so the deer spirit represents the enticing woman. A man who allowed himself to be ensnared too deeply died; but those who did not go so far came through, albeit with difficulty."[24]

The deer woman stories, extensions of the Twin Women beliefs, depend on beliefs about deer taking the form of women and seducing men who are henceforth trapped in unfulfilled erotic passion. Stories told within communities about encounters with deer women or elk men are testimony to the narrative watchfulness people maintain over potentially dangerous passion. How different people interpret these stories reveals the community's responses to risk and change as these are bound up with sexuality. In the images of the deer woman or the elk man, narrative and custom harness the enormous energies of the uncanny and keep narrative watch over them.

As he told these stories, Harry proved his own zest for tales that touch on the uncanny. Nevertheless, his persistent emphasis on the contemporary setting and on exact cultural detail was as strong in these tales as in his stories about his school days. He never narrated tales that were outside the range of his personal experience. Every tale is one for which he could identity when and how he had learned it. His first tale about a deer is set on Turtle Mountain Reservation, where he had relatives, and its events were said to have occurred right after World War II when soldiers were returning home from military service. But this deer being has all the traits of his more ancient avatars. He is resplendent with porcupine quillwork, and the art points us back to all the conceptual complexity bound up with quillworking.

> *When the Indians were somewhere south, they honored some soldiers in World War II.*
>
> *And here they was sitting around the drum when this man came in. He smiles and he smells good—no perfume or anything. He had buckskin-tanned gloves. He always had a gray hat and porcupine-quilled hatband. Sometimes he came there with a horse-tail hatband. He had on a buckskin shirt, buckskin pants. He had boots on, spurs too—all decorated with porcupine quills. He said he had some wonderful songs in the Sioux language. He had a beautiful voice too. All the young women wanted to dance with him, but he always stayed at the drum. Right before they'd quit, right then he'd go out and nobody ever seen where he went.*
>
> *One time they all organized and here is a bunch of boys that had good saddle horses and they were all outside waiting for him. They said they were going to dance until he's going home. They were dancing and having a good time. A lot of good honor songs for the boys, a lot of giveaways.*
>
> *Daybreak comes.*
>
> *This boy comes out. There was a mouse-colored saddle horse standing there at the tie rack. (Maybe you seen tie racks in the TV or in the movies.) Here stands a beautiful mouse-colored saddle horse with a really good saddle on. It was kinda shy.*
>
> *Here this man came out and got on the horse heading for the timber. Here this bunch of boys got on their horses and chase him. Close to the timber, well—here goes a black-tail deer jumping up and down.*
>
> *He went into the timber.*

> There's a story about Belcourt Reservation, or maybe it's San Haven.
>
> There's a hill up there. There's a summer resort up there. There's trees all around the top. There's only one road up. There's a dance every night or so up there. Different orchestras come in to play and people come from all over to dance there.
>
> Here a nice-looking gentleman came there. Fancy suit on, good fancy car. He parks there. He smelled good, no perfume. He just smelled good. The young ladies always want to dance with him.
>
> When he goes out from the dance, nobody can catch him. He goes down the road and disappears. So one time they block the road. He knew it too.
>
> That time they blocked the roads. Here he danced with a girl and put his fingernail in her ribs and on the right side, he put his fingernails right through the girl's hand. She screamed and he went out. And here they said he had a tail on too. They said it was the devil. They said they closed up then. I think this must have happened around 1941 or 1942, right here in North Dakota.

Psycholinguists tell us that our experience of the uncanny attests to an instinctual drive toward representation that invests the semantic with what precedes it in the etiology of human speech. The shiver that is our response to a good ghost story is evidence that there is something that cannot be controlled through direct representation but can only be unleashed and harnessed by the accumulated energy and evidence of instinctual traces that language collects like moss on rocks. And so the uncanny takes us as close as we can get to how human beings react to what they will never be able to capture directly in the language with which they pursue their experiences. Harry certainly knew and delighted in this dimension of linguistic experience, and he was alert to the traces of this particular energy whether they occurred in traditional or in Christian contexts. Another of his stories is remarkable for the way he shows the injunctive power of language in confrontation with dead visitors. For anyone expecting the kind of ghost story to which media culture has accustomed us, the conclusion seems abrupt and without adequate previous development. Yet in its proper cultural context, it makes its decisively powerful point. Language prevails with the dead. A woman commands a ghost to go away and it does just that:

> Back in my mother's time—this is really so although my mother didn't see it—she went to school in Avoka. That is just a few miles from Pipestone, Minnesota. She was going to school to try to learn to be an American citizen.
>
> She also wanted to train to be a nun.

> *Here, early in the morning, about six o'clock every morning she went to the chapel. The priest would come in there and—I don't know what they called the short service—*
>
> *Here now, the priest died.*
> *In the morning, they went to the chapel.*
> *Here now, the dead priest came in there all dressed up carrying the chalice. When he was going to set the chalice on the altar, all the sisters began to cry. Then he took the chalice and went back out.*
> *That's what my mother told. It happened in the same chapel she went to.*
> *Then, some brave young lady asked him why he came back. She told him, "Why didn't he just stay dead?"*
> *So then, after that, he never came back again.*

Some of Harry's stories about ghosts take definite advantage of the closeness between fear and humor and the ease with which these emotions spill one into the other. His hilarious tale of the schoolboy who falls in a grave provides a good laugh and a moment of respect for what adrenaline can do when it hits the human system:

> *Her dad always tells this one. He went to school at St. Elizabeth's Episcopal Mission in South Dakota. Out behind the mission there is the cemetery and a little farther back is the dormitory. One night, he's late so he decides to take a shortcut and he goes across the cemetery.*
>
> *He's scared but he thinks he's gonna run really fast.*
> *And here, somebody had just died and was gonna be buried so they had dug the grave. It was empty, but it was open just like that.*
> *He's running along and all of a sudden,* BOOM. *He falls in that empty grave.*
> *He tries to get out and he jumps and jumps but the sides are too high for him, so he decides he's gonna have to stay all night and he crawls up in the corner and goes to sleep.*
> *All of a sudden he hears footsteps coming. Someone else is taking the shortcut across the cemetery.*
> *Then* BOOM—*he falls in the grave too.*
> *He tries to jump out and he can't.*
> *Her father's real quiet over there in a corner. Then he says, "You can't do it."*
> *That boy heard him and he jumped and he jumped right out of the grave!*
> *Her father had to stay in the grave until morning.*

Harry's sense of humor was a dominant aspect of his personality. He loved stories with episodes of Tricksters, and he could put to practical use the strategies these stories represented. He thoroughly enjoyed telling about the eastern hippie who came one summer to camp in his yard and learn about "the Indian way." Harry says that he went up to his uninvited, marijuana-smoking guest, warmly welcomed the young man, and told him that Indians valued hospitality above almost all other virtues. Therefore they would expect him to eat all meals with them. Harry then detailed foods that he knew the young man would find it impossible to eat. The next morning the unwelcome visitor was gone.

Trickster or Iktomi stories are omnipresent in Native communities, and it would have been strange indeed if Harry had not known and performed some of them. In this respect too, Harry both fulfills expectations and varies their realization. He tells no stories that refer directly to Iktomi, but the Trickster lurks within the structure of most of Harry's tales. In one session Trickster was the model according to which a definite historical character's actions could be understood. In accord with his characteristic stylistic emphasis on the historical rather than the mythical, Harry ascribed Iktomi-like actions to Rain-in-the-Face, who had lived in the region. Harry told several stories in which Rain-in-the-Face tricks the military and outwits those who try to dominate him. These tales were the ones in which Harry took the greatest delight. He repeated them often, needing only the slightest encouragement to tell them to whatever audience was willing to listen.

In his study of Sioux humor, Kenneth Lincoln has penned lines that also apply to Harry Fast Horse's ascriptions of Trickster-like deeds to his favorite figure from recent Sioux history: "And just as the heyoka teaches traditional Lakota the 'contrary' or 'two-faced' nature of all things, so the bonus is a sense of options; nothing is fixed, not even injustice. This bivalent fulcrum divides the tragic sense of end-stopped suffering from comic renewal; the denial of free will is reversed with alternatives, possibilities, recreations. It's an argument between past and future, simplified, an historical determinism transcended by humanist futurity. Iktome, the wily spider, represents one Lakota agent of comic change, a Trickster weaver and medicine teacher who patches torn historical webs and nets the future."[25]

According to the historical record, Rain-in-the-Face was born just west of Cannon Ball around 1835. He is reputed to have participated in a raid on Fort Totten, northeast of Standing Rock. The incidents that Harry Fast Horse elaborates with zest and humor are also hinted at in official history.[26]

The sheer energetic delight with which Harry told his Trickster tales was, in itself, evidence of how their cathartic humor netted in hopes for the future.

> *And again, I'll tell you a story about Rain-in-the-Face. He was taken to the stockade at Fort McKeen.*

> Down below is the cavalry. Up farther is the infantry. That's where he was held prisoner.
> The soldiers were cursing each other at the gate there. Some Indian woman—a Sioux—came up there. Rain-in-the-Face told her to bring some pounded meat and wood ashes in two bags. That's what she did coming up there in a day or so. Maybe she even came back the same evening.
> Here these soldiers always had eaten some of that—they liked it. So when Rain-in-the-Face got some of it, they asked him for some. He told them to close their eyes and open their mouths. Then he put ashes all over them, in their mouths and everywhere. He went out and got a rifle and took five hundred rounds of ammunition. He ran down to the cavalry station and took off.
> So this really happened.

Harry's second story about Rain-in-the-Face is an unmistakable variant of a plot that folklorists have labeled the "Me All Face" plot. It is a narrative with such ancient and widespread European provenance that tracing it gives one an appreciation for the sheer indestructibility of stories, especially when they are funny and a little bit on the vulgar side as they turn the tables on an oppressor. One of the earliest known references to this jocular episode ascribes the incident to Julius Caesar and a Gaul who managed to outwit and embarrass the venerable Caesar, his conqueror. In her study of the incident Cecily Hancock writes, "In America, I have not found the story earlier than the late eighteenth century. It turns up both in French and in English, in the eighteenth, nineteenth, and twentieth centuries and in various parts of North America, but seems to be rather thinly distributed. It is obscurely persistent rather than generally popular. Except for one clear case of copying, the connections between the various appearances of the tale in print in America and between the American and earlier European examples are so mysterious as to suggest common dependence on an oral tradition, rather than direct literary influence."[27]

Harry's use of the plot is adept and fiercely ironic if we remember that local legend continues to name Rain-in-the-Face as the man who killed George Armstrong Custer. With stylistically ironic guilelessness, Harry initiates a slow-paced episode that builds up to the point where Rain-in-the-Face manipulates General Custer's egregious superiority complex until it becomes perfectly natural for him to announce that Custer's face is just like Rain-in-the-Face's arse.

> Another time Rain-in-the-Face was captured again. He was over there. It was in December, about ten below, with a northwest wind blowing towards the south.

> The soldiers were going west to a parade ground. General Custer was leading his men. Rain-in-the-Face was riding his pony.
> They were riding along and here General Custer says, "Chief."
> Rain-in-the-Face had a bare thigh. He had on leggings and breech cloth and his thigh was showing. So [Custer] pointed at that and he said, "Chief, you cold?"
> "No, I'm not cold," Rain-in-the-Face says.
> They went a little ways and Rain-in-the Face kinda reached up because Custer's stallion was higher than his. Rain-in-the-Face's pony was way down. He kinda reached up and he pointed to his cheek and he says, Chief Rain-in-the-Face says, "You cold?"
> Custer says, "No cold, John."
> They went a little ways farther. Custer says, "Chief, you cold?"
> Rain-in-the-Face says, "No."
> It was cold all right. I believe that it was at least ten below.
> Then Rain-in-the-Face looks up at Custer and he says, "White man face like Indian arse, not cold."
>
> This story was told to me by a guy named Casey. He was in the cavalry when Custer was ready to go to the Big Horn to get Sitting Bull. He was left there. He wanted to go along but he was left to watch the camp. (I went to school in Bismarck Indian School. Now it's called Fraine Barracks.) We would always go below the railroad bridge across the Missouri. That was the only bridge in those days and he always gave us candy and cookies. Sometimes he brought us sausage, this boy did. He always invited us under the railroad bridge. He never gave us smoke or drinks. He's a nice man. He was the one that told me this story. He told it to me in 1915 or 1914.

Not surprisingly, General George Armstrong Custer is a regular character in Cannon Ball stories. His journey to the famous Battle of the Little Big Horn began at Fort Abraham Lincoln just north of Cannon Ball. The Custer Battle had preceded my recording of the stories by almost exactly a century. It was one of those historical events that immediately took on a narrative life that had more to do with historical attitudes than with literal events. As Bruce Rosenberg has shown in his study of the legendary process in relation to the Custer story, non-Indians immediately assimilated the event by adapting it to the conventions of epic.[28] The Indian side of the legend-formation process follows significantly different impulses and clearly derives from a contrasting cognitive style. I made no particular point of collecting Custer stories, so I can comment only on Harry's version although I heard many others. Harry tells his story from Sitting Bull's perspective and uses the occasion to tell about the motives behind Sitting Bull's flight to Canada and subsequent return.[29] The story about Custer gives further evidence of Harry's understated and ironic sense of humor, as for instance when he states that Sitting Bull came back but "Custer couldn't make it." Finally we have to note that Harry used his narration as a way to bring the storytelling session back around to his own role in negotiating settlements of Oahe Reservoir legal disputes. This crucial point brings us back to the question of how the broad outlines of a cognitive style affect a narrative structure and unity among many specific items. In Harry's repertoire, any narration of historical events is consistently bound to evidence of their contemporary consequences. Rhetorical transitions depend on the perceived connection between historical cause and contemporary effect. Then expression of this nexus is a prelude to personal speculation about how individuals might act to alter historical consequences and break deterministic chains. And, of course, historical determinations are imagistically bound to physical locations.

> *And about Sitting Bull's coming back. Well, Custer couldn't make it. This old Indian who told me about it, he was in the Custer battle. He was chasing Reno. He was a young guy but he liked to ride, so he did.*
>
> *Now where the decorated Custer battlefield is, well, just south of there is a high hill. There's fine dust there, and there's a group of Sioux standing on the east side of the hill. They saw something shine so they took after the soldiers. But it was quite a ways, ten or fifteen miles. They didn't get there by the time Custer sent some soldiers on the north side.*
>
> *What Sitting Bull didn't like is that Custer went and killed some Indian woman getting water. That's what made Sitting Bull mad. So he told them, "No prisoners. Don't use the bow and arrow. Just knock them off. Go right on, knock them off. We'll clean them up."*
>
> *The Indian who told me this said that in white man's time, it took about twenty-five or thirty minutes. That's why Sitting Bull didn't come back. He went over the border to Canada. He made friends with the government there.*
>
> *When he did come back, he came back himself. No one ordered him to come back. He ordered some boats and he came back and that's why he was here on Standing Rock.*
>
> *The Crows, the Mandans, the Rees, they helped the white man so much that everything they ask in Congress, they get it.*
>
> *But some of them in Congress would rather have a full-blood talk. And that's what I have done. At the time of the Oahe Dam, they wanted a full-blood to talk. They asked me to testify. If I say "yes" or "no," why it would go through. They asked me to do that, this subcommittee there.*

> They asked me so I said, "Yeah, we'll take it. Maybe if we don't, the government will just cut many more millions off."
>
> So that's what I did. And so I got payment for the Oahe Reservoir for the Standing Rock Sioux tribe.

As Harry's historical commentary works its way toward the present moment, the issue of the Oahe Reservoir returns as the overriding fact controlling other narrative features. The reservoir continues as the physical evidence of what history has meant to the people. The building of the Oahe Dam shaped attitudes just as definitely as it redirected a river. We can return to Lawson's quotation from a Sioux leader: "We look back now to see that we lost everything . . . we had the best part of our life in that area."[30] Narrative traditions modify that statement somewhat. The people did not lose the style of knowing and talking that was nourished along the river's edge. That style arises from and attests to a culture that generates new strategies from ancient patterns.

About two years after I first came to Cannon Ball, the appearance of the community changed dramatically. Government-housing authorities replaced the log cabins with prefabricated frame houses, all alike except for the varying pastel-colored exterior paint. The new houses provided badly needed space and other amenities. But beyond that they changed attitudes in the community in ways that I could sense but did not, could not have, should not have documented in their tentative early development. Television made its way into most of the homes and brought with it concrete vivid images from around the world along with all that passes for drama on the airwaves. People acquired new and different hopes and disappointments to go along with the old ones, and they quickly adjusted their sense of their place in the global community. But not all the drowned trees in the reservoir have fallen. Visual evidence from the past is everywhere and the village still requires story as its interpretative guide. Harry's and Lillian's tales were told to the community, not primarily to me. That one locale in North Dakota has the day-to-day knowledge that can interpret the significance of what they told; but the larger global community can appreciate how intimately the life of these stories is bound to the life of that one village, and that knowledge can and definitely should prompt questions about similar tellers in villages everywhere who are adapting history to the quests of a new generation demanding the right to their own local and global powers.

Because Lillian and Harry were such active and conscious tradition bearers, they possessed a communal status that recognized their knowledge as exemplary. As this chapter demonstrates, the cognitive themes that explain the context of their stories coincide with cognitive themes found in other traditional materials if, and only if, one recognizes a similar cognitive style at work in the traditional and the modern materials instead of looking for surface-level continuities. That allows me to assert that the cognitive style I find in Harry's and Lillian's stories is indeed traditional. Other community members who recognize and appreciate that traditional quality mark themselves as passive bearers of the tradition and as appropriate judges of what they believe to be representative of their traditional status. I cannot claim that the cognitive style demonstrated in the Fast Horse narratives was shared by everyone in the community. Much of the other traditional material that I heard in the community was part of a conscious effort to reintroduce old materials to the contemporary context, and it involved retelling tales that had been read in published collections of older tales. Gradually, as such material is told and retold, it should change to reflect the contemporary cognitive style of the community, but when I was there, the process was too near the beginnings for that process to have taken place. Therefore, while I do not necessarily claim to have documented the cognitive style of an entire community, I can claim to have gathered recognized representative material, and that, in and of itself, speaks to a communal process of deciding on the legitimacy of what they want to accept as evidence of their tradition.

I wonder often about the children I knew in Cannon Ball. For those who are finding their own productive paths both within and outside the community, Harry's and Lillian's stories give some crucial clues about the heritage that helped them imagine success. For those who have not found success, history provides another set of clues; for them, the dogs and coyotes no doubt continue to howl their laments, and the people at Cannon Ball probably still tell newcomers that all the noise is about history.

3. Narrative in Transit

During the first years of the twentieth century, each Sunday in winter when the Missouri River was frozen solidly enough to be a bridge rather than a barrier, the Catholic church at Fort Yates on the Standing Rock Sioux Reservation was the scene of one of those startling cultural juxtapositions that prove western history to be a continuing chronicle of the unlikely. Sitting in the back pews, behind the Sioux were German-Russian immigrants who had crossed the ice-bound river in order to attend Sunday mass and to meet with compatriots who lived near the reservation.[1] They meditated (or daydreamed) during Sioux language sermons, and they eagerly joined with the Sioux people in singing Latin hymns. It was as if the deity bringing these peoples together in worship were indulging in a bit of experimentation to see what would happen if two sharply contrasting societies each had to rediscover their identities after being transferred into an ideological environment so strange and so unresponsive to their questioning that maintaining the life of the social entity depended on an enhanced awareness of a few basic cultural strategies. For both groups that meant using the authority vested in kinship roles to consolidate positions from which to negotiate the historical and political currents that drove them into an unpredictable future as forcefully as the strong, deep currents of the Missouri River conveyed goods, people, and ideas from north to south. And, for both groups, sustaining their basic cultural momentum also meant that they had to refashion narrative traditions in order to marshal collective resources in relation to new social coordinates guiding group identity through the historical breaks that left everyone in that church reaching for the level of hope needed to pray to a God in three languages.

The people that the Sioux saw in the back of their church every Sunday were ethnic Germans or Alsatians, born in the Ukrainian colonies near Odessa that had been established throughout the Black Sea region under an agreement with Czar Alexander I approximately a hundred years after Catherine the Great had created similar colonies along the Volga River.[2] From the rich and climactically kind lands of South Russia, these people came to the cold, semiarid regions of central and western North Dakota and Saskatchewan. Migration began in the late 1880s and lasted until well into the twentieth century. These people were lured by promises, most of them false, in brochures sent out by railroad companies seeking immigrants to develop the American Great Plains. James W. Long writes, "It is no exaggeration to state that the Atcheson, Topeka, and Santa Fe and later the Burlington railroads initiated and organized the colonization of Kansas, Nebraska and the Dakotas. . . . Interestingly the last great surge of expansion and colonization by the Burlington lasted from 1901–1905, a time when many colonists left Russia. Coincidentally, between 1882 and 1887 the Great Plains experienced an extended period of higher than average rainfall. . . . Railroad recruiters boasted of this and the abundant harvests in their promotional pamphlets, with some even asserting that the climate was changing."[3]

During that same historical period, changes in the status of the Russian colonies were signaling the end of the social experiment that in the course of a single century had transformed the ethnic identity of German immigrants even as they turned previously uncultivated regions of the steppes into vineyards, orchards, fields, and towns built on the models of their homes in western Europe. By the end of the century, these emigrants could see the limits of their social experiment—definite changes in government land policies limited their access to added acreage, and that drew attention to other limitations on their willingness or their capacity to adapt to the social environment of an imperial Russia caught in the nationalistic cross-currents of European modernization.

What the colonists in south Russia saw as they scanned the political scene convinced them that their way of life was at risk and led them to making plans to extend what they had begun in the Ukraine to other parts of the world. Their land use policies had included the establishment of "daughter colonies" first in the Ukraine, then in other places where they could imagine optimistic prospects, until finally, when all the mother colonies had been destroyed and the people forcibly dispersed or killed, they had to rebuild communities wherever they could, in Siberia, Central Asia, China, or the Americas.[4] But when the immigrants came to North Dakota at the turn of the century, no one could possibly have foreseen the massacres of colonists left behind in Russia in 1919 or the famine and starvation that followed for survivors of Russian revolutionary conflicts. Cautious American immigrants, looking back on their experiences in south Russia, trusting no government (including the American one), generally summed up their responses to the antiminority, specifically anti-German Russification policies of Alexander II by saying simply that they had no longer felt "at home." Others were slightly more explicit about how Germanophobia had introduced anxiety. As one person told me, "In Russia they were looked on as outsiders or as you would call it 'aliens' and they knew it would be better to get out."

After 1919 immigrants in other parts of the world waited in fear for news from the Ukraine. Those who were in North Dakota had their own struggles with ethnic prejudice, drought and near starvation, unfavorable banking and taxation policies leading to their own radical takeover of state government, a deadly influenza epidemic, and a climate that never compared favorably with the Black Sea region.

Their efforts to build and maintain communities generated their own kinds of narrative that found their particular event structure and cognitive style as they were juxtaposed to tales of relatives' dispersal to Siberia and Central Asia. This developing narrative tradition had a job to do. It had to convey the immigrants' understanding that however little they had, they were still the inheritors of a way of life that had been born on the steppes near the Black Sea and was becoming something new in the Dakotas whether or not they had wanted that to happen.

The experience of double migration and Russia's clear colonial policy, which, in theory at least, had allowed for cultural independence and religious freedom as long as a single religion ruled a single colony and everyone submitted to that rule, had also developed a collective identity that distinguished itself by way of its independence of any national entity. In addition, Russian colonial rule had proven how willing national powers can be to revise their own promises, and this experience left the colonists unwilling to trust any national government. With that distrust came a determination to maintain communal bonds strong enough to survive yet another foreclosure on a lifestyle that had achieved its particular features as a consequence of their migratory history and their proudly nurtured capacity to replicate an agrarian lifestyle. The process of maintaining these intense communal bonds is the generative source for the cognitive themes determining the cognitive style of narrative in those German-Russian communities in North Dakota where I lived and whose narratives I recorded and studied. But the propositional content of narrative is seldom about this process. Instead, what we find over and over again is that narrative that is most important to the maintenance of community dynamics is itself bare, stark, as nearly static as narrative can be. Narrative scheme dramatizes an order that makes a process transmissible and transportable. This purpose seems to require an almost mathematical clarity that leaves interpretation to the communal imagination and memory. I interviewed individuals in hopes of finding direct articulation of the emotion and evidence of reflexive speculation that the scheme excluded. I rarely found such directness, though, even when the people that I interviewed were my own parents. What I learned about this reflexive dimension to the culture came about indirectly, accidentally. It was a consequence of living that could not find its way into any interview context.

Analyzing the cognitive style of any community begins with surveying a body of historical data in order to discover relevant presuppositions for narrative. The German-Russians have not written novels about their experiences. Even shorter forms like poems are rare. But they have been eminently faithful in recording local and family history. Perhaps because of their global dispersal, they have formed active local historical societies and they are ardent genealogists. The written family histories have taken on a conventional form that reflects the forms of those oral histories that the first generations of immigrants repeated, sometimes passionately and obsessively, to their children and grandchildren born on American soil. Because I grew up in an exclusively German-Russian village, I had heard most of the oral forms long before I understood them as anything other than predictably repetitive elements in adult conversations.

Eventually my professional interest in oral literatures and histories drew me back to the forms that had shaped my own experience of how a community had marked its members and their memories. Or perhaps I should say that I realized that I had to explore how a particular community had taught a particular style of remembrance. I therefore began the series of formal interviews on which this chapter depends. The interviews, in turn, made me read many of those family histories that had originally seemed too amateur to have much value for anyone outside the immediate families for whom they were written as an accounting. Finally, even the most tedious and ordinary details began to take on significance in relation to how history had placed and replaced the people who were speaking and writing. I began to see how a style had arisen out of ambitions, hopes, conflicts, and oppression and had assumed its place in history as the evidence of individual and communal desire shaping the memories of historical experience. That style had assumed a role in the workings of my own memory without any conscious intervention on my part, but when conscious analysis gave me an understanding of why it worked the way it did, that style revealed how it could identify belonging. The limitations of my data are such that all I can demonstrate is the workings of that style in a selected group of narrators. Nevertheless, a pattern emerges, a cognitive set shows up in each instance of collected narrative, and cognitive themes emerge that tell us how a selected group of individuals used the impact of history to shape a narrative style.

The written family histories gave me a basis from which to gauge variations among repeated motifs that were, I slowly realized, rituals of sorts in which linked elements signed an identity that had no name beyond the very unsatisfactory hyphenated one that addressed two national sites. On rare occasions collective experience could and eagerly did claim both sites. More often people asserted their difference from both Germans and Russians. That, of course, did not stop Russians, Germans, and Americans from insisting on one or another identity or loyalty without much consideration for how local colonial life had brought about something new with no national label.[5] And, as history proves, this refusal to recognize the emergence of a specifically colonial experience did lead to the destruction of the colonies and to genocide during the European national conflicts of the first half of the twentieth century. No one among the emigrants to the United States thought to add a third noun to the national linguistic chain, although the question of how all three national contexts for experience relate to each other remains very much alive and unresolved for any who can claim it as their own. Therefore, the third unnamed element in a national progression seemed to imply its own radical choice, namely the choice about whether to declare a clean break or to work with the historical questions bound to each site. The narrative and cognitive style that I was studying had developed in response to that third unnamed American site, and to acknowledge it is to assume awareness of how nationalisms converge to shape the consciousness of ordinary people.

One frequently repeated event structure reminded me of the contexts in which I had first heard it from parents and grandparents. This pattern was a brief evocation of the Ukrainian setting with its fertile vineyards, orchards, and ordered towns whose recall made them the reflection of an ideal order that no town in North Dakota was ever likely to reveal. And certainly no one in North Dakota could cultivate vineyards to produce those remembered wines that grew finer with each passing year in North Dakota. Nor could the people reproduce the orchards they recalled even though they tried to protect fruit trees through the long winters and watched sadly and commented with regretful recall when the blossoms froze practically every spring.

Occasions for recalling this patterned device that was a structure of Edenic images custom-designed to set against the hard facts of North Dakota life arose with more frequency than children born in the United States had patience to appreciate. Second-generation listeners were inclined to view it all as a nostalgic backward look that had no place on the American Great Plains. But the sheer force of repetition was such that what may really have begun as simple fond remembrance gradually took on qualities that made the resulting narrative pattern and device into a mark of transitional identity. To be sure, it is a mark that invoked achievements in communities that no longer existed. Like the biblical Eden, these were sites from which the people had been driven and that made them, in every way, the landscapes of desire in which the facts of historical reality and defeat could be hidden but contained and retained as the basis for all that remained unspoken in a new land. Set in the past, this idealized pattern, nevertheless, introduces the energy of desire into its every performance, giving it momentum toward a future whose geographical placement was always in question, at least during the historical period when the motifs were consistently performed.

If American children and grandchildren heard only useless nostalgia, that fractured hearing and understanding were evidence of a changing pragmatic context, a changing cognitive style. Their parents who had emigrated as adults used the simple set of motifs as a way of affirming that there really was a point and purpose to all they had experienced; there was some historical or divine destiny that they recognized more by way of what they excluded from their idealized image than by what they included. However individuals may have felt about their communal situation, the power it had to distinguish them from other groups in that ethnic patchwork quilt that was turn-of-the-century Dakota society was a dominant factor in identity formation and, therefore, in shaping relationships to the landscape in which their social identity was invested.

Slowly I began to realize that any approach to the symbolic economy shaping the cognitive style that the German-Russian immigrant cultures had developed as a result of their double migration required detailed historical analysis of how the idealized spatial references to the towns in the Ukraine functioned as the introduction to the story of their life in the United States. It was also a figure shaping the event structures of oral history. We can find uses of this figure that prove that some colonists, at least, had consciously understood the biblical Genesis as the interpretive frame for their own historical evocation of ethnic identity. One example, taken from a collection of family histories, has astonishing clarity and shows the sensuous immediacy of imaginative care: "When all those fruit trees, and the famous acacia trees, orchard after orchard, colony after colony, were in bloom, the air, as it were, was filled with perfume, and a person sensed a little bit of the garden of Eden. Serenely and calmly flowed along these orchards and vineyards, the Dneister, one of the longest, finest and cleanest rivers of the Ukraine, abounding with a variety of fish, and that empties into the Black Sea."[6]

Although this statement is pure description, the action of leaving this Eden is the implied element that makes it a narrative event. Generally such descriptions are embedded in family histories so that the conventionalized descriptive event sums up the historical past. As I worked with event structure as well as propositional content in German-Russian narratives, I gradually developed an appreciation for the emotional intensity with which the immigrants, usually women, transmitted these conventionalized motifs. My own father recalled his grandmother's preoccupation with the Edenic themes. During her last years, living with her son and his children, she had tried obsessively to imprint on the minds of her grandchildren the image of those beautiful towns, lush gardens, and vineyards in the Odessa district. She told vivid tales of managing her large household and of attending communal festivals. All of this was narrated in a North Dakota setting where drought was so extreme that her son had devised a sling so that he and his children could help lift the cows to a standing position in order to milk them because the animals were so weak from eating a combination of thistles, straw, and molasses that they could no longer get up without help. But if life in North Dakota was largely focused on physical survival until into the 1940s, my father also knew that all the people in the villages his grandmother eulogized had been dispersed; thousands had been killed. He knew about the relative in Ukrainia who had been an intellectual and had had his hands cut off to demonstrate that ideas have power and that individuals have to pay for propagating any deemed wrong by the current government. Therefore, my father was understandably impatient with what he saw as useless nostalgia for what no longer existed. He knew that she was talking about a people who no longer belonged anywhere.

Yet a great deal more was at stake than mere nostalgia and complaint; or, perhaps, we might say that affect which might be labeled *nostalgia* was the transitional emotion supporting the development of the more precisely articulated cognitive structures needed in the new setting. The colonists' communal identity, still operating according to the explicit social logic that linked daughter to mother colonies, was naturally drawn toward the distant "mother" so that the literally reproduced buildings, the efforts to maintain social and kinship patterns, and the struggle to reestablish religious organizations were all upheld by emotions that became more retrospectively positive as time distanced them from the facts that had driven them from those towns and villages. And the ways in which a communal condition established choices for individuals also established the points of passage between this tradition and any others undergoing radical change. The act of cultural reproduction from one national site to another is a particular kind of task, one that has continued to gain significance as the twentieth century has advanced and has put more and more refugees on the move, requiring us to learn more and more about a process that differs in significant details from group to group even as the sum total outlines a comparative historical task, one that expresses some of the psychological, cognitive, and linguistic resources at work within those groups that retain, for a time at least, a stubbornly determined drive toward coherent and separate communal identity. Emigration continues to test that vital reflexive process that brings individuals into social consciousness amid communities that are, themselves, crucibles of continuing role redefinition and reintegration.

The spatial references that structure these narratives were the primary features allowing me to align the implicit narrative deduced from pragmatic presuppositions that guided the performance of these motifs with the dynamics of subject formation that all narrative performance supports. Of course, working with the narrative tradition in order to reveal this dimension of cognitive style requires a means of theorizing and thereby generalizing connections between history, community, landscape, and self in ways that go beyond the straightforward descriptive level. Derek Gregory in the conclusion to his study of space and social theory, as developed in Lefebvre and as compared to Lacan's notions of subject formation, provides an extraordinary summary that allows me to strategize this part of my own work with cognitive style against the background of these twentieth-century understandings of individual subjectivity, community, and landscape.

Gregory uses Lefebvre's arguments about how "the intelligence of the body," definite sense knowledge, allows us to constitute a visual field within space, and Lefebvre represents this process as a generalization of the mirror effect in which social space itself becomes a collective mirror. Gregory then makes the crucial connection with Lacan that indicates how my work with cognitive style can be situated:

> *Unlike Lacan, however, the importance of the mirror for Lefebvre is not that its reflection "constitutes my unity* qua *subject" but rather that "it transforms what I am into the* sign *of what I am." In much the same way, therefore, Lefebvre suggests that within the "symbolic imaginary" of social space the sign-bearing "I" no longer deals with anything but other bearers of signs; In effect, "space offers itself like a mirror to the thinking 'subject,' but after the manner of Lewis Carroll, the 'subject' passes through the looking-glass and becomes a lived abstraction." This collective—and historical—passage marks the transformation from absolute into abstract space.*[7]

The towns, gardens, and vineyards evoked by the German-Russian immigrants are remarkable evidence of remembered social space operating as a collective mirror that transforms the individual into a social sign whose narrative purpose, at least, is to maintain a position that sustains the integrity of the whole collective image. That was the message all those first-generation tellers tried to imprint on the minds of their descendants. Surviving the early years in the United States required an emphasis on communal well-being that nearly obliterated individual aspiration. The instinct that shaped narrative, reminding individuals that they are collective sign bearers, was an instinct arising from the most fundamental human capacity for using narrative as survival strategy. Viewed simply as texts, these evocations lacked artistic embellishment. But they were a definite articulation of what Lefebvre has called a conceptual grid allowing users to appropriate space; they were textual evocations of places other than the ones currently inhabited, and these evocations recall a former social landscape, a collective memory in the process of acquiring new significance.[8]

Gregory's comparison between Lefebvre and Lacan gets directly to the question of the relationship between collective strategy and individual experience. How could narrative that was so easily ignored or discredited by listeners play a role in their lives that an analyst can dare to link with fundamental dynamics of subject formation? Here is where the matter of *style* comes to the forefront. The Edenic motifs are simply the clearest and most frequently performed evidence of a public style that drew a line between public and private, between what should be talked about and what should be censored from public speech acts. This style is evidence of a whole body of pragmatic assumptions that shaped the interpretation of individual aspirations over and against communal beliefs. The passage through the looking glass of ordered narrative space that the Edenic motifs represent is also a passage that divides abstract space into a public narrative pattern and a whole series of private ones. This sharp division is one of the distinguishing characteristics of this cognitive style. Different social spaces orchestrated different voices. Each space had its history and each history had had its effects on the symbolic and imaginary that guided the individual subject in process. In the course of one or at most two generations, the descendants of immigrants learned that failure to understand how distinctive histories had worked their indirect ways into their own and their parents' lives could result in an experience of alterity within family networks. Because this otherness was not easily labeled in terms of national origins, it seemed beyond expression. It seemed cut off from the very history that had engendered it. Few would have stated the realization as I just have. Nevertheless, many second- and third-generation immigrants would instantly recognize what I address. One man recalled his first experiences with outsiders who called him a "Roosian" (an ethnic slur). His childhood response was to go home and announce to his parents that from that point onward he intended to speak English. For the most part, he did. His family recognized that it gave him an edge in an American setting and quietly encouraged his resolve. That is an ordinary enough immigrant response. But by the age of about fifteen, he had also resolved to learn what he considered to be "proper" German, assuming that linguistic control would help him separate the various national strands that had gone into his identity. The mixed colonial experience, though, represented something to be sidestepped, its traces eliminated from behavior even though he remained close to the family that had so quietly allowed him to switch his languages, and that family loyalty meant taking over the family farm so that colonial experience was, finally, the dominant influence in his life. For many, the foreignness that inhabited personal memory became the most intimate awareness of how a cognitive style operates to bind or sever or to do both at once as it binds experience through memories that are severed from a style of retrospective understanding.

    Family histories written for local audiences may be consistent in their evocations of the Edenic motifs, but they also provide variants proper to each family that bring us closer to the way the social history summed up by these motifs affected individual subjectivity. Among the oral versions that I recorded, Joseph Vetter's is the clearest in its negotiation of various boundary distinctions, especially as these define his ethnic identity.[9] Vetter's language evokes the imagined Ukrainian ideal set in another landscape where "once there was nothing," and we can see how it establishes a closed narrative loop that is both product and pretense of a carefully cultivated ideology of stability set against the severances of migration. His language performs an understanding of an identity that developed in opposition to national settings even as it confirms the importance of these same literal geographical spaces in relation to transferring elements of what developed there to an American setting, to the "over here" with which he ends his evocation. The motive for immigration transforms a mere Edenic description into a narrative event in which transfer from country to country is the implied action. The event ends with the telling contrasts between "there" and "here," which encompass all of colonial history. "In Russia, the German colonists were independent; they could have their own schools and churches and they became prosperous. The Russians became jealous. . . . The Germans were good workers. They had good land; they could raise anything, apricots, peaches, grapes. They raised a lot of grapes; they made a lot of wine. But that took years too. When they got there, there was nothing, just like over here."

The *nothing* to which Vetter refers need not be read as failure to recognize prior claims to the land on the part of indigenous peoples on either continent. Such failures did occur among individuals, but there were so many similarities between what these immigrants had experienced in Russia and what the Native peoples were undergoing in the United States that the comparisons were lost on no one, and occasionally public family histories include some speculations on the parallels. *Nothing* is a term that has a conventionalized narrative significance within this discursive community, and it applies primarily to the immigrants' capacity to read the new landscape as constitutive of ethnic identity, a fact that was brought home to me on another occasion when I heard the term used by an elder in another German-Russian community well to the west of where Vetter had settled, the community where I had spent my early childhood.

I had returned to visit relatives and I went with my aunt to the church that was, for the moment at least, still the center of community life, although everyone knew that no pastor would be assigned to replace the one who had been there for decades. After the service, one of the village elders, dressed in the formal long black coat and top hat of a previous era, approached me, shook my hand, paused dramatically, and then asked, "Why are you here?"

I answered with more truthful economy than I would have had I not been so surprised by the question. "I want to see what is here."

He gestured to the field in front of us and proclaimed with all the apocalyptic solemnity I had just heard in the pastor's sermon, "There is nothing here."

His grandson, whose appearance suggested his status as an agricultural entrepreneur, laughed and replied, "Don't listen to him; this is still a good place to live; we are all doing fine here."

I knew that both men were right. In that moment I understood that three different understandings of community had unexpectedly been superimposed one upon the other, with our view of the fallow field in front of us holding all three in brief equilibrium. The oldest among us knew that the community his family had tried to transfer from the Ukraine had transformed itself into something he could barely recognize as descendant from what he had known in his youth. My former schoolmate had acquired vast stretches of consolidated prime acreage that grew enough spring wheat to pay for frequent trips to nearby towns or even to distant cities any time out of growing season, and he had little need for the vision of communal cooperation whose absence caused his grandfather to look at the landscape and see a loss that betrayed history. There were still traces of the remembered way of life that could stand against the immigrants' sense of loss, and those traces included the abandoned store and post office, the town hall and meeting house that had once centered the cooperative institutions and beliefs that served most practically as the means to acquire land on which to live at a time when banks were more interested in foreclosing on loans than in helping immigrants survive. The literal placement of buildings in these villages, as in the Native ones that neighbored them, reflected a history of relationships translated into a sign system that had originally served as a myth of ethnic origins, only to be shifted back again into historical categories by virtue of the very success that the young celebrated.

That nearly deserted village was one of my most important reality checks for a lot of theory and academic speculation about cognitive style and narrative. It allowed me to assess the instrumental value of metaphor and metonymy that make language operational in processes of individuation that shape communities and not just individual persons. Or at least that is one of the hypotheses guiding this entire book. And the relation between personal and communal individuation processes is the one that matters for the study of cognitive style. That village, mute testimony to a colonial history that had played itself out on every continent except, perhaps, Africa and Australia, made me question any social theory that could not address the particularities of distinctive national and ethnic formations. Occupied or not, it still anchored the abstractions that might characterize the cognitive style of German-Russian immigrant narratives.

Certainly, for a short time at least, the literal construction of villages had been a means of simultaneously holding at bay the alterity that the American landscape represented and of devising the images that would allow colonists to come to terms with their new site and situation. The colonists quickly discovered how deceptive the railroad publicists had been. The 1890s, when most of them arrived in the United States, were times of far less rainfall than the abundant early '80s. Joseph Vetter lets us glimpse the early confusion of settlers who feared that they had wagered everything and lost because they had come to a desert. They looked at the dry soil, ran it between their fingers, and questioned whether it could even absorb rain in the blessed event of a long soaking spell of moisture. To keep alive some degree of belief and hope in their newly adopted landscape, they dug holes in the resistant soil and filled them with water to see if it could transform dry sand to nurturing mud. As they waited, though, they planned yet another move, possibly even another migration to another nation. Argentina was an obvious place to go because relatives had already settled there. Vetter said, "No rain in 1889. The first rain they got was June 1, 1890. At that time, my dad had already gone out west to Oregon to look for a place where it rains. He said he would never stay in a place where it doesn't rain. They knew that. That summer never a cloud would come up, but lightning would strike and start a prairie fire, so they made fire guards around the land to save some grass for the livestock. Anyhow, after two years without rain, then it started to rain in summer and snow in winter again. So they stayed but they had to go three miles in summer and winter for water, so they got tired of that and moved to where I live now."

In spite of the first-person reference, "Where I live now" are words that account for a communal effort in which a collective vision was the means of survival. Most of the immigrants from the Black Sea region were prosperous, but the cost of immigration and the purchase price for land that often had to be sold at a loss quickly depleted any financial resources they had. Often enough, especially during the recurrent drought periods, they were refugees on American territory, dependent on the community to help them find farms to rent and means to construct family shelters.

Joseph Vetter's presentation includes some of the most revealing responses to the experience of living at the edge of all hope on land where rocks seemed to grow but little else. He tells about one man who left a Sunday family gathering without any explanation. When he did not return, his children looked for him and finally found him in a field, lying on the ground, arms outstretched in the shape of a cross, weeping and praying to the God who had crucified him to the dry land. What draws the analyst's attention to this vignette is not just the anguish of the man/land/God triangle but the utter privacy of this emotional expression. The incident lives in family memory not because the emotion itself is so surprising but because it was the only time the family observed their father expressing private emotion, and, for them, the simple fact of expression was as dramatic as its mode. The incident represents a rare witnessed crossing of the boundary between public and private, and as such it attests to the power of that boundary.

Vetter also described people standing on the roofs of those early sod houses, watching the occasional passersby simply because they needed to retain a visual connection with other people. His reference to *nobody* echoes the cognitive themes summed up in the ways immigrants used the word *nothing:* "Those people were used to being among other people. Over here, there was nobody. When the people saw a team, they would crawl up on the roof of the house and look and look and look where they go."

Vetter's personal comment on this memory is an understated retrospective wonderment. "Well, you can imagine, over there, they had colonies and over here, well it was hard for everyone." Not surprisingly, he ascribes the expression of emotion to women, talking to each other in private, away from the hearing of men. "They liked the government better here—but I heard my mother say that a lot of them cried a lot and a lot of them said they would walk back to Russia if it weren't for the ocean."

Vetter's brief passing reference to "the government" points to the occlusions of the idealized references to life in the Ukraine. The oppressive facts of previous colonial life were definitely excised from the propositional content of performed identity. Nevertheless, they remained the generative source of the dominant presuppositions guiding the interpretation of that content. Konrad Keller's published records for the Ukrainian villages show some of what the colonists managed to censor from their performance of historical memory. One such incident inclines the reader to smile for a microsecond before reacting to its stunning message of repression; it is an entry for January 10, 1810. "Stupid people are not to be so bold as to hold discussions about political affairs, especially about war, in either inns or in private houses. Any who act in opposition to this, will be delivered up to the district office under guard."[10]

One can easily imagine how an adjective like "stupid" used as a justification for legal action might give free reign to prejudice. And the chronologies give repetitive evidence that prejudice pursued its predictably cruel course. The watchful eye of judgmental civil authority penetrated even the privacy of homes. Keller notes that the deputy president of the Social Welfare Committee, a man named Hahn, "had the unusual habit of closely inspecting the women's domain: kitchens, cellars, larders were all inspected closely."[11]

This pervasive coercive control existed in spite of the fact that the official documents establishing the colonies emphasized freedom. The contradiction between promised freedoms and the experience of repression adds to the skepticism and distrust that shape the actual structure of narrative and, even more important, the interpretation of narrative meaning. Colonists in the United States did not speak of what had gone on in the Ukraine because they did not trust the Americans. Cultural insiders could bring unauthorized knowledge to their hearing or reading of authorized history. Cultural outsiders, though, would hear only the conventional exaggerations of what once was without realizing what that carefully constructed idealized surface hid. As we study available texts, we can watch the divisions and contradictions multiply, but only if we recognize how the surface structure pulls us into a play of metaphor and interpretation. Keeping this pragmatic dimension in mind, we can see that the remembered facts of relentless authoritarian surveillance really did have a determining effect on the American context of interpretation. Memories of repression and of a society in which any open talk was dangerous guaranteed a context of reception in which astute awareness of how the experienced facts had negated official promises gave a figurative dimension to the entire narrative scheme. The endless repetitions of conventional ideals were really demonstrations of the power of the collective imagination to project a way of life worth migrating for.

One of the surprising aspects of the German-Russian narrative tradition to which I have had access has to do with how little oral or written records preserve about details of actual migrations. Their transatlantic journeys surely must have had dramatic moments that prompted speculative thought, even discussion. Then there is that first migration from western to eastern Europe when they traveled by wagon train. Joseph Height has recorded facts about that initial migration to south Russia that let us go well beyond what the formulaic statements of oral history evoke. For example, he notes that by the end of 1804, more than 5,000 colonists had arrived and that, due to overcrowding and poor living conditions, 366 people had died.[12]

Almost exactly a century after these events, the grandchildren and great grandchildren of the first settlers set out again from towns and villages that were by then prosperous replications of those they had left in Germany and Alsace. In their oral or written histories they tend to note the fact of the first migration as though arrival and only arrival mattered, and they repeated that narrative gesture when they came to the United States. This narrative device is the most striking evidence we have of a cognitive style that seems to empty time out of narrative and replace it with spatial images. One family historian gave us slightly more detail, from which we can deduce more of the historical presuppositions guiding the pragmatic level of these narratives.

Gregor Seelinger came from the colony of Rastadt in the Ukraine. Several members of the Seelinger family were noted musical performers and composers. But we learn none of this from Seelinger's own narrative, written for his family and translated into English by his daughter.[13] He adheres to the public narrative pattern as he gives the obligatory but passing notice to the ancestor who migrated from Germany to Russia. Then he lists his siblings with their extended families, one still living in the Ukraine, one in Canada, two in the United States, others in places unknown. One brother had opposed the Bolsheviks in 1919 and was presumed dead. This sort of diasporic mapping characterizes all German-Russians of his generation. Even though the German-Russians had, by the late nineteenth century, given up any patriotic ties to their first homeland, those who stayed in the Ukraine after 1900 were victims of the anti-German sentiment that was part of Russia's early-twentieth-century response to the German nationalism that followed Bismarck's rise to power.[14]

But if the colonists were reasonably indifferent to what was happening in Germany, they understood as their own the colonial cultural traces that outsiders thought to be German; they saw these customs as neither German nor Russian, although they acknowledged specifically local regional ties to western Europe. Therefore, the colonists resisted most aspects of the legislated Russification policies, especially those regarding language and religion. Nevertheless, in the midst of political confusion over who they were, they tried to assert their loyalty to the Russian government that had recruited them to their new homeland; and, as Seelinger's narrative shows, they easily incorporated the patriotic czar and fatherland slogans into their public speech. Of course, that very support of the czar put them in opposition to the Bolsheviks who first plundered the colonies and then, during the famine years, requisitioned what food the colonists could grow, leaving them to starve. In the meantime their American immigrant relatives were engaging in their own political struggles that placed them in a position where the Americans were calling them Bolsheviks and doing everything possible to nourish the immigrants' fears of expulsion from American territories.

The language of Seelinger's account barely hints at all the historical complexity it subsumes. His language shrinks political conflict to the size required by the public narrative pattern. Not surprisingly, given the way this public pattern excludes the personal, we find almost no evidence of how people responded emotionally to the obliteration of their culture and to the killing and disappearance of all their relatives left behind in the Ukraine. The towns in the Ukraine whose remembered images had been transformed into narratives of ethnic identity were finally left completely abandoned. Only one telling reference to a court jester suggests to us that Seelinger was inserting private evidence of bowing to fate into a form that resisted anything private.

As I studied what Seelinger had written and juxtaposed it to what I had heard from other family members, I hoped for some direct statements that would give me a better understanding of how historical choices and accidents had shaped interior reflection. I wanted articulate evidence of self-reflection to help me piece together the broken messages that had found their way into our generation. Knowing the power of the public pattern, though, I was not really surprised to find that Seelinger resolutely held to the required rhetorical tone so that individual understanding and interpretation come through only when content seems momentarily to slip the rhetorical traces.

Some of that brief slipping out of imposed structure occurs when Seelinger talks about his brother's anti-Bolshevik activities. Using standard patriotic rhetorical flourishes, he emphasizes that his brother deliberately chose to struggle on behalf of the common people by fighting for "the land of the Czars." How much should be read into the relationships set up by land and czar in this phrase remains a question that cannot be answered from within the context of what Seelinger wrote, and it is precisely this kind of evidence of severance from pragmatic presuppositions that complicates the study of the cognitive style of this culture. On the one hand, because I know the family, I believe that adverbs like "deeply" and "loyally" probably really do suggest how closely the family had bound their identities to the Russian setting that sang through the musical compositions for which several of them were so well known. On the other hand, such expression may be no more than evidence of safeguarding speech in an environment where armed peasants could attack a town and randomly kill presumed enemies of the fatherland. Seelinger wrote, "He [the brother] was deeply involved in politics, loyally in support of the land of the Czars, and he eventually gave his life because he wanted to help the common people in Russia."

Later, the narrative lens zooms in on the barest of details indicating what it was like to be one of the German-speaking "common people" in colonies in early-twentieth-century czarist Russia. As soon as that happens, more of the contradictions of that position become part of the narrative momentum. We glimpse a young man's anger and growing awareness that his status left him with no options but to emigrate, yet he continues with rhetorical references to himself as a Russian subject, not German, and his phrase "already, at that time" is only the barest hint of how much he knew about the devastation that followed his departure: "As a Russian subject [I] had to endure a great deal of (indignities) already at that time."

The unexpressed, stealthily implied facts of all that Seelinger sums up with that strangely parenthesized word *indignities* were powerful enough to maintain the motivational impetus behind migration to the United States even though the struggles of the earlier migration to Russia were still very much alive in communal memory. Along with authorizing laws that enacted the Russification policy, which affected all ethnic minorities in Imperial Russia, Czar Alexander II on June 4, 1871, had issued a decree that revoked many of the specific rights and privileges initially granted by Catherine the Great and then by her grandson Alexander I. At the time Seelinger emigrated, the people still had hopes for improvement in the Russian political climate, but they had no intention of assimilating, and the new land policies designed to benefit the Russian peasantry were equating colonists with peasants, a situation that effectively ended their capacity to purchase new lands for daughter colonies.

The public narrative pattern to which Seelinger adheres takes on added significance when we realize that while individuals clearly had their private motives for leaving Russia, this personal initiative had little or no place in the communal scale of values. Seelinger's narrative gives some slight personalized evidence of how communities made sure that a younger son, determined to strike out for brighter prospects, would endorse the communal motives that justified migration. Predictably, this was done by means of the obvious mechanism of marriage even though colonial standards judged him too young to marry. In spite of what he says in his narrative, family history reveals that, even unmarried, he would not have had to "go into the wide world" on his own, although he may well have shown some inclination to do just that. Other relatives were emigrating too, so he could simply have gone along with them, as was the custom when establishing new colonies. But his family in the Ukraine was not about to run the risk of his becoming an individualistic adventurer in the Americas, and they were certainly not going to leave his marriage to American chance or choice. They made sure that they had bound two segments of an existing community before sending the young representatives of those linked families to the other side of the globe.

Seelinger's own language hints at awareness and even pride in the way his understanding of personal identity was bound stage by stage to communal necessity:

> *My father died when I was ten years old (my mother was forty-five years old at the time. She never remarried) and I lived with my mother, working with my brothers (farming) until I was nineteen years old. Because there was little chance that I would ever acquire an economic farming unit, since I only inherited thirty acres of land and about $300.00 from my father, I was subject to be conscripted into the Russian Czar's military service in which no compensation was received, and as a Russian subject I had to endure a great deal of (indignities) already at that time, I decided to migrate to America, even though it was a difficult decision to leave my mother. My mother didn't want me to go into the wide world alone and she said that if I were to get married she would not object to my leaving. So it came about that I was married when I was eighteen years and eleven months old, on February 11, 1898. This caused quite a stirring among the people and considerable murmuring when the priest announced from the pulpit that Gregor Seelinger, son of Anton and Katharina nee Klug and Anna Wandler daughter of Anton and Magdalena nee Fischer were to be married. It was a rare occurrence that any man was married at such a young age.*

Referring to the first part of the journey across Russia to Bremen, Germany, where they boarded ship, Seelinger states, "We weren't treated as human beings but were handled as living freight and transported in the same way." My grandmother was even less direct about the transatlantic journey. She remembered falling into the water as they boarded ship. Her brother immediately dived in and rescued her. All she ever said to me about the rest of the trip was that she spent most of it wishing that he had simply let her drown.

As he continues with his family history, Seelinger does write about the poverty and near starvation of the early years in the United States, and it is in this context that the telling reference to a court jester appears. But there had to have been a certain hard-edged fatalism in the comparison to a jester's games during those years in which family obligations really did hold individual members to the newly acquired but still unproductive lands even as they dreamed of being anywhere but where they were. Seelinger understates one incident of near despair: "On one occasion, however, it happened that I did not get the money for the hay I hauled to Dickinson; I had to turn it over to the store owner in payment of interest on money I owed him. I had taken the hay to Dickinson because we didn't have enough flour to bake bread. That day I had to return home with empty hands, even though we had nothing to eat in the house."

The poverty of the first years in the Dakotas was consequence of a devastating mix of bad weather and bad government policy. The immigrants simply had to endure the weather, but the policies could be changed, and all the people, no matter their country of origin, knew that one way to help feed North Dakotans was to spend less money getting produce elsewhere, and this led to the rise of radical politics, what the state historian Elwyn Robinson called "the great socialist experiment" that characterized the beginning of the twentieth century in North Dakota. Robinson states unequivocally that "the rise and fall of the Nonpartisan League was a part of the agrarian discontent of all the western states, a part of colonial revolt wherever colonial status prevailed."[15]

The rise and fall of the Nonpartisan League remains one of the least understood aspects of twentieth-century political history in the United States. What began as an organized program against outside domination of the state's institutions ended as a class war within the state, a conflict that was manipulated by East Coast business interests to denigrate socialism by any means necessary. When Minneapolis grain dealers blocked legislation that would have created a state grain elevator and market in North Dakota, angry farmers, protesting railway taxes on market-bound grain, were willing audiences for Socialist Party organizers.

The details that Robinson gives in his history of the state present a political picture that few North Dakotans would recognize today and almost no one outside the state admits as part of American history:

> *The Socialists had considerable success. They brought in many outside speakers; Eugene V. Debs spoke at a large antiwar rally ("red to the core" he called it) at Garrison in 1915. By 1912 there were 175 Socialist locals in the state. Many Republican weekly newspapers had "Socialist departments"; Rugby and Hillsboro elected Socialist mayors. In 1912 the party established a weekly paper, the* Iconoclast *at Minot. It attacked and ridiculed the National Guard, the Reserve Officers' Training Corps at the University of North Dakota, the Boy Scouts ("hired hessians of capitalism"), and a deity which presided unfeelingly over capitalist injustice. It upheld the violent Industrial Workers of the World.*[16]

Socialism took on a distinctively North Dakota cast when Arthur C. Townley got involved. In 1912 an early frost and a break in flax prices wiped out his farming profits. He went bankrupt with debts of eighty thousand dollars. An embittered Townley turned to socialism. In 1913 the Socialist Party hired him as an organizer in the western North Dakota counties. As Robinson says, Townley had "phenomenal success," but party officers, probably jealous of the charismatic Townley, ordered him to stop. He refused and they evicted him from the party. Then he observed the 1915 state legislative session in Bismarck that defeated the bill that would have authorized a state-owned grain elevator. Already irate farmers, most of them immigrants, were angered at the defeat and the insults thrown their way by American supporters of urban business interests. Townley recognized the volatility of the situation and seized the chance to coordinate a new farmers' organization named the Nonpartisan League. As the sheer force of political discontent escalated, the new organization proposed its own candidates for state elections, and what began as a farmer's organization became a political party.

According to Robinson,

> The Nonpartisan League was a blend of socialism and high-pressure salesmanship. It stirred up and used the old hatreds and feelings of exploitation, but it also succeeded because Townley was an unusually talented agitator. . . . by the winter of 1915–1916 the League was riding the crest of a wave of almost fanatic enthusiasm; when snow flew, it had some twenty-six thousand members. Its headquarters at Fargo was sending out topnotch speakers to dozens of meetings all over the state; farmers were driving miles over the prairies to hear them. They were shouting the League slogan, "We'll Stick," and meaning it. Farmer solidarity was Townley's great achievement and the key to League success.[17]

In the November elections of 1916 the League candidate for governor received 79 percent of the vote; 81 of the 113 members of the house and 18 of the 49 senators were League candidates. The League also controlled major state newspapers. The organization had national and international aspirations. Townley addressed the American Federation of Labor in Buffalo, New York, in 1917.

In 1918 opposition to the League set up the Independent Voters Association, which also supported producer cooperatives and tried to draw moderate voters away from the League, which was drawing national attention and opposition. The IVA was particularly popular with the German-Russian immigrants. In spite of the break between the League and the IVA, the 1919 legislature managed to enact the laws laying the framework for state socialism, creating a state Industrial Commission, State Bank, North Dakota Mill and Elevator Association, and a series of constitutional amendments. This drew the attention of outside business and banking interests who began to organize the opposition and manipulate the tensions that men like Townley had aroused from the very beginning.

In 1920 the Independent Voters Association endorsed the popular William Langer for governor, declaring that "the real issue in the campaign in the state is between Americanism and socialism."[18] Langer was defeated that year, but his career was launched and the IVA had become a major force in state politics, and Langer was definitely a folk hero in the German-Russian communities. By 1921 the eastern investment bankers had begun to boycott bonds sold by the North Dakota Industrial Commission. Soon they imposed severe restrictions on the Bank of North Dakota. League enterprises could no longer expand, and League organization was falling apart. The socialist spirit animating the whole venture remained very much a part of state politics until the 1950s, but the radical institutional experimentation and the sense of adventure and control over their own destiny that had motivated farmers across the state dissipated rapidly in the 1930s. While it lasted, though, it had established peculiar conjunctions between state and ethnic politics, and those conjunctions are the basis for the story Leo Sticka tells about the father-son political career that spanned those dramatic years in North Dakota politics.

Leo Sticka was related by marriage to Gregor Seelinger. Leo was the son of Ignatz Sticka, whose first wife was Gregor's sister. Ignatz, his wife Theresia, and their three children emigrated with Gregor and his wife. Soon after their arrival in the United States, Theresia had a fourth child. A few months later she died of pneumonia. Everyone in the community knew that Ignatz needed another wife. So they sent him a young woman whom he interviewed, once. He introduced her to his children. Then he offered her the job as his wife. Many years and several husbands later (she outlived them all), I interviewed her. She laughed about that first marriage and said firmly, "I knew I could do it and I did it." She was Leo Sticka's mother. I asked him if he would let me record his memories of local history, but he said he preferred to write something for me.

Leo Sticka wrote a brief family history in which narrative structures exhibit a discernible homology with sociological strategies for communal participation in state and national politics. His father's role in the community was so taken for granted that his name and his role were identified. People often referred to him simply as "the politician." Leo inherited his political career from his father, who had little difficulty getting the community to accept his personal designation of his son as his successor. Votes of course followed paternal endorsement; nepotism was a sign of communal integrity and stability based on familial status. Together the tenures of father and son in the North Dakota state legislature spanned thirty-two years.

The extent to which the father determined the political career of his son was remembered by a half-brother who describes how the father decided which son would be his designated successor. It was a choice in which paternal wishes were paramount, overriding even the ambitions and hopes of his sons. One of Leo's older half-brothers, Ralph, had shown genuine interest in a political career. Ralph was the one who the father had pressured to learn English; Ralph was the family member assigned to read all available newspapers and discuss the news with his father; he helped his father write political speeches in German, and he then translated them into English; and, not surprisingly, he had his own political ambitions. The statewide German language newspaper published political debates, and the young Ralph began a written debate with a seasoned political analyst. No one outside Ralph's own community ever guessed that one participant in that published debate was a mere boy. When that fact was revealed, everyone predicted a brilliant future for the young political writer. But Ignatz decided that his own frequent absences from the family farm made it imperative for Ralph to concentrate on farming. A younger son, Leo, was the one chosen for politics.

Leo does not directly mention any of these family politics in his memoir written for me a few months before his death and grandly titled "The Venture of Ignatz Sticka into the Political Life of North Dakota, 1870–1939."[19] That 1870 is the year of Ignatz's birth in the Ukraine and not the year in which he entered American politics might be taken as stylistic evidence that the epithet "the politician" applies to a lifetime and not just to a legislative career. The conflation between career and life is also evident in the metaphor that provides the central figure controlling the cognitive style of Leo's entire narrative, and, no doubt, that of most political discourse in these immigrant communities. Leo refers to the state as a "household." Almost obscured by standard political pieties, that household metaphor brings otherwise pedestrian observations into line with the workings of an entire field of practices based in the interactional dynamics of family authority. That crucial and telling metaphor occurs in that part of the narrative where he accounts for his own decision to follow his father's lead into politics: "By observation and study, I felt that all of us have not only a right but a duty to serve when called upon for service in the conduct of affairs of the state's household and this should not be limited only to the affluent of society."

Leo Sticka's written account is divided into two sections. The first tells about his father's career, the second about his own. His father's entry into political life coincided with the years of socialist activity, and Leo's narrative is brief witness to the story of those turbulent years. This testimony reveals several stylistic features that can be linked directly to the cultural history. In North Dakota, ethnic prejudice demeaned German-Russian immigrants' ability to understand anything American. In the way he sets himself up as witness to his father's consuming interest in politics, Leo's style is an implicit response to that ethnic history. But it also reveals the communal process of achieving consensus, then working that consensus into a political position.

> Ignatz Sticka always managed a keen interest in governmental affairs, as evidenced by the fact that whenever a congressman or governor would come to the area, almost without fail, he would dispense with the work load, just to listen to these people in order to be better informed about the affairs of state and nation. I know this to be true, I was with him on these occasions, either as his chauffeur or his companion. As time went on, there appeared on the political horizon a new front composed of disenchanted politicians and some farm people and they organized The Nonpartisan League. This took place during 1916.
>
> The platform of this group emphasized the ownership of state-supported industries, such as the Bank of North Dakota, Midland Elevator, State Hail Insurance Department. This group was successful in electing their main slate of candidates in the succeeding elections. It is to be noted here that at that time, the candidates endorsed by the Nonpartisan League ran on the Republican ticket thereby creating a factional fight in the primary elections, with the candidates of the Independent Voters Association (IVA, for short). The IVA people were a prominent faction in those days in North Dakota Politics. Ignatz Sticka was somewhat sympathetic towards the NPL but not in toto. He had many good friends among the IVA group.
>
> In the spring of 1932 a group of Stark County citizens, among them Ignatz Sticka, met in Dickinson. The purpose of this gathering was to discuss the possibility of organizing a new party to be known as the Stark County Farm Labor Party, and as such a discussion was held about the possibility of endorsing legislative candidates to run under this banner. The consensus of the group was that the organization of the Farm Labor Party became a reality and they also endorsed candidates for the legislature. Ignatz Sticka participated in all of these discussions and in subsequent meetings found himself as one of those endorsed for this post; in the ensuing elections he and his running mates won election soundly.
>
> Ignatz Sticka was elected to his first term in the state legislature in 1932, he did not try in 1934, won election again in 1936 and again in 1938. He served with honor and distinction until February 18, 1939 when he succumbed to a heart seizure during his third term in office at the age of 68.

The second section of this narrative begins with a rhetorical bridge that is precise and strong evidence of the way the culture set up divisions between public and private. Leo Sticka begins by referring to himself in the third person, and by way of such reference he situates himself in the village. Only then does he switch to first person narration. That same move accommodates his understanding of a political hierarchy. His first stated interest is in county politics, and that local point then opens out step by step to the national. "Leo Sticka was born and reared near the parental farm one mile east of the village of Schefield, attended public and parochial school there. While attending school, I developed an interest in the civic and governmental affairs of our county and later in the affairs of the state and nation."

The daily facts of local and familial interactional dynamics gave cognitive depth to the figurative significance of the household as a political metaphor. Historical experience was bound to the household metaphor, endowing different customs with significance deriving from interlocking spheres of authority, and, in the process, the immigrants' narrative of family life developed into a paradigm for all institutional development, which progressed from family to parish to county to state—the nation seemed a paradigm-breaking entity. The Sticka family tested the political power of the household metaphor. Along with community votes, Ignatz obviously got community moral support, but he also got hate mail and other kinds of harassment from outsiders. As his son notes, he died during a legislative term. Many in his communal "household" decided that the stress of trying to find a place for his community in the larger state and national contexts had caused the heart attack. Nevertheless, Leo continued working the boundaries between the communal household and that of the state, and during his lifetime the household metaphor ceased to be the operative political one, but Leo's close ties to the community made him a dependable exemplar of different facets of the communal style of language and action.

Leo's farm was next to ours when I was a child. Leo was also the local auctioneer, and my younger brother remembers him well. When we were selling all our belongings after a series of bad crops that drove us to searching for a new home in Wyoming, Leo noticed the four-year-old boy who had been watching all the action with wide, intent eyes. Leo then pretended to auction off the boy. He brought an enormous price as the delighted community went along with the game. Everyone was too preoccupied, though, to explain to the child that it was all a joke, so he spent his last days in that home expecting to be picked up by his new parents. When finally our heavily loaded family car crossed the state line into Montana, my father told us all to say goodbye to North Dakota. That moment is lost to my memory, but it is intensely vivid to my brother's because he was sure that crossing a state line meant he could keep his immediate family. He also acquired an acute personal awareness of how communal pragmatic presuppositions determine communication.

For the most part, narratives that I group under the rubric of "public" were told or written by men whose personal uses of authority individualize the content controlled by the general scheme. I interviewed women too, and these interviews took different directions from my interviews with men. Undoubtedly, my own gender and communal status affected all the interviews. Women slipped easily into the anecdotal, partly because our relationship was generally that of equals even if I tended to be younger than the women I was interviewing. But apart from the conditions established by the dialogical context, I found that women regularly claimed that they did not really know much about history or politics. Such disclaimers on the part of so many women have more to do with the discursive boundaries between public and private than they do with the general state of women's interest in history. Telling about history was a public act that was culturally assigned to men. Women, as primary agents in household politics, told highly condensed and truncated versions of the public story, but they eagerly elaborated on the private detail in conversational genres that were part of the texture of daily life, hence the almost compulsive anecdotal tendencies that caused so many to remember grandmothers as women who talked whether or not anyone was there to listen. The boundary between public and private divided men's and women's language into different sectors of permissibility and possibility. But no matter how verbose or reticent individual men or women might be, all believed themselves bound to silence on many topics. I interviewed one woman whose words were shadows of the shapes of all those culturally imposed silences.

By the time I met and interviewed Walburga, she was more than eighty years old. No one seemed sure of her exact age. My first glimpse of her occurred as she came to meet us from one of her large vegetable gardens. She was small; she had probably been about five-foot-five at her tallest, and she was by then stooped and thin as only the very old can be when even the bones give an impression of lightness. She extended one hand to greet us, and with the other she dragged her hoe along the ground. Naturally her gardens were our first topic of conversation. They were not doing well; the weather was too dry, so she had to carry water to them with a pail, and she had to keep the ground well hoed to prevent precious moisture from simply running off the hard surface. All this she told without the slightest note of self-pity. In fact, her speech was so rapid that its very animation almost detracted from its content. I paid less attention to what she said than I did to the overall effect of her personality, reflected everywhere on the farm she shared with her sons. The farm was a visual wonder, astonishingly colorful even though no lawn grew in that yard, no flowers that I remember (someone like Walburga would not dream of using precious time and energy or water for a lawn or more than the occasional flower). The color came from painted decorations on several buildings that seemed bound to the soil by the fact that most were constructed of fieldstone.

The brightly painted pastel designs on the wooden eaves, roofs, and shutters on the stone buildings gave a definite jauntiness to the entire scene. As I looked around, I could see why people went to Walburga's to imagine stepping back in time. The original sod house, built just after the family came from the Ukraine, was now covered with white wooden siding. Window frames were painted red, while the doors to the house were green with yellow trim. The one obvious concession to modern technology was a tape recorder with an amplifier that animated the entire yard with lively polka music. Walburga claimed it made the chickens lay more eggs and the plants in her garden grow bigger. The yard had other evidence of her ability to shape her surroundings to reflect her innate aesthetic sense. She had asked her sons to build an equally colorful miniature of the entire place for birds so they could use it all as busily and productively as she did.

Although old, the farm equipment was the best that she and her sons could afford; in this respect, she was not deliberately rejecting modernization. In fact, as I reconsidered my short visit, I doubted that she was actively rejecting anything. She had little money; she had put what she could into purchasing and working the land. I came to believe that she lived as she did because she saw no reason to change what did not need changing. As our talk went on, I caught glimpses of how Walburga had lived with her memories by keeping her sights fixed on practical ends, on definite tasks with a beginning, middle, and predictable end.

After the customary rituals of greeting and introduction, during which Walburga changed her black babushka and gray apron for more brightly colored ones suitable for company, we finally settled into a room where photographs of family members covered the walls and most of the available space on tables. Of course, there were also reproductions of religious paintings to remind all of us of the mix of beliefs and facts that are the background for Walburga's story. We casually began the process of recording her story of emigration to the United States.[20] She had found her own kind of victory on this terrain, and with an instinct for the way ethnic history has shaped the categories of memory, she started her story in a manner that dramatizes all the limitations and challenges of her situation in relation to the agricultural cycle. "When we came to America, it was spring—time of the year to clean wheat. We stayed with my brother who had a mud house. They met us with horses and sled."

Her family arrived as the agricultural cycle began, and the sheer speed with which her narrative links arrival to the spring duties of preparing wheat for planting by separating weed and wheat seeds is strong testimony to the deeply pragmatic impact of the public pattern on the economy of personal memory. She does not stress the wintry weather that must have been worrisome for these immigrants from a southern climate, but she did retain the concrete image of being met in a sleigh. As a distinct visual image it is eloquent in its implied significance. In those circumstances, cleaning seed wheat becomes an act of desperate hope that was severely tested during the first years in the United States. That affective charge is emphasized by the fact that it occurs out of the temporal sequence that controls the next segment of her narrative. After Walburga frames her entire presentation with that opening image of arrival and cleaning wheat, her reverie moves backward in time as she sketches the journey from Odessa to North Dakota. "We came abroad by ship, which took us one month. To get to the ship we traveled by train. Also when we got to this country, we traveled by train to get to our destination. On ship we got very sick. The only thing we had to sleep on was a mattress. I was six years old at the time."

As with everything she told us, she presented this event shorn of all detail and limited to its clear, clean lines of purpose—the action of getting to the destination, the point in space where she and her family have chosen to remain. I wanted more detail. But no one dared to interrupt her for fear she would not resume her story. Even her sons were amazed that she was saying this much about memories that she had apparently never articulated before. Her sons teasingly remarked that they were shocked to see her sitting for "so long, just to talk." Her sons' sense of "so long" was definitely relative, because from my perspective her tale is brief. It may be argued that that brevity was merely an effort to conclude the interview so that she could get back to watering her gardens, but to Walburga the tale might not appear so brief. Her sons may have given the real clue with their amazement at "just talking." My presence with a tape recorder prompted the instinctive reflexive work on the temporal origins of her position; she was not just talking. She was giving verbal definition to her place in the community, and she was instinctively trying to piece together what she could of the public pattern that she knew as the model for the proper sort of talk for the occasion. In more academic terms, we can say that she was performing the discourse of emigration as it had defined her.

As I continued my extremely limited vicarious participation in her story, I realized more and more how much is summarized by that simple statement of arrival, of having emigrated and then having established a position from which to talk about it to someone who viewed the fact of that continuance as having value for a broader audience. Walburga's historical memory affirms the fact of arrival in a new and strange locale as equivalent to establishing a community; she does not understand emigration in individual terms; the shared effort itself had been the purpose for living and for telling; but she had outlived that moral view and she had found herself in a social context that valued individual achievement. Her narrative, though, cannot, does not address that change. Its clear lines follow the old patterns of her way of life; the personal and the subjective aspects of her life and experience are completely subordinated to the facts of acquiring land so that relatives could live near each other. "When we first came here, we lived next to my father's brother.

We lived three miles apart. We did field work together and helped each other in various ways. In Strasbourg, North Dakota, we could buy two quarters of land for twenty dollars. We built a sod house. My father worked as a hired hand for farmers in a twelve-mile radius. He worked for one summer for two horses and a cow. When we first settled here, the only food we had was bread and milk. Soon after, we owned livestock we could butcher for beef, chicken, and sausage."

Walburga gives no detail about her marriage beyond the fact of where her home stood in relation to her in-laws. Marriage places people. That belief is redundantly narrated in this tradition, and the fact of placement is all that belongs in the public narration of history. As Walburga sat back and allowed memories to lead her back to the past, conflict and pain soon emerged. Walburga's tone of voice and her facial expression altered just slightly. First there was the simple, almost humorous memory of communal conflict, viewed through a child's eyes. "Where we lived at first we had a very mean neighbor. He would get upset if cows got out of our fence. He sometimes would come to the yard and fire a gun. Usually everyone would hide because they were afraid of him."

On the face of it, this incident seems quite typical of farm life anywhere, but this memory shard opened the way for fiercely suppressed memories of trauma and loss. As they emerged, emotional intensity burned away language, leaving absolutely minimal reference and then silence. Immediately after the tale of a cantankerous neighbor, Walburga stated, "We lost two children, very young, due to illness, one boy at age fifteen."

For a moment the animated conversation stopped. Then a niece wanted to know how they had died. The boy had had tooth infections. They could not get to a dentist, and he had died of septicemia in extreme pain. Walburga's niece had never heard about those deaths. That segment of family history had had no previous place in the standard family narratives. A child's pain had overwhelmed the narrative impulse, but now it had broken through into family remembrance. The silences that punctuate any narration work in this case to hint at everything else that may have fallen into narrative gaps. The niece, like all of us, responded by letting the silence envelop us until Walburga herself broke it in her own chosen way. That silence was our mark of respect, our recognition of our meager imaginative resources for really grasping what Walburga was telling us. No one asked about the second child, apparently a daughter. We all sat there momentarily adrift in memories we would never pass on to the next generation.

We left the past after that, choosing to test present moments for their possibilities of lightness and humor, and we succeeded soon enough, aided by the familial habit of having the right diversionary line, the right touch of humor. I forgot to turn off the tape recorder, and much of what I later carried home with me is an indistinguishable mix of repartee and laughter. Walburga arrived back into the present where she has her remaining children, her grandchildren, her garden, her chickens—her own household anchoring her own story. Returning to Derek Gregory's metaphor that allows him to connect the work of Lefebvre and Lacan, I can say that for Walburga, arrival really is a passing through the looking glass of collectively organized space. Her farm is her looking glass. Its signs are her signs of agency.

Understanding a cognitive style that performs subjectivity by way of references to communal spaces that are signs of communal history really does turn out to be the quality of understanding that lets the American children and grandchildren of immigrants glimpse the human experience behind the seemingly bare and definitely schematic narratives that are this culture's discourse of emigration.

That schematism draws attention to itself. Historians and folklorists tell us that the colonists in Russia made their own adaptations of the rich Russian folktale traditions. While most of them valued education only for its practical purposes, most were literate in German and in Russian; many also knew French, and the Polish clergy who served their religious and educational needs added elements of Polish culture to colonial life. Members of my own family speak of a neighboring colony of Greeks from whom they adopted various minor customs, even a few loan words in the local dialect. The ethnic diversity of the Odessa district nourished a rich cultural life that seemingly withered on the American Great Plains.

Many factors undoubtedly affected the new directions for narrative in the American immigrant communities. Common sense tells us that the Americans themselves made for better tales than some folkloric hero from the Russian past. My own father recalls his childhood fascination with visiting storytellers who plied their craft after a generous dinner. My father's voice takes on a tone of genuine appreciation as he claims, "He told stories; oh, he could really tell stories; trouble was, I believed him." But the stories that my father recalls were all about the marvels of an America that the immigrants in the North Dakota plains had little hope of ever seeing and that made a listening child dream of jumping on a passing train and joining the hoboes who, during those years, were the best storytellers of all and the most grateful for a good meal.

The immigrants' narratives of their Russian past were definitely not devised for entertainment or even for cultural appreciation. History, as an idea generating an ideal, did not exist for these people. They were fascinated by the past, anyone's past, simply because it was interesting and diverting. They tracked aspects of their own history because the identity and location of the extended family was, in an authentically experienced way, the source of their perceptions of individual identity. But if history was subordinated to culture, the social bonds that held people to communal loyalties were survival mechanisms, and narrative had to imprint this fact on the minds of individuals. The public pattern had a definite job to do.

But what about the private voice? Religious discourse supplied the terms for the inner voice in its responsive dialogue with the externalized (public) discourse; and this provided everyone, but especially the women, with occasion to develop a subjective position that other contexts denied. It enabled the turnabout from public to private, and it provided the imagistic expression of emotions that were excluded from the public pattern. This role was a direct effect of the fact that religious expression was itself so obviously divided along all the lines that characterized the rest of the culture. Therefore, performance directly associated with beliefs became a dependable context for making belief structures into transitional expressions. Obviously, such performance can enforce belief and the practices associated with it. Certainly the pastoral rhetoric of the time derived from prescriptive discursive patterns. Any culture nourishes resistance to its own prescriptions, and in these cultures, history had strengthened all the mechanisms of resistance to authority, including religious authority. John Shanley, the Irish bishop of North Dakota, may have been impolitic, even prejudiced, when he called them "ruffians" and refused to assign clergy to those "hard-headed and stubborn immigrants," but he was definitely picking up on actual attitudes that his replacement, Vincent Wehrle, recognized for their true historical worth when he encouraged the linkage between ethnic and ecclesiastical politics.[21] Yet even his considerable patience was tried at times. These "hard-headed" immigrants had developed unusual critical insight into uses of ecclesiastical authority, and a range of practices, generally classified as "religious," demonstrated their resistance to any outside influence over this critical dimension of their cultural development. For example, well into the twentieth century, women maintained healing practices based on religious beliefs that are likely remnants from pre-Christian times. Whatever else was achieved by way of these practices, they certainly maintained a social context in which private matters could be addressed in religious terms without, however, involving religious authorities. The practice of "brauchen" was passed on from individual to individual. Prayers to the four directions and to natural elements such as water and fire were combined with prayers to the Trinity. These healers used a variety of therapeutic practices such as massage and herbal infusions, but the general belief was that they had direct access to some power other than human. Priests often harangued against them, insisting that these powers were diabolical. The women steadfastly countered that they were the gift of the Trinity and, as such, could not be harmful. Patients were generally too practical to take sides. One woman told me that when babies got sick, her mother took them to one of the healers, leaving them for "babysitting." The babies got better and the woman had nothing to confess to the priest, although the occasion gave many of them a chance to talk about priestly rhetoric and pressures. What resistance there was to the firmly paternalistic authority structures developed in settings like this.[22] Both women and men were practitioners, although it was definitely a cultural realm in which women's authority was dominant and women's agency was steadily nourished. That authority was passed on through hundreds of years in quiet defiance of all established ecclesiastical authority.

The divisions within ecclesiastical authority were pervasive and so evident that their performance could nourish critical thought. The Russian colonies had all been established as religious entities whose boundaries were carefully and rigidly drawn along the lines of religious affiliation. Clergy staffed the schools; they governed the intellectual life of communities. As mediators of virtually all institutional expression of symbolic authority, they could blur the lines between the will of God and their own will, or that of the czar, or even, for that matter, that of the town mayor. They could play fast and easy with all the sanctions at their disposal, and they often did just that.

The political organization of the Russian colonies had provided the perfect setup for any and all excesses of ecclesiastical domination, and to detail a century's worth of history would be to tell a tale of rampant opportunism and exaggerated pietism. The authority of ecclesiastical institutions was undermined by administrative incompetence so extreme as to approach parody.[23] Disillusioned colonists added skepticism toward religious authority to their growing skepticism toward civil authority. In spite of their downright melodramatic religious history, though, the Russian colonists did not opt for widespread secularism. A rather more complex process occurred. Widespread loss of confidence in ecclesiastical institutions effected a division, or rather a series of divisions within the dynamics of sublimation and idealization that linked religious beliefs to the concrete business of building communities.[24] Religious faith, always an abstract quality, took on an increasingly transcendent function in relation to authority invested in specific social roles. Well into the mid–twentieth century, the German-Russians had a reputation within the Roman Catholic Church for being robustly anticlerical. Faith and the authority it channeled increased in inverse proportion to evidence of institutional mediation. Mysticism flourished as ecclesiastical prestige declined. One priest in North Dakota held his German-Russian parishioners in thrall for his entire pastoral career by giving apocalyptic sermons about "three dark days" that were coming soon. Sinners would die; pregnant women would die; only blessed candles would give light. But after three days, the redeemed would rebuild society. His parishioners did not really believe all this, but as far as they were concerned, visions credentialed a priest, and as long as knowledge of the visions could act as a marker of their village distinctiveness, few found reason to object.

The abstractness of a concept like faith made it an adaptable focus for transferences of all kinds. Whatever their degree of skepticism about ecclesiastical politics, the immigrants needed the symbolic structures supplied by religious discourse with its particular aesthetic and psychological resources, its metaphoric language and its cycles of celebration all bound to ancient symbols of accomplished psychological investments in agrarian rhythms. These structures subtend the highly focused familial (paternalistic) authority; but beyond that, they set up relations between public narrative and all that private experience that was excluded by the cognitive structure and style of public narrative.

The insecurities of migration intensified the need for all transitional strategies, not the least of which are the metaphoric strategies that allow for psychological transferences between familial and extrafamilial authority, which was mediated by way of religious authority and discourse. The metaphors supplied by religious symbolism could accommodate all the contradictions that history supplied. Therefore it is not surprising that upon arrival in the United States, these immigrants immediately wanted to use scarce resources to build churches, concrete reminders of a religiously articulated continuity based on an idea of a God who transcended the political machinations of those who claimed to be speaking His will. The actual church building stood for a local conjunction between public and private that supported psychological options along with social ones.

All of this history can be brought back to the image with which this chapter began. Two distinctively different peoples are brought together in one church by political forces beyond their control. Members of both communities are attuned to the interior voice, communing with all that exceeds it and seeking at least enough security within their own understanding of their historical situation to act effectively within a rapidly changing social context. The interior voice of the individual is coached and guided to public expression by communal narrative, which, in the case of both these social groups in that one church, was so active a force for adaptation that calling narrative a primary means of survival is no overstatement.

4. Narrative Redirected

Tracing evidence of cognitive style as it operates across a range of different oral literary genres uncovers those local variations on available means for orchestrating cultural themes that depend on a history of language usage within any community where customary events are, in effect, the performance of features of communal identity. Such performance is always immediate; it updates cognitive style through the way participation and interpretation play on the differences and options that open between semantic givens and the available communal means for expanding or reinterpreting or just plain subverting the significance of past performances. When participants in a performance come from more than one cultural background, performance should reveal a range of different points of passage between traditions. But what about the move from oral to written genres? Does the method explored here open any significant critical horizons for novels? The easy affirmative answer applies in those instances wherein a novel is explicitly an attempt to represent or otherwise to participate in the signifying dynamic of oral performance.

Writers everywhere experiment with ways to bring some of the responsiveness of oral performance into written action. Texts can represent the oral process (i.e., they can be about it), or they can attempt to mime the process (i.e., they can aim to be dynamic doubles). In either case, the writer seeks a connection with a particular community that depends on identifying traces of historical memory at work within the structures of intentionality nurtured by that memory. Nurtured by the oral, these structures of intentionality can affect every aspect of a novel; they are an effect of ongoing local interpretation. The novel thrives on close participation in this process, gaining flexibility and vividness. Such writing obviously has to address a broader audience too, and that broader audience might remain unaware of all but the most obvious aspects of its local significance. The way in which a novel participates in the coming-into-being of communal identity is a critical story in its own right, quite separate from the many other critical stories that we construe in relation to novels. In our contemporary world where most people do not live in traditional communities, novels that say something important about how the individual might connect with the communal call for a critical response that enhances that dimension of its possible significances. Global mobility means that people seldom have the chance to settle in a place and let the slow, ordinary process of building community achieve its integrating purpose. Now most people have to accelerate their capacity to establish communal bonds and connections to the local, and it has made them conscious of their need for conscious understanding of interactions between the individual and the communal. Novels have their own role to play in developing this enhanced consciousness.

In my own work with connections between Native oral and written genres, I have argued for attention to a range of intermediate genres, that is, to written texts that are obvious efforts to adapt oral forms to the exigencies of print media and that may, sometimes, be closer to the transcription of oral genres than to fully realized written forms.[1] Texts illustrate all points along the continuum, and the point of studying them in their intermediate stages is to illustrate the determination to preserve certain ideas, forms, and images by whatever means possible. We get a good sense of what people value most by following each step of the transformation from oral to written. Staying within the field of Native literatures, I have also tried to draw attention to ways in which the event structure of superbly accomplished novels like N. Scott Momaday's *House Made of Dawn* and, even more clearly, Leslie Silko's novel *Ceremony* show signs of the authorial effort to adapt the event structures of oral forms to the demands of novelistic writing. As many critics have noted, Momaday uses the Navajo Night Chant as an infrastructure for his novel, whereas Silko works out a multifaceted set of connections between the traditional oral plots, presented as poetic divisions in the text, and the modern action, presented in ordinary prose, which exemplifies a search for a connection to the traditional.[2]

The relationship between the oral and the written has been a major theme in critical studies of Native literature. In her work with this literature, Catherine Rainwater refers to the incorporation of oral strategies into written literatures as a means of demonstrating changing power relations between Indian and non-Indian. The aim of Native writing, she says, "is not domination and empire, but social reform through relocation of non-Indian people from positions of authority to positions as listeners and receivers of knowledge." Rainwater envisages the entire process of experimentation in terms of a semiotic counterconquest reversing the earlier semiotic conquest of the Americas.[3]

In the general field of narrative studies, questions about relations between oral and written have been in the forefront since the work of the Russian Formalists. One of the primary goals of the Russian Formalists, namely to develop techniques for talking about the history of the novel, remains part of contemporary research agendas even if the means of going about the task and the purposes for pursuing it at all have changed significantly. Monika Fludernik has called for a reconsideration of the place of oral narratives in general narratology studies. Her goal of giving a diachronic dimension to narratology brings her to questioning anew the narrative status of medieval texts, which show their close ties to the oral forms preceding them. Her experiential approach to narrative means that she focuses, as I do, on the context of reception. She examines how narrative consciousness reflects the means by which narrativity achieves its cognitive goals. Some mediating consciousness has to achieve this self-reflexive role. It may be a consciousness situated in the fictional world in the voice of a protagonist or an authorial voice, or that role may be transferred from the text to the reader. She isolates the traces of consciousness that are part of a mediational process that "results in the establishment of the mimetic illusion, of narrativity."[4]

Looking at narrative from this perspective, there is no reason for postulating sharp breaks between oral and written. However, the functions of various devices change when the means of presentation change, and those functional changes can give us a particularly productive take on the history of the novel and on comparisons between what is happening in the field of Native literature and other kinds of novelistic study. Fludernik's point about a functional continuum between oral and written goes well beyond examples that are conscious and/or explicit efforts to integrate the two. Her entire project is an effort to "emphasize the receptional and creative aspect of narrativity, discussing the generation of narrativity in the process of narrativization," and this generation of narrativity occurs by way of natural oral contexts such as conversational storytelling just as it does by way of efforts to integrate more formal oral literary genres like the folktale.[5] This emphasis on natural narrative allows for discussion of relations between oral and written even in relation to novels that are not obvious experiments in aligning the two, and that is the situation of the novel I have chosen to illustrate cognitive style at work in literature dealing with immigrants.

For my examples of cognitive style in written works, I choose to analyze the work of two Montana novelists, James Welch and Mildred Walker. Welch is a Native writer while Walker depicts an immigrant experience (although she is not herself an immigrant). Welch's writing shows us that even when people try to ignore or escape history, the landscape in which that history took place can insist on a reckoning of one kind or another; and when history is a powerful mix of pride and pain, the reckoning is no easy matter. Welch's early characters do their best to avoid it, but eventually history finds its way into their lives, and confronting it becomes a matter of do or die. Their learning provides an exceptional fictional example of cognitive style keeping up with the times as it enables a contemporary take on the past that lets ordinary people live with the knowledge of what has happened. Walker's novel, by contrast, illustrates how characters learn that the breaks between landscape, history, and cognitive style caused by immigration—either from nation to nation or region to region—cannot simply be ignored or repressed. The lack of local implicit narratives is experienced as a psychological and linguistic deprivation that drives a person instinctively toward pragmatic reorganization of the relationship between place and identity as a prerequisite for allowing the local a real purchase on individual identity.

My choice of Montana as a region is a matter of personal interest. Comparable questions about literature and landscape and narrative arise everywhere, but there is no doubt that the American West has some strategic advantages as the region of choice. If we pause to imagine Montana's geographical as opposed to its epistemic spaces, the mind conjures up stunning natural scenery where the human contribution is pretty well limited to a few medium-sized cities and a lot of haphazard towns with a here-today, gone-tomorrow kind of look. But the visual artifact that I want to evoke as a concrete guide to this analysis is the barbed-wire fence snaking toward the distant horizon. I choose that minimal image because it can recall a history of divisions and separations accompanying beliefs, variously proclaimed, that something new in human affairs was about to get going even though the names on all the casualty lists still represented immediate griefs. This was most definitely the case for the Blackfeet about whom James Welch writes. In a very different way, it was also true for all but the wealthy and powerful within the immigrant world that Mildred Walker depicts in her novel *Winter Wheat*. For the Blackfeet the fences were, and sometimes still are, evidence of breaks in the culturally woven coherence linking human experiences of body, mind, and place. For the immigrants they represented a series of divisions that were inevitably a part of their new start, which was wild promise or lonely threat or both at once.

Examining the configuration of text/location/community from a Native perspective seems at first blush like a rather obvious sort of thing to do, a task deriving from what is somehow securely, integrally just there. Tribal enrollment does indeed link person and place, granting a legal identity that has origins in sovereign rights anterior to state and federal rights; but any intellectually responsible approach to the knowledge coordinates that go with this linkage gets fractured by the incommensurable variables that history has relentlessly introduced. In the wake of a colonial history of dispossession, we can understand why Vine Deloria talked about American Indian exile in the very spaces of home many years before postcolonial theorists put the dynamics of exile and diaspora in the general critical spotlight.[6]

Welch's writing has proven to be a continuing dramatization of just how right Deloria was. But Welch has not just been writing about what went wrong. He has written his way toward communal options and prerogatives that show how vital the tradition still is even when his heroes may not be aware of that vitality. If we look at the progression of the writing we see that it crosses historical divides, brings the exiles home, even when the journey away has never been other than a journey in spaces of mind that had ceased to be spaces of home for reasons that the novels demonstrate. Therefore, critical understanding of this journey requires enough historical detail so that reference to breaks, divisions, and gaps has concrete legitimacy. In a Blackfeet context, any choice of a privileged historical moment from which to gauge change immediately raises the question of whether the chosen historical marker occurs before or after the winter of 1883–84. Why is that one year such a crucial dividing point? Because it was a year in which approximately a third of the people died of starvation while Congress stalled the efforts of Indian rights activists to get them to authorize needed funds for food. It was a year that concluded a decade that had begun with smallpox epidemics. It was a year during which extremity seemed to override the symbolic codes that linked social continuity to the signifying potential of location. I fall back on that word "seems" in recognition of the fact that during the summer of 1884 a woman did pledge the Medicine Lodge Ceremony in which the people proclaimed and performed their beliefs in the continuity of their historical responsibility. Whatever fears the people may have had about the future, the very fact of the ceremony speaks to belief in their communal possibilities. Yet the ceremony itself represented an absolute risk because the woman who pledged that fundamental ritual had to enact the fact of the historical break by substituting the meat of domesticated cattle for buffalo.[7] Her risk merits being called "absolute" because the ceremony derived from the belief that a woman's error had caused the original suffering that the ceremony countered; therefore, any woman pledging the ceremony risked bringing death to loved ones, possibly to all the people, if she made any ritual change or error.

Every woman who pledges the ceremony is the historical representative, the ceremonial daughter, of the prototypical woman in the origin narrative who learned the ritual as a consequence of her error in judgment. This mythic woman's experience of human contingency also established her son as a fixed point in the heavens. Her son is the North Star, which allows humans to calculate their relations to time and space by the same terms that reveal the moral consequences of basic human relationships.[8] The cognitive themes summed up by the Medicine Lodge Ceremony and its founding narrative are directly comparable to those discussed in the two preceding chapters about Sioux understandings of gender roles. But other dynamics are also at stake in Welch's novels, and they go well beyond comparisons of traditional elements. Welch's writing lets us see how the contemporary need to understand traditional themes is a motivating force that adds its own elements to the tradition. Need to know is a conditioning negativity. Present motive redirects the cognitive styles of the past.

Critics can speak in the abstract about how traumatic historical disjunction displaces without naming and shifts language into interpretive registers for which traditional beliefs no longer automatically provide the codes. But creative writers who try to tell about the home territory have to be more concrete about the causes of "winter in the blood," to use the memorable phrase that is also the title of Welch's first novel. And, in Welch's case, the concrete demonstration stands as both a novelistic and a critical accomplishment. Not that he intentionally set out to write cultural criticism but that, like Toni Morrison, he seems to have followed through on his writerly instinct that "something is missing there . . . something else you have to figure in before you can figure it out."[9] What Welch figures out in the course of figuring in five novels, an early book of poems, and a nonfiction book works as superb evidence for thinking about the problematic of cognitive style and localism. The transition to reservation life and the loss of the buffalo meant that the Blackfeet had to achieve radical adaptations of all they knew about how to live in their own country; and they are still engaged in political struggles that one of Welch's more recent characters, a smart, young, almost-too-good-to-be-true lawyer, understands as a paradigm for what is happening to the entire Rocky Mountain West as the multinational corporations square the historical agendas of the nationals. Welch's novels require a contemporary perspective before they allow the historical reflection that no one, including the heroes of his several tales, willingly takes up. Like all of his reluctant heroes, readers have to work out the conditionality of the enunciative present. Or, stating it all the more casually, we can say that readers are pulled into a narrative quest for workable equations between what history gives and what present circumstances require. For Welch that has meant bringing into the narrative present the mythic prototype for those women whose annual ritual activities dramatize a precise cultural understanding of how people in actual places access the significance of epistemic spaces in order to maintain or redefine the relationship between geographical locale and historical identity.

This turn to mythic memory occurring in Welch's third novel was a surprise to readers and critics, although as I will show, he had clearly given us characters who demonstrated a need for what the historical novel makes explicit. We could have noted the early clues about how the sheer force of belief with most of its content forgotten will demand an articulation of the missing content to overcome the displacements of history, both literal and psychological. We could have; but we did not see that what is missing always comes back pragmatically redefined. The important clues in Welch's first book, *Winter in the Blood*, were so easy to overlook because this novel had a distinctively modern edge to it that signaled Welch's talent and provoked altogether relevant comparisons with the likes of Samuel Beckett and Saul Bellow.

Critics were more than happy, were, in fact, downright relieved to recognize Welch as the writer who let American Indian novels take on a plausibly antiromantic (i.e., nonmythic) contemporary form. Therefore, critics minimized the significance of the event that lies at the heart of that very first novel and invokes the winter of 1883–84. That story within the story involves the unnamed hero's grandparents. A feisty old curmudgeon tells the hero the secret past of his grandmother. The hero thinks of his grandmother only as someone who terrifies every woman he brings home. Yet the old man tells him about a woman his wildest imaginings would not have conjured. His grandmother was once the youngest wife of a leader. With all her considerable advantages, she had aroused widespread jealousy. Then, when military defeat coincided with starvation and the people looked for a scapegoat, jealousy turned to blame. Only one man stood by her, found food for her, and saved her life. Unknown to the hero, the old man narrating the tale in the bleak present is, in fact, his grandfather. So far, the subplot has all the standard romance elements. But Welch does not pursue that obvious direction, or rather, he ingeniously reroutes the romantic theme. What astonishes the hero is that once the two determined survivors get settled on the reservation, they appear to end their relationship. But that is only a cover-up designed to help them maintain it secretly even though there is no obvious reason for such secrecy. Key questions never find much of an answer in this novel, but they are posed with enough compelling interest to keep readers coming back for more. Why would the grandparents keep family history a secret, and what does that revelation from the past mean for the unnamed hero?

Several novels later, readers can backtrack and see that when Welch wrote his parable from the past, he was pointing toward ways of crossing the violently imposed gap between past and present. He was giving some very concrete clues about how the structure of intentionality, always implicit in cognitive style, sets up conditions for the emergence of contemporary significance. In his novelistic vignette, the cognitive features are implicit in the performed positionality of the mother, father, and grandson because the significance of these positions has been so consistently addressed in traditional story and ceremony. The Medicine Lodge Ceremony is the continuing historical enactment of how and why so much significance became so tied up with understandings about distances between family members, a point to which I will return.

If we stay, for the moment, with the obvious facts that Welch gives us in the first novel, we note that each family member is placed at a controlled distance from the other, a distance that inaugurates a whole series of choices and actions because it requires them to enact the terms of an ancient pattern for organizing temporal meaning in spatial terms. The importance of such choices would not have been lost on people who participated regularly in the customary or ceremonial enactments that taught them to understand how crossing the literal distances of the Montana landscape could be a way of achieving spiritual as well as practical goals. But it is definitely lost on Welch's hero, and learning the identity of his grandfather does not really make that much difference. Other heroes in other Welch novels would gradually get the point, though.

In an interview Welch has talked about the reservation as a place where secrets seem hidden everywhere, waiting to be discovered. That is certainly the way the past functions in his books.[10] If his first hero does not ever learn what to make of the way his grandparents chose to live out their lives, it is because he does not know how to interpret what is right there to be seen and known, even though he does pick up on the fact that others around him seem attuned to something he is missing. Therefore, it is not mere academic reductionism to claim that there is a real sense in which Welch's realistically characterized couple reenacts origins. When they enter the reservation era, they go back to human and cultural fundamentals. What makes all this good literature is the fact that this transfigurative element is narrated as a secret that is withheld from the reader until the publication of Welch's third novel, *Fools Crow*. In the first two novels, the not knowing, the powerful negativity that characterizes the grandsons who simply do not get the message sent by grandparents is what drives plot. Readers learn about the jagged power of not knowing.

In Welch's second novel, *The Death of Jim Loney*, only nightmares come from the past, but these nightmares, like the secular ritual of two old people, situate a mother, father, and son as a dialogical triangle that depends on beliefs with form enough to shape dreams but without sufficient content to allow the waking mind any interpretive hold or respite. Awareness of the past sets up recognition without understanding, submission without contribution to the establishment of a contemporary efficacy. This second novel gives us a hero with a name at least, but little else unless you count a lover who is obviously too sensible to hang around for very long. As the tale advances, the nightmares prove more important than the lover. By the end, Jim Loney is dead, having set up his own father to arrange that death. Yet he ends his life in his hometown, and the novel is constructed to make the reader believe that this is important. If we take the novel on its own terms, we have to look at arguments for staying in the middle of nowhere with nothing to do, and the arguments, in this case, point toward the absent mother. Loney's dreams project each member of his family onto the stage of his visioning mind, and we learn that the light of his dreaming self is focused on people who have placed him where he is and then left him to cope all alone. Loney's mother had abandoned him. But for a time, he—and he alone—knew where she was, and that strange fact bears all the narrative weight, so much weight that we know it points well beyond its realistic import. "And he had never sought out his mother, nor she her natural son. It had been enough for Loney in those days to know that she existed" (119).

The simple fact of the mother's existence in a known locale assures the son his orientation in space and time, and finally with Welch's third novel this absolutely minimal maternal role is linked directly and clearly to traditional beliefs about space, time, and affective investments in kinship categories. At the time of its publication, this historical novel surprised practically everyone because it was so different from the taut psychological first works. This third novel retains its importance, though, not so much for reasons of its literary merit as for its critical significance. Taking the risk of engaging in excessively weighty labeling, I will claim that this novel is an act of discursive institution: that is, it achieves a contemporary discursive representation of socially operative differences that in their continuing action are evidence of a community's power to institute by way of reinterpretation or innovations. In this third novel Welch tries to name what had been unnameable in contemporary terms and which, therefore, eluded his previous fictional characters. In other words, this novel gives us the terms we need to identify a traditional cognitive set realized through contemporary action. We can argue about the artistic merits of his effort, but what he tries to do can, I believe, show the power of novelistic discourse for naming and for valuing the import of what would otherwise be affect without conscious object. That having been said, we need to ask exactly what it is about this novel that justifies such weighty commentary.

Briefly stated, we can say that through it Welch reclaims the most basic of all foundational narratives in the Americas, the Star Husband myth in its Blackfeet realization, which is also the foundational narrative for the Medicine Lodge Ceremony. In the past that one narrative summed up a foundational archive of pragmatic presuppositions; and Welch's historical novel raises the question of the present status of this entire archive even as it narrates a tale about the historical past. Welch crosses the historical divide when he takes this overdetermined source as the model for the maternal figure who can require his hero to read about and therefore to endure the knowledge of the winter of 1883–1884. The fictionally evoked woman stands as embodied memory, and she frames the post-reservation conditionality of historical memory.

In writing his historical novel, Welch does not just fill in human detail to flesh out the known historical and mythical frameworks. He does not just give us sympathetic characters to make history seem real. He achieves a more intimate and dangerous creative identification as he imprints his characters with an emotional marking that first specifies and then redirects universal instincts through reinterpreted symbolic representations and ceremonial (hence pragmatic) realizations that establish the foundations of Blackfeet culture. He follows his historical reflections all the way back to symbolic origins, where he discovers something no one noticed before, something implicit in mythic resources but unexpressed, an invisible writing behind the mythic text. He shows us the mythic culture mother in a new narrative role, one that reinstates her in the emotional economy of history. With a novelist's freedom and instinct for what story can do, Welch seems to have confronted the nexus of creativity/femininity/transgression, and his novelistic writing realigns the narrative's relationship to history.

In *Fools Crow* the implied and/or lost historical content of the other novels is reconstructed. The novel depicts the last years of the traditional life before confinement to reservations. Its hero, unlike his novelistic predecessors, is destined for leadership. We first meet him as a hesitant young man overshadowed by his best friend's good looks and quick tongue.

The particular directions of young Fools Crow's adolescent development depend on details of his visions and the corresponding psychology of dream interpretation. Unlike Jim Loney, he can rely on the knowledge of traditional dream interpreters as they listen and guide him.

At the beginning of the novel, Fools Crow is worried because he has not received a vision that will make him a powerful leader. All that changes, though. This character becomes a vehicle for presenting a carefully nuanced study of how visionary dreaming allowed for the interpretation of symbolic options in daily life among the Blackfeet. In and of itself, that cultural dynamic has a definite contemporary interest, but Welch is doing something more. In the way that he develops the character Fools Crow, we see him as the novelist's avatar. Fools Crow eventually has to learn a particular kind of reading that plunges him into historical knowledge before the actual events have even occurred. This mystic temporality works in the service of contemporary cognitive goals.

Working this plot element for its pragmatic significance, we can say that it splits *what is known* from *how it is known,* and the space of historical responsibility is thus established. Both sides of this division are problematic. In the character of Fools Crow, Welch manages two things: he dramatizes how the traumatic breaks in cultural continuity can thrust the one who looks at history into unimaginable cognitive space where events overwhelm the emotional resources a person might have for confronting them; and he sets up a source of empathetic awareness in the person of Feather Woman, the founding mother from the Blackfeet tradition. In other words, Welch dramatizes an emotional economy to support the cognitive transitions required by people in a postcontact culture.

Welch details the various aspects of Fools Crow's learning in ways that show it to be a fit model for a novelist's apprenticeship. The young Fools Crow tells his vision to an elder, a culturally appointed dream interpreter. But this mentor is unable to decode the dream with any degree of certitude. Historically among the Blackfeet, such interpretive vagueness endangered the teller of the dream tale. According to Blackfeet beliefs, as stated in the novel, dreams require accurate interpretation to prevent the spirit inspiring it from roaming freely about, causing harm to those responsible for giving concrete historical reference to its significance, its power. This connection between verbalization and agency stands as important evidence about cognitive themes in Blackfeet culture—but more of that later.

Once Fools Crow learns that the exactly told vision is also the appropriately internalized human responsibility, he must begin to live according to the consequences of that knowledge. In keeping with the mythic structure that seems to lie behind virtually all that Welch has written to date, this awareness of responsibility for dreams is regularly articulated in relation to bird imagery, as we can see in one passage in which Fools Crow doubts his own abilities: "The flashing wings and cries were all around him now and he knew that his power was gone, but he walked ahead as a man does who is dreaming. And like the dreaming man, he did not see the geese, for they were all within him and they consumed his power, and he walked among the gray trunks of the alders in the false dawn" (314).

This passage occurs near the climax of the novel, just after Fools Crow has begun to glimpse the social chaos and historical tragedy of non-Indian domination. Deeply depressed, he asks, "But what good is your own power when the people are suffering, when their minds are scattering like horses in the four directions? Was Sun Chief laughing at them, not content just to abandon them? Why must he pull them apart? Why must he make them abandon each other?"(314).

The overwhelming fear that holds earlier Welch heroes hostage has been voiced in this novel too: abandonment. The divinity seems to have abandoned the people who abandon each other. Abandonment breaks all bonds, including those between person and place. The stage is set for the extraordinary role that Welch creates for Feather Woman, the mythic mother.

Welch gives Fools Crow a vision in which he is taken to the home of Feather Woman, the heroine of the Blackfeet Star Husband tale. The energy of the scene is signaled by all the bird imagery clustered in the section. Readers find themselves remembering all sorts of puzzling details in Welch's earlier novels. We cannot help thinking of the bird in Jim Loney's dream or the silly yet strangely portentous ducks in Welch's first novel. And those who know their comparative traditions will remember that the Sioux Double Women are also associated with birds, as are countless other beings who prefigure gender roles. Whatever is going on in this section of the novel, it involves the separation of mother, father, and son, a separation that provokes stunning grief and surprising anger:

> *Just then the woman began to sing. . . . Three times she sang this, then three times more, and when Fools Crow looked up at the horizon before her, he saw Morning Star and his son Poia, against the deep blue of the false dawn. The woman began to wail, and her wailing filled the bowl with the voices of a thousand geese, and Fools Crow closed his eyes and clapped his hands over his ears but the sound was once again in him and he was outside of himself, a child again, staring at the wintry lake and the flashing wings. . . . Fools Crow wanted to go away, to shrink back into the trees, but he could not bear to leave her this way. He walked quietly into the clearing, and when he reached her he touched her shoulder. He squatted beside her and looked into her face. The tears had dried, but*

> something in the face told Fools Crow of a grief so deep it would always be there and no words from him could help.... On the other side of the peak, it would be winter, and his people would be there, waiting for a direction or a sign. Would they wait forever? Fools Crow turned back to the woman. "Who do you mourn?" He was surprised by the anger in his voice. "Who are you?" (336–38)

When Fools Crow confronts her, Feather Woman tells him her story, and it is not quite the tale he has always heard in camp. She tells him that she did not really die. She exists in a middle place, between earth and sky, which is also a temporal middle ground from which she can see backward and forward in time. What she sees is the basis for her art; she paints her mediating vision on a yellow hide. That pictographic prophecy is what Fools Crow must read. He is required to read his way into the future, confront coming misery, and absorb the shock so that Feather Woman's writing can become his historical responsibility. As a consequence of what he reads, he will be able to give appropriate leadership to his people, and this leadership is indirect evidence that Feather Woman has not abandoned the people; she has her chosen connections. "Fools Crow sat for a moment and looked out at the blue river. Somehow he knew that the point of his journey had finally been reached. He was in no hurry as he crept around the fire pit and knelt and looked down at the yellow skin. It was a well-tanned skin, creaseless, without thin spots or cracks" (353).

As he reads, he slowly realizes that he is seeing his own community as it will be during the times of starvation, smallpox epidemics, and postreservation confusion. "Fools Crow shrank back from the skin with a small cry. He trembled and he wanted to run away, to leave that place and the strange woman, to return to Red Paint and his family. He was no longer eager to complete his journey, to learn the fate of his people.... Why did he have to see this thing?" (358).

Having seen what is to come, Fools Crow has to learn to live with his knowledge. That is the message and purpose of the novel. He learns that Blackfeet children will be "alone and foreign in their own country" (386). Welch, at this point, takes a turn away from what many readers might expect. Fools Crow's grief over all that is to come is sharpest when it is a response to the loss of historical memory. He agonizes over children "who will not know the life their people once lived.... They lose their own way." On this score Feather Woman can comfort him. She assures him that "they will know the way it was" (359). This watchful care over the transmission of history is an aspect of the maternal role few have really applied to contemporary life. It implies that the maternal function includes vigilance over the conditions that safeguard the life of knowledge by making it endurable. That is an affective and not just an epistemological responsibility.

Welch places Feather Woman in a green sanctuary between earth and sky. That middle ground is Welch's own insight; it seems to end a long narrative journey. It is certainly the image and locale of a particular kind of reading and interpreting. It implies a unique manner of knowing. This reading occurs within a dream that is within a myth, and the double descent into mythic structures implies its own commentary on the altogether realistic history that is represented. By means of this double symbolic spiraling to the spaces of the past, Welch the novelist can recover the affect that the mythic structures and symbols once mediated. As he does so, he also interprets that affect for a modern audience. Feather Woman, the mythic mother who inaugurates the Medicine Lodge Ceremony, is given her role in a postreservation emotional economy. Welch creates a character who has already responded to the postreservation fears of psychic abjection resulting from abandonment. As he reveals Feather Woman living on in her middle ground, Welch presents someone who experiences the entire range of human emotions as she inscribes the outlines of her knowledge about what is to come, drawing pictographs on her yellow hide, achieving the transferences that give definite reference to the changing symbolic economy and to the affective one that allows humans to endure the changes.

However one reads that narrative message, it works as a way of breaking out of the circle of unrecognizable human responses to life at the edges of new societies. It connects the new, its terrors as well as its advantages, to the old. As Feather Woman makes events "readable," her transcription anticipates one part of the novelist's role. She opens herself to the emotional impact of all those historical events that she knows before they happen so that her preexperiencing can be a prefiguring that contains what is needed when it is needed. What is more, she knows that who she is has something to do with how things are in a particular place. She has to live with her responsibility, which she turns to the benefit of humankind by inscribing the nature of things in texts whose reading she forces on leaders who accidentally find their way to her middle ground. Fools Crow, well disciplined to tell his visions with enough exact detail to give them a place in history, anticipates the other half of the writer's job. He has to read what she writes and get it right so that he can continue her telling, adjusting it to particular audiences. Both parts of the task begin with knowing what neither wants to know even as they inaugurate a discursivity that assures the continuity of knowledge of what it is to be Blackfeet. They represent the historical task of daring to imagine what had been unimaginable. Welch's novel takes the emotion invested in beliefs about origins and extends them from genesis to apocalypse and beyond. That trajectory gathers history into its momentum, and, in the next novel, it interprets the present historical moment.

In the way that Welch retells the myth of Feather Woman, he makes it into a means of representing a new departure for the culture by way of understanding something new about how the past connects with the present. Feather Woman affirms a symbolic place—a space of mind (and psyche, and myth)—toward which the visioning powers turned toward interior distances draw the individual. Extreme historical trauma blinds the eye of the mind. Myths in culture after culture confront this psychological fact. The blind Oedipus, able at last to confront the real historical and political arena, is but one among many mythic beings carrying the message that reading the times requires transitions to new psychological spaces. History provides its own evidence of this dynamic. Survivors of all kinds know that trauma creates a division in memory that is also, in some sense, a redefinition. Trauma ejects the individual beyond the entire symbolic order. To return (and the alternative to return is psychosis) is to gain a new reading of that entire order and a new place within it. This fundamental dynamic must be a symbolic—hence mythic—process.

In the story of the woman who went to the sky and came back, we have a mythic survivor. Of course, the story has rarely been understood that way, even though it is one of the most analyzed plot structures in the world. Welch, by choosing the variants of this plot that remain indefinite about whether the woman lives or dies and by creating the novelistic middle space as Feather Woman's own site, has established a new historical role for this ancient mythic structure, and he transfers its functions from the oral to the written modes.

We are in rich semiotic territory with this narrative complex, whether we work from a comparative perspective or narrow the focus to a single culture—whether we look at the book-length analyses of Claude Lévi-Strauss, who can tie the myth to everything in the Americas, or we turn to a poet like Joy Harjo, who says that the woman with the star husband is from "the family of myths who would give anything if asked."[11] And academics have certainly asked a lot of this extended mythic family, beginning with the careful mapping and syntheses that gave the historic-geographic method its raison d'etre.[12] Studying it from the perspective proposed here, we see that the variations from tribe to tribe can be interpreted as historical evidence about processes of localization. Among the Blackfeet, this narrative is explicitly bound to women's ceremonial assumption of responsibility for Medicine Lodge Ceremony, the Blackfeet Sun Dance.[13] What are we to make of that linkage?

First, I propose that specifying the cognitive set that establishes the most rudimentary spatial and temporal coordinates evoked through the Blackfeet narrative of the woman separated from her husband and son can show how this narrative simultaneously implies a cultural logic and the existential, human impact of this logic. It certainly coincides with the way Welch uses ideas of distance between mothers and sons to imply the nature of a relationship to an entire tradition. The earthbound woman representing humankind is in several concrete relationships to celestial phenomena, thus setting up the categories of time in relation to space so that her earthly movements can chart her relationships to her husband and the son from whom she is forever separated because she could not fulfill a promise to her husband. He is Venus the Morning Star, whose celestial movement appears to make him the solar front-runner. What is more, his movement is controlled by the Sun, his father. The woman's son is the North Star, the celestial body whose fixity, the myth tells us, is a consequence and continuing reminder of the woman's transgression. Those who move about freely on earth can calculate their physical location and the time of day or season by reference to these celestial phenomena, which thereby provide the most basic terms of ordered movement. The kinship designations, of course, link movement through time and space to moral obligations. Thus time and space tell a family tale, and we have the first layers of a series of ever-more-differentiated series of overlays of cognitive categories that elaborate the broad kinship categories according to different pragmatic registers. But that is the logical bottom line, which does not tell us much about why the woman's transgression is epistemologically necessary or why the narrative has such a central ceremonial function. If we go back to my earlier point about the hierarchies and entailments of cognitive features that give a local calibration to universal significance, we get a little closer to historical understandings about this mother whose descent from the sky is the inaugural mythic event for a way of life.

Several connections point toward what may be basic cognitive themes. There is reference to the two levels within the maternal role, the ceremonial and biological. The woman loses her son but the same events that culminate in that loss also compensate for that loss because they result in her obtaining ceremonial means to overcome human error, and she passes these on woman to woman through the generations. By virtue of her ceremonial action she establishes relationships to those who annually enact her role; as each woman passes on her rights to the ceremony to her follower, she also assumes the role of mother to that woman.[14] Generation after historical generation, a woman who exemplifies the mythic mother performs the ceremonies that maintain the maternal prerogative and keep communal bonds intact. All this comes about because a woman broke a taboo. Before we make this mythic woman too close a relative of the biblical Eve, we should, I think, go back to that consistent linking between features of location, volition, and transgression that we find in many Native cultures. Here is where the transformation of perspectives that can come through the empirical and technical work of linguistic pragmatics once again proves its capacity to fine-tune interpretive processes, whether we are thinking about the communal significance of some oral genre or the written works of individuals who may themselves be trying to find the secrets of their connections to the community that sustains their artistic impulse.

In her linguistic analysis of the Papago creation story, Madeline Mathiot notes how the fact of error during creation results in deprivation of voluntary mobility for one originary being, and that fact divides all beings into subcategories of agency (the cognitive theme under analysis). In other words, deprivation of mobility sets up the first step in a local system of categorization that proves to be the basis of an entire philosophical system. Some of that linguistic detail deserves attention in this context because the same cognitive theme can be found in many Native cultures even though its narrative realizations are significantly varied. As Mathiot documents the theme, she allows us to follow from afar a configuration of ideas that opens out onto a horizon of significance that stands as a powerful contrast to systems descended from European cultural categories. And that difference is a good part of my point in making the following brief foray into cognitive territory where mobility, voluntary or involuntary, is primary evidence of agency. Voluntary mobility is contingent on habitational conditions, and that is a point we discover over and over again as we look closely at different Native languages and the narratives that arise from distinctions within those languages. As Mathiot explores how the semantically distinctive features with respect to the category of person relate to the associated conditions of animateness, she notes that co-occurrence patterns yield four sets of features defining animateness, not the logically predictable three. For one, voluntary mobility is unconditionally present; for the other, it is conditionally present; and for the last, it is unconditionally absent, with this last category being divided into entities for whom it is absolutely absent and those who through association with entities for whom it is present can achieve it by extension. The categories of conditional mobility and mobility by extension are the most interesting because of the way they stand in contrast to the categories of European philosophy. Unconditional voluntary mobility characterizes humans and animals. But what is "conditional voluntary mobility" and what might be its philosophical significance? Mathiot says that the Papagoes grant conditional voluntary mobility according to degrees of association with whoever possesses unconditional mobility. The same is true for voluntary mobility by extension. All of this is powerful evidence of thinking that is fundamentally relational. Movement, the sign of life, is itself qualified by relationships with sources of willpower that control movement. For her example, Mathiot mentions a mountain that can shake or move in response to the will of a being in close relationship to it; but she says that Papagoes would always refer to such action as originating not with the mountain but with the being whose will is revealed by the moving. As Mathiot analyzes the distinguishing features of entities in these cognitive subsets, she comes back to Papago understandings of motivation (movement of the mind influencing the movement of other beings) and relationship as expressed through voluntary movement across spaces of all kinds.[15] Agency is conceptualized in direct relation to distinctions made in the capacity for voluntary mobility, which, in turn, is affected by places where action occurs.

What evidence allows us to transfer cognitive themes found in Papago culture to Blackfeet materials? First of all, there is linguistic evidence that points toward similarly configured cognitive themes. Among the Blackfeet as with many other tribes, features of location entail volitional features, and this entailment is the linguistic requirement for agency. The following grammatical statement by Donald Frantz is as intriguing as a good lead in a spy novel: "Transitive verbs of Blackfoot require subjects which are animate, and this animacy must be real i.e. it is not a gender requirement but a requirement that the subject must reference any entity which is capable of exercising will."[16] Then there is evidence that comes from explanations of ceremonial action. The woman who pledges the Medicine Lodge Ceremony has to be a woman of irreproachable fidelity. One explanation for this requirement invokes the theme of volition and presence of mind, and because it does so in the context of the culture's central ceremony, we see how insistently the culture emphasized the theme of woman's willpower. "The Blackfoot assume that many women have at one or more periods of their lives been invited by a man to commit the offence and that often the occasion is one of great temptation or calls for great presence of mind and will power," Clark Wissler writes.[17]

The emphasis on volition in the ceremony that commemorates the Star Husband narrative invites another look at that familiar story to see how its local variations play on the distance theme in relation to willing and transgression. The first event, one with widespread distribution, narrates the woman's choice of the Morning Star to be her husband. It is a choice with literal consequences because her choice results in her being transported to the sky. Once there, she marries the Morning Star and acquires the Sun as father-in-law and the Moon as mother-in-law. In another event with broad distribution, she is given a digging stick and forbidden to dig a certain very large turnip. While the event itself is found elsewhere, details of its event structure are local variations. In this case, the mother-in-law gives the digging stick to the woman, thus establishing a woman-to-woman pattern of transmission for this ceremonial item. In another event with limited distribution, hence localizing significance, the woman's willpower is tested every time she eats because there is a short supply of food, and if she eats it all, her people on earth will starve. The details of the woman's transgression also have some distinctive local cognitive features. She decides to dig the forbidden turnip, but when she tries, she discovers that the digging stick will not move. Its movement is beyond her control. This has to be a basic clue to reasons why transgression is epistemologically necessary. As it turns out, through her transgression, she acquires the power to control its action and transfer that control from the sky world to the earth. A crane woman who has always been faithful to her husband has the power to release the digging stick from its forced immobility, and she transfers that power to the woman from earth, who then moves the turnip, sees her people, and learns from her husband that she can no longer remain in the sky world; she must return with her son to her own people. The son, though, cannot immediately make the transition from one world to another. He must remain in an intermediate stage, a middle ground, his feet never touching earth, for a specified period of time. The Morning Star tells his wife that since she broke one promise, she will inevitably break that concerning the conditions of her son's coming to earth. The event that leads to the son's becoming the North Star is clearly structured around the woman's inability to control the destiny of her son. She leaves him briefly in the care of her mother, who does not understand the taboo, and through brief inattentiveness lets him leap off his bed and touch the ground. Earth is territory he is not yet equipped to inhabit. The son is transferred to that place in the sky left blank by the turnip that the woman had dug while she was in the sky world. She keeps her digging stick, though, which remains on earth as part of the medicine bundle for the Medicine Lodge Ceremony. She loses her son but acquires daughters whose willpower is strong enough to empower them to plead for the welfare of the people, year after year.

The mythic mother's journey to the sky world makes her into the figure who, through her varied positions in different locales, embodies both the significance of unconditional voluntary mobility (her initial human state) and that of conditional voluntary mobility (her state when she is in the sky as wife of Morning Star, the same role assumed by the woman who pledges the Medicine Lodge for the time of the ceremony). The story, working in the richly contextualized manner that characterizes narratives of origin, makes the important point that unconditional does not mean inconsequential. Event after event uncovers conditions and consequences. The mythic mother tests relations between locale and volition, and her experience endows charted distances with emotional and moral significance. The son, who becomes the fixed North Star when his mother accidentally transgresses the will of his father, is an exemplar of mobility by extension. His capacity to move (actually an inability to move) is entirely dependent on his father. But the father's will gives a stable point from which humans can chart their movements.

Mythic narrative lets us understand voluntary mobility as the fundamental human condition, and it teaches conditional mobility as the human status in a solemn ceremonial setting. Unconditional immobility characterizes the entire nonhuman world, which can, however, still be affected by human willpower. Human agency participates in all three conditions. Seeing what there is to see, making the right deductions, connecting what needs to be connected. These actions assure continuity of life. But the myth also reveals that the human condition is such that something is always unknown and overlooked. That is why ritual is necessary.

What can we transfer from this traditional configuration of mythic connections between mobility and agency as affected by place to contemporary life? We get some of Welch's answers to that question by looking at *The Indian Lawyer*. This novel moves away from myth to the daily stuff and muck of contemporary politics and tests the usefulness of the mythic reinterpretations in new sorts of historical spaces with new problems, namely the legal arena. The style of this novel is completely different from its predecessor. Some critics have read it as lacking the courageous edginess of earlier works. It appears to play to all the most troubling stereotypes of women. But whether or not one agrees with those critical perceptions, the novel still stands as a powerful experiment when read within the critical context explored in this chapter. Welch achieves an impressive novelistic update on issues he has been pursuing from the beginning, and just beneath the surface of this thoroughly modern plot, we see the event structure of the Star Husband tale.

The Indian Lawyer has several scenes that seem to act as signposts telling us where we stand in relation to other landmark events in Welch's literary and historical positioning amid the Montana landscape. Once the cognitive detailing is in place, we can see that we are in familiar narrative territory. With all that previous novelistic conditioning, references to a middle ground stand out like exit signs on Interstate Highway 91. And in this novel, like the previous one, the middle ground is a place of vision that turns inward to spaces of the mind. As in the myth, it is the space where the mother has to leave her son. Only visions, like everything else about the contemporary story, are literalized and psychologized. Most of the visions that frame the middle ground in this novel occur when Sylvester Yellow Calf looks into mirrors and sees the world reflected and refracted through the gaze of self looking at (and into) the self. The mirror scenes have their correlated window scenes when Yellow Calf looks outward from his office or apartment in Helena, Montana, the state capital, his place of testing where he will encounter the woman who will make him read the shape of things he would rather not know or see.

The events dramatizing the main thematic elements are so overtly stressed that no one can miss the fact that they bear the burden of proof not just for the case stated in this one book but for matters that have been four novels in the making. In one of these events we are left with no doubts about the fact that Yellow Calf, like all Welch characters, has trouble with history, or, to be more exact, he has trouble facing himself against the background of history that is anything but comforting. In a fine artistic touch, this event has the noise of a TV game show as its background. Sylvester is visiting his grandmother and goes to his childhood bedroom. His interpretation of his own image in the mirror calls into play the presuppositions about the role women play in teaching men to read an image accurately:

> *He looked at himself in the mirror above the child's dresser. His black hair looked dull and his close-set eyes were foggy with fatigue. He knocked on the scratched, sorrel-colored dresser top and noticed the pouch. He picked*

> *it up and felt it. The covering was soft-tanned hide made hard by the years. The top was tied shut by thin yellowing sinew. He held it before his eyes by the two rawhide strings. It was completely unadorned and heavier than Sylvester remembered. It was his great-great-grandfather's war medicine, the medicine his grandmother had tried to give to him when he went away to college. He held it to his neck and looked at himself in the mirror again. He tried to see in the mirror a Blackfeet warrior, getting ready to raid the Crow horses, but all he saw was a man with circles under his eyes, a faint stubble of beard on his chin, a man whose only war, a skirmish, was with himself. The new warriors. He remembered Lena Old Horn's brochures and articles about Indian lawyers. He wasn't even a new warrior. He was a fat cat lawyer, helping only himself, and some fatter cats, get richer. He put the pouch carefully on the dresser. (167–68)*

If it does nothing else, this event assures us that Welch is still asking just how the past sneaks into the present and makes us take an honest look at ourselves. Of course, honesty is not guaranteed or automatic, and that is what gives some genuine complexity to this plot. The women who teach Yellow Calf do not operate from the omniscient perspective of divine beings; they are themselves caught up in the sorts of confusions that make their willpower into an interesting force in the novel.

The middle ground of this novel is, as in all of Welch's novels, a space controlled by women whose loneliness is both cause and effect of transgression. It is artistically difficult to transfer the mythic force of the Star Husband tale to a political novel about modern Montana, but Welch attempts just that feat. Keeping in mind the puzzles, games, and secrets that lie everywhere in the Welch novelistic terrain, we are bound to respond with delighted recognition to the grandmother's name, Little Bird Walking Woman, commonly called Mary Bird. This bird, like the grandmother in the Star Husband myth, has taken the abandoned son, the abandoned chick into her nest. "Many of her old friends had felt sorry for her when she had taken Sylvester in as a baby. Some who were not traditionalists even thought the baby would be better off if it were put up for adoption. They felt Sylvester might have inherited his parents' ways and would end up breaking Mary's heart. But she knew different. She knew he would be her boy and he would make up for her daughter's wildness" (181).

For anyone thinking in terms of the myth, the associations between Mary Bird and the various birds that surround Feather Woman are automatic. This insistent associative level is directly and delightfully tied to notions of reading and interpreting. Mary Bird can predict the weather by "reading" the landscape. In keeping with the realistic decorum of this novel, Welch gives an entirely ordinary and plausible explanation for Mary's ability to see the coming weather: "Mary pulled her shawl tighter around her shoulders. She wished she could see the mountains. She could always tell the weather by the way the mountains looked. When Earl first got his TV set, he would watch the weather report, then come into the kitchen to tell her the forecast. But she always knew. And she knew when they were wrong too. She used to drive Earl crazy when she contradicted the forecast and turned out to be right. He expected a lot from his TV set, including the right to a wrong forecast" (180–81).

Welch is having fun; at the same time, he manages to sustain his pervasive visual emphasis that binds temporality to spatial specificities. Outsiders don't always get the local forecast right. Mary Bird's way works better. She watches the way atmospheric changes affect local geographical features, and she can read the times. Welch keeps up the visual emphasis by giving us other occasions when characters look at pictures to read what is coming. In a stylistically overdetermined instance, one of Feather Woman's modern sisters, a high school counselor, points to a picture in a brochure as she advises Sylvester about law school for Indians. In a sense the whole novel is about Sylvester's learning how "to get the picture," learning how to read what modern pictographs are telling him, even when the graph is framed by a picture window in the state capital.

But perhaps the most important evidence linking this young Blackfeet lawyer to all of Welch's other heroes—and to Blackfeet mythology—is the fact that he too has been abandoned by his parents and he too grows up with his maternal relatives. All the extensive elaborations of this psychological, mythological, and historical configuration come together in another mirror scene in which Yellow Calf glimpses himself in a middle distance with no escape. He has been maneuvered into this position by a woman whose husband is in prison. As a member of the parole board, Yellow Calf is vulnerable to pressures for favorable parole decisions; and in this instance a husband uses his wife to lure Yellow Calf into schemes that will wreck his political career.

In an effort to outwit those bent on destroying his career, Yellow Calf goes to a bar and, while he waits for his blackmailers, finds himself thinking about his parents—and his nightmares. This event, like others related to reading images, recalls the same cognitive theme of maternal transgression that a son cannot understand. Sons, though, have to recognize that the mothers too were caught up in circumstances that conditioned their choices. This is a tradition in which the limitations of a mother's choices created the most fundamental life conditions. As Sylvester thinks about his mother, he sees that the middle ground in which mothers always have to place their sons can have dead-end implications. He cannot stay in that middle ground:

> *He had nightmares of waking up in the street, stark naked, alone in a crowd of strangers, not knowing where he was or what had happened, alone and naked and full of loathing of himself, his father, the strangers—and his mother. . . . She could have taken him with her, or come for him later if she had to leave in a hurry. . . . Sylvester caught himself looking at himself in the mirror. Perhaps that was the middle distance old barflies found—the mirror image of themselves somewhere in no-man's-land with no escape, no farther to go. He had learned to live with the fact that his parents had abandoned him. He had had a good life with his grandparents and he was proud of them for having raised him up to be a decent human being. He could not be a barfly and he could not hate his parents for whatever weaknesses led them into their lives. Sylvester watched the heavy wooden door open in the mirror and he saw, beyond the two figures that entered, light and snow, clean and dry, and he wanted to be out in it. As he watched the door close, the figures became shadowy. (249–50)*

This passage presses all the critical buttons preset by Welch's previous novels. In the middle distance to which a woman has led him, Yellow Calf sees the limits that set up the spaces of any individual life. Those who can go in and out of the middle space can extend the range of their freedom, but those who have to stay in the middle space teach the transitory ones how to read the pictures of history. Sylvester goes in and out of this space of knowing. Doors open for him. And women make sure of that.

Quite possibly this novel sets a record for fateful door openings. Yellow Calf enters and leaves, enters and leaves, and learns that there is a price to be paid for doing so. The problem is that he does not know how to think about those who stay in the middle space. Yellow Calf tells his lover Shelley: "I can't remember a time that I had to work hard, on my own, to achieve something. There was always somebody there to open another door, to say, 'come on in, it's warm in here,' then they seem to shut the door on the faces of people I came from. Sometimes I imagine Donny Little Dog—that's the boy I grew up with—standing just on the other side of that door waiting for it to open again. But it never will. Not for him. Not for the others I left behind" (58).

Just as Fools Crow has to learn to tell in accurate detail what he sees in dreams, Yellow Calf has to tell what he has learned by "reading" a woman's designs. Only Yellow Calf has to tell his story to his boss, hardly a shaman; nevertheless, the boss, a lawyer and political pundit, interprets the events in a way that turns Yellow Calf toward a new vision of his future, one that salvages his recent learning.

There is considerable difference of opinion over how well Welch manages the difficult task of making all this into good fiction. Readers have particular trouble with his transgressive feminine figure, Patti Ann Harlow. She compromises Yellow Calf by tricking him into a blackmail scheme that ends his bid for Congress; she seduces him with calculated deliberation. Then, after they have managed to defeat the blackmailers and the even more indefatigable energy of all the gossip vultures, she ends up a "loving pal," the perfect person with whom to spend a celibate New Year's Eve (346). It all seems a bit too much when Yellow Calf asks her to help him bring in the New Year, asking her to join him in celebrating "endings and beginnings of one thing and another" (339).

Readerly credibility and patience are further strained when a proven talent like Welch writes a passage that depicts Yellow Calf struggling "to say something, something both exhilarating and sobering, something about what had happened to them, who they were now. Endings and beginnings for both of them. Instead he can only say 'You make me awfully happy. Isn't that the strangest thing?'" (339).

Yet it makes definite and, I believe, powerful thematic sense. Patti Ann Harlow is one of Feather Woman's descendants. What is beyond speculative play is the fact that she gets Yellow Calf into spaces where he learns genuine empathy. And he learns to read the meaning of history. A whole pattern of stylistic details falls in place around this reading of Patti Ann Harlow's role. Feather Woman seems to stand behind the whole cluster of references to women who give Yellow Calf pictures to read and who open doors for him that get him in and out of a middle place. In the thematically saturated last pages of *The Indian Lawyer*, after Yellow Calf has told his story to his mentor and to his lover, the latter walks away from him. "She opened the heavy oak door and turned. There were tears in her eyes. 'Call me—in a week—okay?' Then she walked out, Buster put his arm around Sylvester's shoulder. 'Women. You gotta love 'em,' he said sweetly" (336–37).

Just in case a reader might be inclined to pass over the last events as mere evidence of getting a plot tidily accomplished, Welch sends us one of his ever-present birds. "Buster did say that Sylvester was still a vice-president of the firm and, as such, he should be there. But Sylvester had an image of a dark bird, ever present, circling slowly over the festivities. He had a hunch Buster saw that vision too" (338).

By the time he wrote *The Indian Lawyer*, Welch had developed his thematic concerns to the point where his characters were no longer immobilized by the traumas of abandonment—whether those traumas were experienced in the mother/son relationship or through the abandonment of tradition itself when colonial rule and smallpox set people adrift in history. The woman-centered middle distance is a place of learning how to think about the mother and her secrets. All this is a narrative construction showing how each new narrative seeks its context in myth or in history just as each son seeks the mother. A critic, though, is more or less duty bound to expose the markers along the way and to show the evidence of how a genealogy of narratives establishes a notion of communal identity. People in place still have to learn about how they came to be so placed, and that includes an affective as well as a geographical dimension. As all the complexity of ethnolinguistic analysis suggests, the connections between the geographical and the affective can also reveal an entire philosophy.

The workings of transgression in the Feather Woman episode (and later in the Patti Ann Harlow story) bring us back to narrative origins. In the way Welch retells a foundational cultural myth, he shows how the myth brings people into consistent confrontation with the emotional dilemmas posed by movement into new and strange places, just as he reminds us of the most basic mythic message of all, that such confrontations establish the conditions of culture itself. Through the myth these conflicts are imagistically bound to dynamics of sexual difference.

The middle distance that Feather Woman and all her descendants finally inhabit in Welch's work creates the subject as it constitutes a culturally specific territorial image for the workings of what are otherwise universal instinctual and emotional origins. Welch reveals how maternal cultural space provides the space of radical responsiveness at the same time as it gives a specific cultural mark to universal psycholinguistic processes. The middle space, as Welch develops it with his women and men, is also a place to learn responsiveness that is first of all linked to sexuality. Sexual tension and alertness to possibility are part of what holds each participant to the seeing that reveals the design (the story? the secret?) that woman reveals to man. As the man "reads" events, he sees what is ahead for him and he goes beyond sexual desire to assume the role of the teller and caretaker of the knowledge he has glimpsed in woman's design. Fools Crow and Yellow Calf are both leaders; the latter is a lawyer, a member of a profession that makes eminently pragmatic use of stories that define a mode of action for society.

"You would have to care about the place. Nobody has been here long enough and the Indians have been very thoroughly kicked out." This is the first sentence of Thomas McGuane's novel *Nobody's Angel,* and it helps us in taking a final look at Sylvester Yellow Calf. In the course of one novel, Yellow Calf figures out a lot about caring for Montana. He is an Indian who has been kicked out and then kicked back in again by the women in his life. He has been kicked all the way to Helena, the capital city of Montana. He even lives near Last Chance Gulch, an urban-renewed section of downtown Helena designed to recall the past and encourage tourists to help finance the future. In his swinging-door role as outsider/insider/outsider, he can see only too well how all of Montana now knows the vulnerability to outside control that once only Native peoples knew. He can see all of Montana as one vast reservation. He has not lost the traditional Blackfeet approach to letting women teach him how to find his way through the dilemmas and conflicts of loyalty deriving from risks that have to be taken to transform and sustain the life of the group. The details of that tradition as they inform daily life are women's secret. Its historicity and its role as a middle ground of self-knowledge in relation to the women who orient the knowing it establishes happen to have been Welch's secret. As such, the narrative of the middle ground has been a promising source for strong stories, and that wellspring should continue to yield intriguing narratives about Montana's place in the world.

5. The Stranger's Language

From *Winter in the Blood* to *Winter Wheat* there is only a quick metaphoric step, and James Welch made it when he wrote the introduction to Mildred Walker's novel, drawing attention to the interlocking significances bound up with all that the title implies and the style reveals. Welch kept his introduction to essentials, telling us about Walker's life, highlighting a few stylistic fine points, and giving the reader some deceptively simple advice: "Don't overlook the brilliant metaphor of winter wheat. It is the type of wheat that does best on the high plains of Montana. If planted properly at the right time, if the gods and the weather and the earth are kind, it will yield a harvest as spiritually fulfilling as financially rewarding. But if there is too little moisture in the ground, or too much, if the winter is severe or the wind blows too hot, or a random hailstorm chooses your farm, then the spirit sinks as much as the financial return."[1]

Walker's novel, first published in 1944, was a more or less lost and out-of-print contribution to American regional literature until the 1992 Bison Books edition. The choice of James Welch to write the introduction for that edition was an inspired editorial decision because it brought together two writers' explorations of what the Montana landscape can do to characters from altogether different cultural and historical perspectives. Add the other crucial variable of gender and we can see that the resulting contrasts shape a broad field of speculative play as we compare novelistic moves linking site and self, character and geography. If we choose to make the adjective "regional" a rigorously productive rather than a pejorative qualifier for the noun "literature," then comparisons between Walker and Welch can refine our judgments about what a genuinely situated literary criticism might be like and what the broader theoretical consequences of such criticism might be. Pursuing some of these critical options, we might realize more of what exploring place in relation to plot might yield as a way to gain richer access to the diversity of American literature. In this chapter I combine aspects of the philosophical pragmatic tradition with my own work in narrative pragmatics.

Richard Poirier's assessment of Emerson's impact on American consciousness suggests why the method of questioning what is summed up in the phrase "cognitive style" can be central to any project that addresses linkages among landscape, culture, and language. Poirier claims that Emerson "would have us ask continually the question posed at the beginning of 'Experience': 'Where do we find ourselves?' As

I will propose, we 'find ourselves' it would seem inevitably *in* words. And yet we need not find ourselves trapped and held there by any particular text. Words have a way of opening up gaps in themselves which, like the gaps in Frost's 'Mending Wall' allow two to pass abreast.... [Emerson] writes always from the inside out, not from the outside in. 'The only path of escape known in all the worlds of God,' he says in 'Worship' is performance. You must do your work before you shall be released."[2]

I would give a slight but significant twist to Poirier's important comments by adding that there is a reciprocity between finding ourselves in words and finding words in place. That reciprocity recalls Ricoeur's characterization of the relationship between event and system (see chapter 1). The work or "the path of escape" involves finding a working relationship between event and system, which is the realized linguistic parallel to the working relationship between experience and interpretation, whether personal or communal. Writing or speaking that tends to "the gaps in words" tests all the ways in which language is co-implicated with history, including personal history that the twentieth century has expanded into the history and politics of subjectivity. And, of course, a major theme of twentieth-century thought can be evoked by recognizing the various problematics that go with adding the adjective "situated" to "subjectivity."

Alongside the psychoanalytic ramifications of the phrase, the geographical aspects can appear minor indeed. But we have only begun to explore possible relations between actual physical placement and psychological development. That is beginning to change, though. Personal history has become a favored domain for critical theorizing, so we have a rapidly expanding body of texts to work from as we enhance our understandings of human dependence on natural, environmental factors. As Nadia Lovell points out, we are still in the early stages of scientific and anthropological thinking about nature, not as something to be set against culture, but as a "realm of experience" that "interpenetrates" the human in a mutually interpretive manner."[3] What this might mean in terms of the literal experiences of real people is one of the problems we can bring to bear in a regional criticism.

Twentieth-century literature has been a grand experiment in what can be conveyed by way of stylistic high-wire acts. Walker's text does not belong to this tradition of stylistic experimentation. In all her writing, she stayed with simple language. Yet the simplicity of this work can be viewed as its strength as it tells an elemental American story about finding one's language, one's cognitive style in a definite landscape after migration has placed the individual where space no longer evokes the history that structures the rhythms of a life. That is a process that requires clear telling, addressed to the general public. That is a narrative strongest in its impact when it is most directly told. It is a narrative about how the narrating voice comes to be, how it learns to read a set of circumstances in a particular landscape.

David Huddle, announcing the 1993 National Fiction Prize for Larry Watson's novel *Montana 1948*, could have been talking about Walker's novel when he reminded us all that a truly expressed sense of place is seldom an effect of aggressive technical virtuosity; the reader's perception of complexity might come only as an aftereffect, but it is no less real for all that. Huddle writes: "The unusual qualities of the book are not immediately evident: the writing is clean, clear, and unpretentious; the structure is traditional; the beginning sets forth circumstance, time, and place in a familiar fashion. . . . I can neither purge from my mind the truth it delivers nor ignore the deliverance its truth brings to my mind."[4]

If these novels deliver their impact without any technical showiness, then what exactly is going on—besides a plot that a lot of readers seem to enjoy? We can take the critical position that holds together the varied chapters of this book and say that it demonstrates how cognitive style has to be considered in relation to its regional variations. We can turn again to Michael Kowalewski, who wonders why region has been so neglected as a serious critical category even though "cognitive scientists are now suggesting that memory itself cannot function without place, that we have no awareness of past events in our lives without a sense of the place in which they happened."[5]

Walker's novel works as a particularly fine case study for looking at how memory depends on place as it mines the past for future significance. Her plot is carefully constructed to show that when time makes good on its promises, adding level after local level of significance to the way language, especially metaphoric language works in a given place, it establishes that crucial reciprocity between subjective affect and communal language so that the two become mutually interpretive. Therefore, to abandon place as a variable is to abandon that value-added psychological profit that goes under the common rubric "sense of place." With this subtext, Walker manages her own kind of experimentation, one that is not so much technically ostentatious as it is cognitively persistent—as persistent as winter wheat on rocky slopes. Analyzing this novel is more a matter of showing first the impact of decontextualization on narrative. Then, bit by bit, context is drawn in by way of the seasonal temporality of Montana. The primary contribution of the novel is to show concretely how that local temporality paces self-knowledge and how it works to invest the immigrant's language with transitional significance.

Winter Wheat covers the span of two growing seasons, two times of latent development for what grows in early spring. Walker's character Ellen spends the first winter at the University of Minnesota in Minneapolis, where she learns to look at Montana from the outside in. She also begins the process of trying to write about her Montana life, so we can follow her own attempts to understand her life as narrative. She spends the second year at home because she agrees to teach in a one-room rural school; that reimmersion in a life she thought she was leaving teaches her to see the place from the inside out. With that turnabout, she grasps how much she had previously missed about the emotional economy of her family, and that fundamental revision gradually gets linked to an understanding of how the setting in Montana has set up conditions for communication or the lack thereof among family members.

Lacking a conscious grasp of these conditions, Ellen finds herself briefly isolated, even from her immediate family. During her lonely winter in a one-room schoolhouse, she reviews and revises her understanding of several relationships. There is her broken engagement with an architect from Minneapolis who has been drafted into the army; there is her growing friendship with the divorced father of a troubled but beloved student in her classroom; and, most important of all, there is her changing perspective on the struggle that binds her immigrant Russian mother and her Vermont-born American father in a marriage that Ellen comes to view as destructive to all involved. One question echoes throughout the entire novel and finally pulls us back to the role of place as a factor binding these different narrative elements. Walker has her character ask, "Is there any real unity of feeling with such a mixture?" (26). That question, placed early in the novel, is variously orchestrated through all the subsequent events before it is answered by reference to the metaphor of winter wheat and the eastern Montana growing season, the most elementary context of all. As Ellen tries to create a realistic narrative about life in Montana, she also discovers that "unity of feeling" as an effect of narrative. The novel unfolds as a series of events that teach her the conditions under which her life can be perceived as a narrative construct, and these conditions are firmly bound to place even though she does not want them to be.

For the sake of comparisons between Walker and Welch, we can say that both authors have created characters whose only hope for finding some point to their lives involves discovering one or two basic things about how that saving unity of feeling can only be found at home, whether or not the characters want to be there. Of course, "unity of feeling" is itself only a vaguely imagined construct with no obvious significance unless one assumes an affective investment strong enough to gather other textual features to the task of lively specification. As it happens, a fortunate plot symmetry lets us go beyond mere setting as our point of comparison between the two authors. Both Welch and Walker give us maternal characters who prompt questions about what a person's place within a family might have to do with that person's ability to find a place within a landscape and within the narrative whose significance has to be found in that landscape. Is there, as both authors imply, always and necessarily a secret dimension to a mother's love that binds a child to a place even as it frees that child from infantile dependence on the mother?

Psychoanalysts could, no doubt, pursue the question in relation to the dynamics of identity formation; but before such unraveling of what happens in the process of individuation can add very much to our understanding of the novels under analysis here, we need to see how Walker sets up some features of the question that no theory would anticipate. That means exploring how Walker's novel, like Welch's, works its telling way around and through a secret, a blank narrative center, a gap, if you will, in words that shapes character by virtue of its hidden force and places a requirement on that character to find a way beyond its negative compulsion.

Secrets, of course, power any good plot, but Walker's novel plays on the way secrets can initiate a dynamic of estrangement from parents and project a character into new psychological space where all previously known ways of reading the self as a social being have to be revalued or transvalued as relational balances are shifted. In this context, the phrase "reading the self" is a way of referring to the way the novel's events set up narrative expectations that generate further events. By taking away previous supports of self-understanding from the character, the author places the reader in a constructivist position following, event by event, a learning process that is about self in a landscape perceived as alien. But it is also about what narrative is and can do in that situation.

The central event of the novel is that in which Walker lets the daughter Ellen (Yelena to her Russian mother) learn about a parental secret just when she is least prepared to cope with the emotional consequences of what she discovers. She is in a state of extreme vulnerability because her fiancé's first visit to the family ranch has been disastrous. She correctly believes that he decided not to marry her when he discovered how alien her home life felt to him. During the course of his visit, she too adopts his perspective and sees her parents as an urban stranger might. She decides that the perceived tension between them is evidence of what happens to couples who get isolated in the vastness of eastern Montana. After saying goodbye to her fiancé, Ellen is distraught. She needs time to herself, so she pretends to go to bed only to slip out of the house alone, take a long walk, and brood on her loss. On reentering the family home, she overhears her parents' conversation about her presumed engagement and its contrast to theirs.

That accidental eavesdropping is the event that forces several fundamental revisions in her understanding of her own life situation. She learns that her mother had tricked her father into the marriage that brought her from Russia to the United States. Along with that crucial clue about her parents' relationship, she also hears a fierce and stunning emotion in the tone of her mother's voice. Its power is new to her, yet she instinctively knows that it somehow defines her. What is more, it immediately divides her between differing parental identifications. Each parent stands for a contrasting set of emotional and cultural options. Life in Montana is the maternal requirement. Or, as Ellen sees it at that moment, it is her mother's fault. Separate events are fused in mind and emotion so that they exist for her as cause and effect. Her broken engagement is experienced as a consequence of her mother's lie that had exiled them all to Montana:

> *It seemed to me that hate and hopelessness filled our house to suffocation. Maybe Gilbert had felt that hate between Mom and Dad. Maybe that was what drove him away from me, because I had seemed to be part of it. All these years Dad and Mom had lived together, pretending to be fond of each other, even having me, when all the time they had hated each other. . . . Then I came back to what I had just heard. Little bits fitted in together. . . . A feeling of shame, deep in myself, crept out for Mom. If she had really loved him, she couldn't have done that. Suddenly she wasn't Mom; she was Anna Petrovna, someone strange whom I hardly knew. And he wasn't Dad, tired and tormented by shrapnel; he was Ben Webb, a strong healthy young soldier. (93–94)*

A revealing distance of estrangement comes into being as the space of novelistic tension through this event, which revises the meaning of all that came before. This dramatic distance becomes the narrative space within which her secret knowledge of their secret can require and slowly acquire a whole series of new connections, a whole set of differently contextualized understandings about what things mean within that family. A new narrative about the family has to emerge. The novelistic narrative becomes a temporal accounting that reveals where and how and by whom meaning has been invested in actions, people, and places. In this novel, a whole series of identifications are interrupted and redirected after Ellen learns the secret that calls into question what she thought she knew about her place in the family and in the world. Amid all this underplayed internal drama of severance, reintegration, and redefinition, Ellen also discovers how many of the connecting elements she needs have already been invested in the Montana landscape through the way she and her family have experienced its impact.

The critical social space in this novel is entirely familial. Therefore Ellen has naturalized its impact. But once events strip away that veil of naturalness, she has to consider the constitutive elements that went into the making of this seemingly natural social space. Returning to Derek Gregory's fortunate metaphor linking social construction of space with theories of subjectivity, we can say that discovering the secret of her parents' pasts causes Ellen to step through the looking glass of known social space, only to discover that she is a sign in a system she does not comprehend. Social space is transformed from absolute to abstract.[6] She has to find interpretive clues to the system. And that sign system requires powerful emotional signifiers. No immediate explanation can be adequate to the task of giving her a working knowledge of a past that reaches deep into the psyche of each family member just as it derives from histories that developed far from Montana. Only time will tell. That cliché comes alive in this novel and can so easily be used to make the point that the implicit narrative bound to its cognitive style registers the temporality of place as it allows for access to all the connecting elements that are necessary for conscious understanding.

Stated less obscurely, the same ideas can seem self-evident. Every place modulates a person's experience of time. Seasons and the rhythms of cloud and sunlight, times of ease and times of danger, times of being house-bound and times of walking about in open space—all of these so obviously modulate our subjective experiences of time that we naturalize the experience as fully as Ellen naturalized her understanding of familial dynamics. But as Walker's novel narrates, the way in which the temporality of a place paces subjective experience is central to the way in which we work the linkages between knowing, feeling, and the landscapes that condition that knowing and feeling in a manner that we sum up with the word "home." Walker's novel uses the metaphor of reading to get at the learning needed to give her character access to the interpretive skills that will bring her back into the understandings that can give the parent/child bond its particular intimacy. That metaphor now gets such consistent critical usage that it is losing its critical effectiveness; nevertheless, it gets at the learned quality of processing experience. It encapsulates the distance implied between landscape and an experiencing consciousness. It points to the need for narrativizing that distance. Walker shows an interrupted "reading" that is a consequence of migration. Replacement requires new strategies for reading an old story and extended emotional skills for coping with the impact of transferred and transplanted histories.

Ellen takes an elementary school teaching position; therefore she is teaching one kind of reading even as she learns another. She has to achieve her own rereading of the family story. That process of reinterpretation gives a double referentiality to all the novelistic detail about teaching, reading, and writing. Walker uses these processes to figure a pragmatic cognitive reflexivity. While at the university Ellen had begun to write about her family, but her writing had been flat, as unidimensional as her understanding of home territory. So she is every way poised for radical revisionary questioning, and hers is a credible fictional consciousness for decoding and encoding different levels of meaning in an environment where the mundane has to do exceptional signifying duty. Ellen has to learn how to decipher a code that only her foreign-born mother could have introduced as an element into the text of the local American landscape.

The mother may have lied about her pregnancy in her determination to emigrate; she did not lie about carrying a new life in transit from Russia to the United States. As a nurse, ministering to Ellen's father she had understood something quite concrete about how passion and desire require institutional realization if they are to transfer to another nation. Concretely, that meant marriage. In her case, the institutional bond was forged in spite of culture, nation, even language as the sheer power of her determination brought practical realization to an intuited possibility. In this novel, marriage as an institution is stripped to its stark symbolic minimum, and Anna Petrovna knows that she can make it work because she can transfer the energies of sexual passion into the energies of culture building and simultaneously develop the emotional support for it all, creating new life out of whatever she manages to transfer to Montana. In this novel, the family system is shown as the matrix for narrative generativity.[7]

Sexual passion intensified by the extreme needs of a woman whose home and family have been destroyed by war is the founding energy of the social unit that Anna Petrovna shifts into the Montana landscape, where passion is then further channeled into the task of establishing the family farm. In this novel, for this family emerging from the randomness of war, farming is passion realized; it is a way of living out a secret knowledge. It is a plot analogue to the secret love affair that Welch made the symbolic foundation of *Winter in the Blood*.

In both novels, a child or grandchild has to reconsider his or her identity in relation to newly acquired and surprising knowledge about what parents or grandparents have secretly achieved. Welch's novel, with its unnamed male protagonist, plays that theme in all its mythic registers, thereby allowing us to go from no-name or a mass-culture Prufrock spin-off to a definitely named Yellow Calf, an individual whose name symbolizes a recognized place in Blackfeet tradition. Walker, though, tells the tale of a woman alone, or rather two women, mother and daughter, each figuratively alone until she can find the other. Immigration has cut them off from the tradition that might interpret actions and contextualize language. When Ellen begins to perceive the strength of the emotion informing her family history, she sees her mother transformed into a stranger. That image of the mother is in direct relation to estrangement from the geographical landscape, and the power of the novel lies in the way its events link reconciliation of the one with the other.

The newly recognized mother figure is so sexually compelling and so sharp a rebuke to Ellen's own femininity that at first Ellen refuses to deal with her. She withdraws physically to her own schoolhouse and she withdraws psychologically by identifying with her father. Subtending the psychological dynamics informing this feature of the plot, there are intriguing cultural dynamics. The father's Vermont heritage is safe, conventional, undeniably American—and unsuited to life in Montana. The mother's Russian heritage is perceived as dangerous, inimical to Ellen's own hopes for a modern urban life with an American man, impossible to imagine with any but fragmentary, accidental detail, yet somehow the mother's heritage is the power that binds them all to Montana, willingly or unwillingly. This is the dimension of the novel that makes it important for comparative purposes.

Different immigrants brought with them different ways of investing the landscape with communicational power; they did not necessarily bring with them the ability to comprehend how their relationships to place affected interpersonal relationships or how the histories of other nations reverberated within the words they used to describe American experiences. The children of immigrants only discovered that part of the American story bit by bit. If such children also happened to be writers, they told those crucial parts of the American story that we, as critics, are still learning how to read.

Walker's novel keeps to its realistic promises by resisting the melodramatic impetus of its plot elements. Ellen accepts the fact that the newly perceived peremptory and disturbing mother coexists with the maternal persona she has always known. The woman she is beginning to glimpse is no less maternal, just differently and frighteningly so, disruptively entering Ellen's experience of need whether or not Ellen consciously wants any awareness of her. This Anna Petrovna may be an incomprehensible stranger, but she is needed, and Ellen knows that need deeply through her own emotional turmoil, which resists any naming even as her experience undermines and unnames remembered emotions. The mother's struggles with the English language parallel the daughter's struggles to name her psychological state.

Ellen is alone in her knowledge of facts whose significance she cannot judge. Therefore, only events that can break through the aura of distancing estrangement can become part of the narrative of Ellen's subjectivity. This sets up a temporality based on breakthroughs, on intrusions and their subsequent familiarizations when remembered associations reestablish a continuity of feeling. The metaphor of winter wheat controls this process as it reminds us of an inescapable temporal dimension. It establishes event structure as it links the conditions of subjective comprehension to experience of place with its variable weather-related rhythms and its invariable landscape markers to serve as stable figures from which to calibrate destabilized meanings. As the narrative adds level after level of significance to its controlling metaphor, it transforms a simple metaphoric identification into a symbolic construct that configures the mother's immigrant experience for both mother and daughter. Winter wheat needs its time of apparent dormancy before early spring growth.

Giving so much weight to so simple a metaphor seems extreme unless we remember that this particular metaphor is assigned a foundational role in this novel. Ellen has no obvious cultural models as she moves forward from the event that destabilizes her sense of self and landscape. Walker's depiction of the parental figures explicitly eliminates religious, therefore mythic, precedents. For non-Indian characters like Ellen, Montana history is too recent for precedents. Time appears to be as empty as space, but both exist in relation to more precedent-rich areas of the world; this very knowledge of contrasts and options in other places establishes the particular conditions of isolation Ellen first resents and then finally comes to understand as the source of her own capacity to recognize significant elements in both time and space that will enable her to narrativize her position.

Language issues are shown in their peculiarly American complexity by a crucial scene in which Ellen is reading Walt Whitman to her father. This event sums up the significance of all the others built on the themes of reading and writing. Its explicit reference to Whitman's radical poetic agenda seems far from incidental in this novel in which a Yankee and a Russian cultural heritage are fusing into a western one. We are prompted to consider how Whitman set out to Americanize metaphor and to prove that metaphor was a force that could make Americans. To expand on this notion of Whitman's metaphor, I turn to Richard Poirier's reading of Whitman, who, as Poirier has pointed out, illustrates "a theory of entitlements." "While allowing for the common assumption that words are the signs of things, [Whitman] proposes that the reverse of this may also be true: that things are the signs of the words. That is, the things we look at already carry with them a fund of association that empowers, even prompts, the words by which they can then be represented. Things are 'funded' by the previous human uses that have been made of them."[8]

We can read Walker's novel in ways that detail Poirier's argument along lines set up by the conditions of immigrant life in Montana. Walker's plot concentrates first on the absence of any entitlement for words. Then it shows how family interactions occurring in a particular geographical environment with its particular temporality build up that "fund of association" that gives semantic depth to the words by which they can then be represented and that allows words to mediate between system and event. We can get beyond emphasis on language alone by saying that Walker is dramatizing the issue, first of creating, then of transmitting that "funded" linguistic heritage from parents to daughter. Ellen inherits a different bequest from each parent just as she is in line to receive yet a third one, that which the parents have jointly created. As a writer, she can pass on the heritage to a larger community. To inherit, though, she has to learn the cognitive styles (the investments of meaning in language) that her parents have evolved together and separately in Montana. In Walker's novel, the lines quoted from Whitman focus attention on the giving and taking that build up that relational and durational sense of family-centered self.

Walker uses Whitman's unitary language as a basis from which to control a character's awareness of severances that precede new and more conscious connections, thus making duration into a process of conscious placement deriving from the nature of relations achieved in a place over time. Ellen quotes lines from Whitman that have to do with the continuing generational power of families and with making the biological the prelude to every other generative act:

> *His own parents, he that had father'd him and she that had*
> *conceived him in her womb and birth'd him*
> *They gave this child more of themselves than that,*
> *They gave him afterward every day, they became part of*
> *him.*

When she reads these lines with her own family in mind, Ellen has a startled reaction to the text. She realizes how aptly they articulate her family position. She notes first the contrasts in what each parent has given her; then she links that to the novel's central event, that secret knowing of a secret that disconnects and disorients and necessitates the reconstruction that is the novel's real point. Ellen realizes that there is a taking that can be every bit as much a part of the parental role as the giving: "First Mom gave to me and then Dad gave to me. Only that night when I had learned about the hate between them had they ever taken away—but then they had taken away so much" (141).

What has been withdrawn are the props of an idealized primary identification. Once Ellen is forced to recognize her parents as individuals, the relationships between family ties and linguistic investments get worked out in carefully plotted narrative detail. Ellen's youthful narcissistic reading of parental identity dissolves into a mix of questions, resentments, and new identifications; the process repeatedly brings readers back to the question posed early in the novel and in this essay: "Is there any real unity of feeling in such a mixture?" When we try for a sensibly detailed answer, we realize that the question needs reformulation. What can we say about what we perceive as the unity of feeling in this mixture?

In the character of the immigrant mother, the interconnected subtleties by which speaking and doing are elaborations, one of the other, achieve the clarity of precise focus. Although Walker gives Anna Petrovna a tragic personal history, she refuses to endow her with tragic attitudes. Instead she shows how the severing of ties to people, place, and language has rechanneled psychological energies so that Anna Petrovna's farming in Montana is also her way of rebuilding lost connections between doing, speaking, and relating. Rebuilding, however, is not reduplication in this instance. What Anna Petrovna transmits to her daughter is not so much a matter of discrete object lessons as it is a matter of tacit knowledge and skills. Or we can say that it is an approach to knowing that is a style of knowing. Furthermore, the mother has learned what features of that style translate from language to language, from place to place. That active working out of the conditionality behind the extreme necessity of emigration is the secret of this mother's love.

Most of what the child Ellen has learned about her mother is so much out of cultural context that the facts themselves make less of an impact than her mother's style of confronting them. That transferred style of dealing with life is precisely her heritage, translated and made into something quite different as that style is transmitted from mother to daughter, or to return to matters of language we should say that the style of confrontation is transmitted from mother to daughter via objects facilitating the transmittal so that the style of confrontation is thereafter represented by the object. Once while working in the garden, Ellen asks about her mother's parents, and her mother responds in broken English, narrating the brutal facts of wartime murders:

> "My father try to keep his pigs from robber soldier. The man shoot him and burn our house. My mother burn to death."
>
> I stared at Mom. Even to a child my mother didn't hide things or make them seem better than they were. I saw in her face that she could see it all just as it was. . . .
>
> I remember how still it was out there in the garden, and since that day I have always known how red are the veins of the beet leaves and how like soft green leather the leaves themselves. (34)

That crucial event shows the details of transference as the mother's memories are bound through the daughter's hearing to the details surrounding the conditions of that hearing. The beets growing in Montana remind Ellen of her mother's Russian past, but, more than that, they come to signify a way, a manner of facing up to any threatening memories and of living with them. The beets become a metaphor for a way of dealing with the past. Complex knowledge is bound to local and simple phenomenality as it is passed on to the daughter. A parallel scene several chapters later underscores this novelistic point as it serves to illustrate Ellen's exposure to her mother's teaching, an exposure that simultaneously reminds her that she needs to be part of the place where she herself has grown into the conditions of meaning and remembered associations. And this awareness of how place plus duration constitutes a sense of place that can become a foundation for a local knowing is the cognitive point behind the novel with its metaphor of winter wheat. The related event showing the temporal extension of the garden experience occurs during the time Ellen is teaching in her one-room school far from any other dwelling. One of her students has been lost in a snowstorm and has frozen to death. Alone after that harrowing day, Ellen can see the implications of what she learned from her mother in the garden: "I found something out that night; something that made me feel closer to Mom. A thing doesn't hurt you so much if you take it to you as it does when you keep pushing it away. . . . I remembered Mom telling me about her mother and father's death, when we weeded the beets in the garden. I could see in her face that she remembered it all as though it had just happened and it hurt her all over again, but I felt she wasn't afraid to remember it. I wouldn't be afraid of this; it was a time I had to remember; it was a part of my life" (192).

The persistent but unobtrusive novelistic language about becoming part of, taking part in, separating and departing weaves a pattern that finally points to the way landscape conditions human emotions—gauging and modulating broad categories of feeling. Because this narrative calibration occurs in conjunction with the metaphor of winter wheat, we can begin to distinguish a dynamic series of metonymic transfers operating in conjunction with the naturalistically determined significations of the winter wheat metaphor. "I liked the snow falling down on the hardpan soil around the teacherage," Ellen writes. "It was almost a foot deep. I felt the way I do when I see the snow coming down to cover the fields that are planted to winter wheat. I guess you have to live on a dry-land wheat ranch to feel that glad about the first real snow; it seems such an easy way of getting moisture into the soil" (168).

Snow, so predictably ordinary a feature of all northern winters, acquires an associative transfer of meaning that gathers in the commonplace connections between drought and emotional thirst or need, and that complex of meaning is then shifted into a context that undercuts the negative connotations of cold by balancing them against the need for moisture, which is more likely to be met when soil can absorb the wet, slow-melting snow than under the conditions of driving summer rain falling on rocks and hard ground only to run off into gullies and creeks.

The language is simple; its figurative values and transfers are complex; but the experiential immediacy of snow makes it into just the direct metaphoric term that Ellen needs. After her exhilarated run through the early snowfall, she finds that she can finally write to her fiancé and name the separation that she had known but had been unable to verbalize either to him or to her parents. As she writes, her reference to the snow begins as obvious cliché, then it gathers in and explains the whole sequence of separations just as it expresses a fundamental acceptance of them. In all its simple directness the language of the metaphors related to snow encompasses a cycle of experience that eludes the linguistic assertiveness of direct reference. Duration and placement are shown as determinants of a signification that is available only through submission to their requirements.

Ellen writes: "Tonight it is snowing. I went out a few minutes ago and felt the snow on my face and on the hardpan ground. Do you know what I found myself thinking, Gil? I began thinking how green it would be around here in the spring if the snow stayed and there was enough moisture. I wondered if there would be as many flowers as there were last spring on the top of the coulee. I would know better now than to try to show them to you. You have to be more simple and pleasant like my mother and me to care about our wild flowers. But I'm glad we met and that you came out here to see me, even though I lost you that way" (169).

We find here a recapitulation of the progression presented a few paragraphs earlier where Ellen has stated, "I guess you have to live on a dry-land wheat ranch to feel that glad about the first real snow; it seems such an easy way of getting moisture into the soil." Only here, that notion of moisture in soil is already bound to memory that includes a metaphoric extension of snow in relation to painful memories. And here, in this context, Ellen recognizes that she cannot quickly or easily convey that significance to an outsider, even one she loves. Just as it separates her from him, it unites her to her mother, whose style of knowing and remembering is invested in the very same natural imagery of Montana life. The letter unobtrusively gives us the understanding that presages a reconciliation between daughter and mother. When she had shown the wildflowers to the man she loved, even she had not understood why they mattered so much to her. By the time she writes the letter, her losses have given Ellen a self-observant distance that makes her into an alert transcriber consciously sorting out the features of meaning that will let her breach her resistances to what experience is teaching her about how place and time interact to create foundations for a dimension of meaning she can find only by staying where she is.

This farewell letter recalls the last words of Larry Watson's more recent novel about Montana in which an old man, forced to remember events that had driven his family from Montana, bangs his fists on the dinner table and angrily yells at his startled guests, "Don't blame Montana; don't blame Montana."

In keeping with the use of reading and writing as metaphoric activities controlling the retrospective revision of temporal significance, Walker finally presents the novel's resolution in terms of a reading that makes the right connections to let Ellen grasp the meaning of her place in her family and in her landscape. Almost a year after his departure, Ellen learns that her fiancé has been killed in battle. She tells no one; her losses are all too bound to each other for her to tell her parents what is happening to her. She even loses her teaching position when she tries to reach out to the two other outsiders spending the winter in Montana, a child and his father who compensates for his own losses by excessive drinking. Through this character war themes are precisely orchestrated in relation to other features of the novel's unfolding significances.

Finally, her mother breaks through Ellen's aura of isolation with its self-perpetuating misreadings of so many human motives. Not knowing that the fiancé had been killed in battle, the mother confronts Ellen: "He'll never marry you. You waste your time. He ain't nothing you want, anyway" (282). Ellen, in anger, fights back.

The silence is broken. Ellen's accusations compel the mother to tell her own and her husband's story as one in which two people had each gauged the character of the other and had dared the risks of staying together. Then the mother shifts to matters of knowing as a basis for loving. "'You can write that young Gil of yours that he don't know what he think he does. Sure, we fight sometime, but we got no hate here.' Her eyes flashed" (284). At that point, Ellen tells her mother about Gil's death.

Because she has to compare her father's side of the story with her mother's, Ellen tries to get him to talk about the marriage, but he seems to be surprisingly evasive, veering off into talk about farming and Montana, which is, of course, the only accurate way to talk about his marriage. Later, at dinner, Ellen looks out the window at the landscape, and that visual framing provides the right focus for all the other framings she needs. The composed setting allows for a rereading and reframing of memories composing her family story:

> *From where I sat I could look out the window by the sink and see the sky above the roof of the barn. I thought back over the things Dad had said. Even when I had made it easy for him he wouldn't say anything against Mom. He had acted almost as though he had not liked my criticizing her. And he had gone on to try to make me understand her as he did. . . . My own thought startled me. . . . I had to stop and look at it.* AS HE DID!
>
> *I had been so sure that there was no real understanding between Mom and Dad. He had said himself: "Sometimes it's hard to understand your mother, Ellen," and then in the next breath, as though he were embarrassed, he had gone on about this country and how different it was from the East. "Maybe you never quite understand why, but this country gets to be a part of you when you live with it." Could he have meant that he felt that way about Mom too? It struck me all of a sudden, as though I had been trying to read something in the half-dark and now I had come outside where there was light. (294–95)*

Once Ellen achieves a conscious revision of her previous perceptions, what had been a "wall of strangeness" separating her parents becomes a "strange understanding" binding her parents through their mutual encounters with the land. This "strange understanding" is the immigrant's goal and gift, and it is what drives many an immigrant to the kind of linguistic struggle that results in novels and poems, some of them excellent, some failed attempts, but all of them reflective of the "strange understanding" the storyteller tries to bring to the light of conscious understanding.

With this in mind, we can reflect on how carefully the reading reference is structured. Ellen has not understood because she has been trying to read "in the half-dark," and once she starts to "look at" her own thoughts, she moves outside to where there is light. "I began to see." This same passage also includes reference to the novel's emphasis on becoming part of something, some place, someone's life. Interpersonal relationships have to be read in the same terms as relationships between self and place. That "strange understanding" binding her parents is a compact of renewal that requires the externalized form of work realized through time—it requires the farm as evidence of invested understanding.

In a fine novelistic touch, Walker has the mother noticing that something has happened to the daughter, and, employing a reference to Russian custom, she announces that Ellen looks like someone celebrating her name day. Ellen is celebrating her own naming, or, more precisely, she is celebrating her own dawning comprehension of how to read the names of objects and interactions in her own environment.

My critical naming that achieves a reading of Walker's novel assumes that history or, more exactly, histories imply investments of cognitive significance that can be accessed only if the geographical setting of that history is honored. As psychological theory makes clear, the developmental trajectory traced by individual human growth is one marked by breaks rather than continuity, which is an effect of achieved agency. Landscape easily and directly provides the metaphors for continuity. Internalizing those metaphors is far less easily accomplished, though. And it is never accomplished quickly. Walker's novel makes the claim that these metaphors can be internalized only if their natural temporal structure is respected and if there is some conscious transfer of meaning to create a metaphoric field, a cognitive set. Distances in time have to correlate with distances in space, and both have to correlate with the internal distances of the psyche.

The preceding statement can return us to comparisons between James Welch and Mildred Walker. James Welch's statement from *Winter in the Blood* about the distances in his novel can be seen as applying equally to the dynamics at work in Mildred Walker's *Winter Wheat*. "The country had created a distance as deep as it was empty and the people accepted and treated each other with distance. But the distance I felt came not from country or people; it came from within me. I was as distant from myself as a hawk from the moon."[9]

In the novels of Welch and Walker, the internal distances set up a necessity to cross all the varied distances in order to find words that "tumbled meaning into wind."[10] In the novels of both authors, the "quick paces and a space of mind" are the preconditions for getting on with life and getting along with family. But the contrasts in the ways that the authors cross various kinds of internal and external narrative distances are equally telling, not just because they illuminate the works of these two writers but because of what they tell us about regional approaches to literature rather than approaches to regional literatures. Each author tells us something significantly different about the work of remembrance, about the tasks and the skills that make remembering a culturally as well as personally significant act.

James Welch's characters have all had to learn how to revise their own understandings of their own traditions. This knowing is definitely not a matter of mastery over systematized information. It is a matter of learning to understand aspects of the tradition as open systems capable of yielding new understanding, capable of revealing its secrets to those who know enough of the code to uncover the way the system works. And, as I read Welch, even the code had to be found through a novelistic journey into the past that sought those features of tradition that opened out onto more and more distant interpretive horizons. Welch has shown how the history of narrative is a spiral, moving ahead into new narrative territory by turning back over previous terrain to observe what couldn't be seen the first time around. Welch implies that, in order to keep going forward, we have to take a look backward and downward not just in order to see the way we have come but to see what was hidden along the way, what secrets were there that we could not grasp. The secret possibilities hidden in mythic structures give us a needed edge as we look to the future.

Walker, by contrast, does not give her characters any of the comforts of a narrative tradition, not even the "freedom and justice for all" kind that turns conventional narratives of American history to mythic advantage. Yet she too sets up a spiral movement. Her characters have to look back over previous tellings, previous interactional contexts that planted the seeds of narrative significance. Their growth is just as secret as that which occurs in the grander frames of the Native American mythic traditions, and they create a level of significance bound to basic metaphors. In a word, they are the "seeds" of myth, undoubtedly a secular myth but nevertheless one deserving of the appellation reserved for narrative structures that continue to generate other structures. Furthermore, the secret growth of these fundamental familial interactions depends on other more traumatic secrets that generate a forward momentum for characters, even as they compel the backward look along the spiral. In this novel, she describes a very limited social space—the family. But the novel also insists on its action as the beginning of a new kind of reading and writing. By way of narrative, the discoveries that take place within the familial institution can be extended to other institutions and social spaces. Walker's family is a secular mythic unit.

The kinds of narrative possibilities that Walker establishes for Montana farm life may never achieve full-blown mythic flowering for many people. But I have no doubt that I could go to the Montana plains and talk to farmers and find many for whom winter wheat has taken on mythic significance, however we may choose to quibble about what myth means or how it affects culture and cognition.

Memories break into new settings; the resulting associative significance is a renewal and/or inauguration of meaning-in-place. Walker's novel insists on this configuration comprising the historical fact of immigration and the advent of significance in a new place that goes well beyond translating the semantic content of one language into another. All those cognitive features deriving from relationships between person and place need their own mode of translation, and this translation depends as much on duration as it does on rational comprehension. Crucial features of meaning derive from what landscape evokes within the subject during all those temporal variations that slowly become the transferential basis for establishing preverbal analogues for affective states. Emotion gets invested in landscape. From landscape to language is an easy semantic step, but it is a complex cognitive one if the intent is to communicate the rich and dynamic play of transferential significance orchestrated by duration within a particular setting. Anna Petrovna's daughter, Ellen, eventually finds herself part of Montana because and only because she has inherited what her mother has invested in the details of Montana farm life.

Reference to culture and cognition brings me to the crossovers among disciplines that inform this study of cognitive style in regional novels. Carol Worthman, in an essay exploring relationships between neurology, psychology, and anthropology, cites biochemical evidence to support her assertions that the way we learn to account for our experiences is bound to a whole complex of reactions that include such factors as timing and the event structure leading up to an experience. She claims that "the learning of schemata for interpretation and organization of experience occurs not just through internalization, but also by forging linkages between physiologic states and interpretive-organizational schemata. Thus physiologic states have both direct and indirect (via schemata) effects on affect and behavior. Physiologic states alter the threshold to certain cognitive states, affective states and behaviors. Further, physical states can trigger or evoke schemata that, in turn, entrain their cognitive, affective and behavioral components in the individual." She asks, among other things, for "a profile of operative criteria for access to experience."[11]

Studies such as Worthman's, concerned with finding a place for comparative cultural data in the disciplinary frameworks of psychology and neurobiology, also suggest the importance of concentration on cognitive style in regional literatures. Language has its place within the economy of measurable behaviors. Pragmatic features of linguistic reference are variable but also verifiable. They exist in changing, creative, productive relationships to semantic features and to semiotic elements that derive from individual subjectivity. Studies of narrative and cognition generate profiles of "operative criteria for access to experience." If narrative studies use fictional sources, the results, of course, are hypothetical. But good regional fiction can generate strong hypotheses about how local elements shape schemata that "in turn, entrain their cognitive, affective and behavioral components in the individual."

If the technical detail of narrative study or of psychological anthropology seems too great a set of disciplinary distances for literary critics to cross, the spaces of the mind can be narrowed to the literary critic's more customary metaphorical spaces, and we can indulge in some quite ordinary attention to character as we appreciate how Walker dramatizes a series of transferences, each different in quality and scope, but each qualifying as essentially maternal creations, as basic to culture building as child care is to creating a family. But that basic quality should not eclipse the importance of what is linked to specific times and places, for it is a style of managing these specificities that is the real maternal creation.

Conclusion

"You tell the stories you need to tell to keep the story tellable." This is the sturdy pragmatic conclusion toward which this book has been moving chapter by chapter as I focus the critical spotlight on narrators who choose fundamentally different modes of narration to work their way toward just the right connections needed to keep the story of who they are tellable to their audiences of choice. Novelists, poets, professional or amateur historians, all in their own way call attention to the fact that keeping some story tellable in real time and space is its own kind of job; it is often a trust that is handed on from generation to generation across distances of all kinds, and, as such, it has political as well as artistic implications. Assuming that the central stories that a community conspires to keep alive all lead back eventually to questions of identity, we can see how the process of constant updating is a primary ideological necessity. It is the necessity that leads us to ask about the different points of passage between different spaces of the mind as these are traversed, mapped, and translated into further narratives whose performative potential makes narrative into a renewable resource. All of this persistent updating generates an energy that feeds the political imagination.

Postmodern thought focused persistent attention on master narratives in an effort to undermine their political power and simultaneously drew attention to the multiplicity of local language games and the rules that gave them power to organize a cultural field and shape identities. All of this coincided, of course, with the rapid increase of new communications technologies and the growing power of multinational corporations that made globalism the general theme of the 1990s. The conflicts and contradictions arising from new relations between the local and the global are shaping the decisive questions launching the twenty-first century, questions that will inevitably bring a new emphasis to narrative studies and to the various formalisms that narrative studies engender. By surveying the current theoretical scene, we can discover the questions that link various strands of narrative studies to the primary philosophical and literary questions of our time and that are motivating new approaches to various kinds of formalism.

The complex relationship between universalism and particularism, connected to the kinds of analyses undertaken in this book, are debated at length by Ernesto Laclau, Judith Butler, and Slovaz Zizek.[1] Laclau argues for setting up relations of equivalence among categories that derive from different ideological contexts, different language games, Butler for a form of translation among these categories, and Zizek promotes a quest for the "kernal of the real" that exists in differing categories. Other scholars are taking comparable questions in slightly different directions, but whatever these directions may be, they require some form of close analysis of local categories as the first stage in a comparative project that has as its goal a global imaginary that does not override or deny local claims and rights. How to proceed with this analysis is a question of some urgency. The cognitive sets that I have been examining should be seen in relation to these current projects in understanding the importance of local categories for global projects. This is the project of the new formalism. Standard general analysis usually relies on the theoretical or conceptual, but microanalysis of local cognitive sets is fundamentally dependent on study of the poetic or mythical traditions for the simple reason that many cultures have retained their critical heritage primarily through performance of their imagistic heritage rather than through the development of explicit conceptual or philosophical systems. Those cultures cannot and must not be excluded from the debates surrounding a global political imaginary, and their representation within these debates should be one that sets forth the genuine complexity of their own aesthetic-philosophical positions.

Because my opening quotation is a line taken from Richard Powers's novel *Galatea 2.2*, which is about a group of scientists placing bets on whether it is possible to program a computer to do textual analysis that would be other than formulaic, it is an indirect commentary on my purposes in calling attention to a renewed and updated formalism in comparative studies. In this novel, the computer has to process the English literary tradition, and that tradition is starkly revealed as a call for alternative categories, hardly an insight unless one thinks about the fact that such a conclusion is arrived at by way of mechanical processing of details. The computer experiment shows that formalism allows us access to the details of cultural categories, but it can and should do more. Enough detail always reveals questions and sets up a momentum toward a future in which those questions will seek answers. That is the energy that I have sought to find in the narratives I have explored here. It is not just a matter of showing something about the past but of showing how stories told in the past have generated narrative that keeps certain basic ideas tellable. And I have insisted that one kind of story that keeps the others tellable is theoretical. That is an unusual insistence, not because anyone questions the need for theory of narrative but because there is good reason for denying theory the right to be called narrative in the strictest sense. Yet I hope in the preceding chapters I have pushed theory into new relationships with narrative so that theory is shown in its narrativizing capacity.

That particular conjunctive between theory and narrative is why my critical maneuvers never really turn into an exact formula that others can apply directly, although I believe that my steps are retraceable and should motivate related studies in other communities. The first steps follow quite faithfully what other theorists have done. Behind it all are the abstract strategies like those of the great narratologists in the tradition of Teun van Dijk and of A. J. Greimas, who gave us logical formulas to apply to our narrative of choice in order to reveal structures of both mind and narrative and which have been sufficiently close to mathematics to support work on artificial intelligence. And certainly the influence of Paul Ricoeur and Michel de Certeau is everywhere. Then too, Claude Lévi-Strauss has been a pervasive influence, especially in helping me devise those initial formalistic moves. But where I have deviated more or less from all of the above has been in my effort to go beyond formalism, not to high theory but to narrative, and that leads to an unusual blend of objective and subjective, emphasis on the empirical and on the poetic, the literal and the imaginative.

I have devised my notion of implicit narratives as a way to show how the cognitive sets generate narrative as they relate to the literal detail of the local. The literalism that undergirds the structure of each of my chapters arises from the specific sociohistorical status of each represented community, and it builds a controlled design that guides the critics in the quest for signifiers that allow for movement between the particular and the universal as we now understand such movement.

Reconstructing the cognitive sets that structure a context of interpretation starts with gathering literal detail about what is obvious to participants in that context. The question is always "How much is enough?" My practical answer in this book has been that we need enough detail to show how the process of narrativization works in a particular context. What historically based core of experience is being performed by way of narrative? The answer to that rarely lies in the explicit content alone. Yet the implicit is never ending. And that prompts me to point out that I use "implicit" as mere modifier. I quite deliberately attach that to the noun "narrative" to indicate that my critical enterprise has been one of creating a controlling critical story that does more than just point to selected details. It shows how those details configure sets of narratives in particular communities and how narratives link up one to another.

My implicit narratives specify central features of cognitive sets. I have examined the performance context of narratives and have done the research that lets me see some of the "wants, wishes, preferences, interests, tasks, purposes, attitudes, values, and norms" that make up the pragmatic context of the narrative.[2] The evidence I use to justify my emphasis on particular wishes, wants, and so on is that they generate continuing narrative. Following how narrative calls to and links up with other narratives gives us a certain confidence that we are following a path that is significant for a particular group. And I want to emphasize again that it is *cognitively* significant. We are following an epistemological path, a point that cannot be overemphasized because our current political condition still leaves whole groups of people in positions of epistemological vulnerability. Their ways of knowing are in danger. It is difficult to be optimistic about a future that encourages epistemological alternatives, but we can try to show the power of those alternatives through the way that we approach the past.

Cognitive sets change, and I have tried to show how history can account for some of those changes. The dynamism of cognitive sets requires performance, and as they are performed, their vitality is revealed by way of cognitive styles. Even the least complex bit of narrative is always evidence of macroprocessing, and, as such, it always incorporates an enormous range of variables. Dakotas in Cannon Ball, North Dakota, maintain the conversational use of basic historical references because they live according to a whole configuration of beliefs about how the human mind accesses physical and spiritual resources invested in a particular landscape. What is more, historical reference accounts for a distinctive political identity. Novelists like James Welch create characters to explore how individuals might have to find their own devious paths to beliefs that shape communal identity, and that quest involves achieving individual agency by way of all that academics sum up with a hefty label like "cognitive social psychology." Of course, immigrant experience necessarily tests the ties between community, individual, and landscape.

The different ways in which people reassemble the cognitive connections that let us link these focal points of cognition make for some of the most critically important and fascinating conjunctions between social scientific and humanistic research. Reorganization of cognitive sets and connections between different sets occurs, at the individual as well as at the communal level. But, as my chapter on Mildred Walker's novel is meant to show, when individuals wake up to how social ties are setting up their individual options, they have to manage their own conscious and responsible alignment within the social story or cut themselves loose until they can find some other conjunctions between self and communal placement. In actual daily practice, most of us, I suspect, go on hoping that this ongoing process of alignment will be smoothly imperceptible, blessedly dull. We would like to leave the drama and trauma to artists and scriptwriters so that we can let the virtual do the work and let educators explain that work. If the work really gets done, though, it will cause us to reflect more comprehensively on our own experience and discover that some of those ordinary interactions we might have passed over in a hurry and judged insignificant were, in fact, really quite dramatic evidence of individual and social adjustment. Much of what is in the chapter on narrative in transit qualifies as this sort of evidence.

The use of formalized cognitive sets as the basis for differing cognitive styles that characterize different times and places and communities gives definite, historically based content to my critical narratives. However, if I were to have a narrative rather than just a formulaic summary or critical device, I had to severely limit that content and I had to add some catalytic element to bring it all to narrative action. I used as my catalyst the question of *where* action was taking place, and I trace the effects of placement on narrative development.

Asking the question *where* lines up all the factual content along the vectors that plot our current understanding of individual and communal identity, and it turns the story into one about how the continuing quest for narratives about identity leads to the historicizing and psychologizing of landscape. That gives me a lot of concrete detail that is a definite cognitive set in the making. I have used Derek Gregory's exceptionally helpful conjunction between Lefebvre and Lacan with its reference to passing through the looking glass of social space in order to turn absolute into abstract space that makes the individual a sign within social space, someone who can use the entire sign system to alter the significance of positions within that space. But my contribution is to show the actual details of the process, and that means listening to what people say about their positions. It means paying close attention to ways in which people formalize their understandings with or without knowledge of how academics achieve such formalization.

All of that allows me to indulge any dreams I may ever have had of being a novelist. I have had to let each of the narrators achieve a carefully imagined reality in my mind and memory, one that I always backed up with historical realism. Most of the narrators in the first part of the book are friends and family. Some are close family members. I have let all of my academic speculation flood my memory in wonderment as I listen to my mother's tape-recorded voice explain how her favorite game as a child was to build models of villages. Her voice takes on the tonalities of contented pleasure as she tells how she and her brother spent happy hours outdoors in summer working with mud and twigs and designing exquisite villages that the wind swept away each night. But that did not matter. Their play satisfied their need to construct models, and I definitely believe that this need corresponded to what the adults were doing as they made narrative models of villages in the Ukraine that had less to do with the Ukraine than they did with the fact that those narratives were transportable and could be renewed with each telling. I also have my mother's old school notebook with its careful maps of the state. No erasures are evident on the yellowed paper. Her pencil lines, set down when she was about twelve years old, are as exact as any surveyor's drawings. Then she carefully lists important dates in North Dakota state history. That notebook is a concrete cognitive set in the making, and my mother clearly intuited that such making matters.

Then there is Lillian Fast Horse, whose short narrative response to a concrete social situation reveals an entire array of cognitive themes whose history is bound up with the expressive potential of a particular language, the Dakota language.

CONCLUSION

The distinctions that have characterized Native languages are a basic resource of inestimable and irreplaceable significance, and narratives that work these distinctions to the advantage of particular textual communities are powerful testimony to the historical continuity of these communities.[3] Beyond that, they are fundamental evidence of relationships between community and language that go well beyond the rather obvious relationships that linguists and discourse theorists have managed to document to date. By observing how distinctions operate within narrative we can begin to access a cognitive archive that lets us back up our general assertions of alternative epistemological territories superimposed on geographical territories. Such assertions are most definitely not versions of essentialized radical alterity. Nor are they mere replays of debates about the Sapir-Whorf hypothesis in its weak or in its strong form. Debating whether language or culture is the greater determining force interests me far less than showing where and how we find interrelationships between the two that do not make for easy translation from language to language, place to place. Cognitive sets are adaptable. The language of a particular place is always marked by adaptations to that place, and the macroprocessing that narrative always introduces orchestrates the adaptation, giving it the pace and rhythm that, so far at least, remains bound to specific communities. The mass media adds its own rhythms of adaptation, of course. But to date, we have no reason to give up on the transformative and adaptive potential of any community that can gather in and orchestrate influences from anywhere else without losing its own distinctiveness that will show up as narratives of all sorts in coffee shops or around the coffee pot at work, in beauty parlors and barber shops, in telephone gossip, and, these days, in Internet chat rooms. The means multiply, but the end remains pretty much the same—communities work out their own interpretations of outside influences, shift their own boundaries a little, bring some new individuals in and shun some others, adopt a few new premises about communal identity, and adapt countless others to keep that identity recognizable in historical terms.

I now turn to the vision of group communication implied in the following passage:

> Another important aspect of a cognitive analysis of macrostructures pertains to the various structures, systems and representations that influence the various macroprocesses. Not only our knowledge and beliefs are involved, as we saw earlier for the assignment of global structures to discourse and interaction, but also such factors as wants, wishes, preferences, interests, tasks, purposes, attitudes, values, and norms. The set of factors that in a particular context of action or discourse processing, influences macrostructures is called the cognitive set of a language user or participant. Thus it is plausible to assume that if a language user has

> specific interests or tasks, the formation of topics during comprehension of discourse may be different from that of other individuals with a different cognitive set. The assumption is discussed briefly in this chapter but without the necessary extensive treatment of the nature of the various factors in the cognitive sets themselves. We pay attention primarily to the role of knowledge and beliefs in macroprocessing. Theoretical and experimental work about the interaction between the other factors of cognitive set and macroprocessing is a major topic of cognitive social psychology, which needs treatment in future research in that area.[4]

Every part of this paragraph stands as a technical plot summary for all my implicit narratives, for all my continuing efforts to find the right detail and link it to others according to some plan that keeps all the connections and cross-referencing from becoming simply my version of idiosyncratic historicism. The idea that a critic could actually specify all the variables set up in van Dijk's paragraph should be considered as a critical dream at least as grand as any that the most ambitious novelist might devise about how machines can be made to mimic consciousness, and that is why I want to decontextualize this paragraph, take it out of its empirical setting and treat it like a utopian dream that can be questioned and criticized like any other such dream. The book from which this quotation is cited is presented as "an interdisciplinary study of global structures in discourse, interaction and cognition," and its writers do recognize that setting the parameters of a task is still a long, perhaps an impossibly long, way from actually achieving the task. Still, the parameters suggest how many variables would be in play in any truly comprehensive implicit narrative based on any actual pragmatic reconstruction of cognitive sets. Therefore, they also show the limitations of any actual project and the need for continuing collaborative work.

I call attention to the way the phrase "during comprehension of discourse" highlights the act of communication. We are concentrating on what happens during performance and what can be learned through performance that would be impossibly fleeting if it were not for the fact that communities depend on telling that captures what matters enough to merit retelling and reshaping that will benefit the specific interests that keep a community going. Some specific interests are obviously more important than others, and members of communities determine this hierarchy. The ongoing determinations create the textual community.

The term *specific interests* can easily slide by popular association into special interests. Linguistic rhythm can nudge us past technical empiricism to politics. If there is some rhetorical sleight of hand at work here, it has its purpose. Power politics always shape specific interests in ways that bind members of a textual community. Whenever and wherever the community is threatened by the power politics of outsiders, that fact will obviously have an impact on cognitive sets, and resistance will show up in the way cognitive styles hold off whatever threatens the community. None of this is news to anyone, but linking it to linguistic pragmatics introduces some connections between politics and community responses that are not routinely made. Studying how cognitive sets and implicit narratives shift under pressure reveals the political imaginary at work.

Specific interests require a whole range of different alignments in relation to contemporary academic agendas. The current critical enterprise establishes its own cognitive sets that keep it going full speed ahead. Critics definitely use language to situate themselves in their own textual communities, and keeping up with the boundary negotiations of these communities can be a full-time job. Conferences have become the academic equivalent of ethnographic fieldwork in theoretical communities. Finding the central themes of the cognitive style in these intersecting critical communities is a matter of catching the current overtones of professional jargon. Situating this book in relation to the critical times is a process that could go on and on, and various facets of my ongoing dialogue with critics of all persuasions find their way into the text and into the sometimes exceptionally long footnotes that work as a kind of countertext.

But one particular development in the theoretical community has to be redundantly acknowledged. At the present time, interdisciplinary groups are giving increasing attention to new distinctions within the language/landscape configuration. Nadia Lovell sums up several of the distinctions guiding these new developments:

> Landscape, as it is presented here, provides only one tool among others through which interrelationships between humans and nature, and between humans in social and situated communities, are produced and reproduced. Landscape, in this sense, does not stand as an absolute geographical site conquered once and for all, and the sitedness and belonging is therefore constantly re-enacted in order to transcend (and simultaneously allow), the vagaries of migration, of movement and of existential uncertainties. Rather than view the local as firmly situated through myth or ritual, the performative aspects of religious activities are considered essential in anchoring belonging and making it (temporarily) tangible through social practice. . . . Landscape, as it is treated in this volume, is thus closely associated to myths (of creation, of origin) and ritual performance.[5]

Imagining a symposium in which the narrators quoted in this book each respond to points raised in Lovell's general summary is the kind of mental exercise that allows me to make this conclusion into an opening and a request for collaborative work and response. It also brings me back to my opening citation from Richard Powers. Each narrator, whether historical or fictional, oral narrator or novelist, has clearly worked out a sense of belonging that is strong enough to tap into a communal narrative style. That belonging gets performed on a regular basis. Except for the novelists, the narrators presented here are not particularly inclined to use terms like *absolute geographical site[s]* as a way of expressing contrasts to social sites, but they are enacting the process that the critical language subsumes. And all of them, novelists included, have found in the landscape a means of giving figurative form to uncertainties that have to be translated from the absolute to the abstract, from fate to concrete figure. That translation occurs by way of narrative.

All that is the long road back to the defense of the implicit narratives that are part of the promise of this book. In the chapter on linguistic and narrative theory, I explicitly set out to label features of the pragmatic component of the language model. It is an ordinary enough goal, and I assume that a few key features of cognitive sets can be reconstructed and that this reconstruction will give us one kind of social map.

A key point I want to make here by way of a novelistic parable about our contemporary, computer-aided hyperawareness of language and intelligence is that Powers uses all that awareness to insist on a radical present tense. The adjective "radical" is justified by the way each narrative occasion with its specific temporal and spatial intersections always demands a new telling that requires a new take on "the story," which in Powers's line is singular. While I am not at all sure of his reasons for such singularity, I will appropriate the syntactic emphasis as a reference to the way cognitive sets are always ready-made but by no means custom-fitted. Finding an individual fit and/or giving us the specifications of what is ready-made is what keeps individuals and societies going, along with all the disciplines that are the support networks of these societies. And teaching all of us how to tell what is appropriate to any given time and place is what the humanities are supposed to be all about. We scan the past so that we can be responsible to the radical present.

Narrators like Harry and Lillian Fast Horse knew that their stories had a definite place in a political agenda that depended on each generation's recognition of continuity in the traditions that they were performing with their updated commentaries on how that tradition had shaped their own positions in a community that was their home and that they hoped would be home for their descendants. Their narratives live on in a political context of Sioux sovereignty that places their community in a particularly defined relationship to the United States government, which gives a definite pragmatic edge to the ways in which those who identify as members of the community think about their history and its impact on their individual identity.

CONCLUSION

The conditions that allow for the continued vitality of their community are also the conditions that make their story tellable. Therefore, in presenting their story, my task has been to show how these two sets of conditions overlap and to show it in a manner that witnesses the necessity of that story in the more general struggle to ascertain what enhances the chances of global justice.

The German-Russian narrators pose rather different questions for contemporary audiences. While their experiences and the narratives they generated can undoubtedly have a certain comparative illuminative power for other groups caught in historical circumstances that require communities to focus their persuasive resources on holding individuals to local loyalties, that condition does not characterize the common awareness of the present. It seems to me, though, that the German-Russian examples speak to a cosmopolitan condition more through their specificity than through their generality.

The chapters that address novels have a different kind of complexity. The creative writer is in a position to require the past to make good on promises to the present. Questions can have answers; or, perhaps more to the point, they can be posed with far more clarity than most of us ever manage outside fictional worlds. Good novelists are tough teachers when it comes to holding individuals to their responsibility to account for a presence that makes a difference, and good critics take their cues from the writers. And that raises the question of what kinds of cues a critic should take from writers and how much of a critic's own creative work should go into the writing of a critical narrative. There are, of course, as many answers to this question as there are critics, but the one that matters here addresses the "implicit narrative," the narrative arising out of the way I establish a radical present for the cognitive set that operates in any given chapter.

"You tell the stories you need to tell to keep the story tellable." Now I really have worked my way back to Powers's wonderful line about narrative and our human propensity to take it apart, then check out the technical aspects of those elements that make narrative such a complex reflective mechanism for the human mind.

The end of Powers's novel takes the surprising turn that makes it a work of literature and not just an elegant theoretical tour de force. The fictional novelist programming a machine by reading it every book on his literature master's examination list finally wakes up to what the project has been about all along:

> "You think the bet was about the machine?"
>
> *I'd told myself, my whole life, that I was smart. It took me forever, until that moment, to see what I was.*
>
> "It wasn't about teaching a machine to read?" I tried. All blood drained.
>
> "No, it was about teaching a human to tell."[6]

All the programmer's concentration on finding and making explicit the key connections between texts and life eventually convinced "Helen," the artificial intelligence par excellence, that it could not comment on life. The machine shut down. Formalism reached its limits. But the whole experience of trying to find all those connections gave the novelist-programmer a new start, a new take on what narrative and cognition really amount to.

Using the terms of this study, we might say it taught him that cognition involves style and that while style may be dependent on the view of life that Powers characterized as "a chest of maps, self-assembling, fused into point-for-point feedback, each slice rewriting itself to match the other layers' rewrites," it is nevertheless not explained by or reducible to all that feedback, connection, and recursiveness.[7] Finding an individual voice amid the communal style is the cognitive task and finest trait of conscious individuals who, in turn, use that finding to link up with communities in definite places and play on that belonging. Ending with Powers's extraordinary language, I would insist that cognitive style is evidence of "faith's flip side." We always need the language of communal narratives to get us to pay attention to that other side of faith, the side that is right here, in the daily details and the formal categories by which we communicate those details to the community.

Notes

Introduction

1. Nichols, "Form Wars," p. 489. This article is a critique of David Bordwell's *Narration in the Fiction Film* (Madison, 1985). It is useful to note that Nichols concludes his criticism by addressing cognitive issues. "In this context, assessment of use-value might come more appropriately from asking how that dimension of ourselves whose task it is to learn how to learn (how to learn which strategies and assumptions serve us best in given circumstances) may benefit from the methods, tactics, and results we employ" (p. 512).
2. The link between historiographic discourse and narrative constraints imposed by culture and revealed by discourse has been part of general historiographic method at least since the work of Louis Mink *(Historical Understanding)*, who summed up the issue thus: "Insofar as the significance of past occurrences is understandable only as they are locatable in the ensemble of interrelationships that can be grasped only in the construction of narrative form, it is we who make the past determinate in that respect. If the past is not an untold story but can be made intelligible only as the subject of stories we tell, it is still our responsibility to get on with it" (p. 202). The notion of cultural field is a standard ethnographic notion currently being popularly developed by Pierre Bourdieu, whose methods of situating narrative within the field of cultural production provide basic working principles. Randal Johnson's introductory comments to Bourdieu's *The Field of Cultural Production* achieve a crucial theoretical situating. "Like Foucault, Bourdieu sees power as diffuse and often concealed in broadly accepted, and often unquestioned, ways of seeing and describing the world; but unlike Foucault, in Bourdieu's formulation this diffuse or symbolic power is closely intertwined with—but not reducible to—economic and political power, and thus serves a legitimating function. Bourdieu's work on the cultural field constitutes a forceful argument against both Kantian notions of the universality of the aesthetic and ideologies of artistic and cultural autonomy from external determinants. He provides an analytical model which reintroduces, through the concept of *habitus*, a notion of the agent—which structuralism had excluded from social analysis—without falling into the idealism of Romantic conceptions of the artist as creator (or *subject*) which still informs much literary and art criticism today. At the same time, with the concept of *field*, he grounds the agent's action in objective social relations, without succumbing to the mechanistic determinism of many forms of sociological and 'Marxian' analysis" (pp. 2–3).
3. Wlad Godzich has noted that the distinction between the way the storyteller, as described by Walter Benjamin, endows experience with meaningfulness and the way the analyst reduces meaningfulness to diagrams and schemes is one which invalidates the claims of narrative. Explanatory regresses can render all but impossible the experience of meaning implied by narrative. His arguments, though, do not address the issue of cultural difference. If such perceived difference is operating as a dominant motive for

discourse, it opens its own space of narrativity. This space may be mapped initially by way of schematic analytic devices of the sort devised by Greimas, but the critic too can subsequently move closer to Benjamin's position, one in which the lived experience of the narrator (or the critic as a narrator of a particular facet of the text) renders the schemes meaningful again. See Godzich, "After the Storyteller."
4. See, for example, Bhabha, ed., *Nation and Narration*; and the more recent Moore-Gilbert, ed., *Postcolonial Theory*.
5. Joseph Carroll, "The Ecology of Victorian Fiction," in *Philosophy of Literature* 25, no. 2 (2000): pp. 295–313.
6. Doig, *Heart Earth*, p. 3.
7. Jahner, "Cognitive Style in Oral Literature."
8. Jahner, "Quick Paces and a Space of Mind," *Denver Quarterly* (1980): pp. 34–47.
9. Kowalewski, "Writing in Place," pp. 182–83.

1. Theoretical Foundations

1. Mathiot, *Approach to the Cognitive Study*, p. 143.
2. Hymes, "On Typology of Cognitive Styles," p. 441.
3. Chatman, "What Novels Can Do," p. 117.
4. Propp, *Morphology of the Folktale*; Dundes, *Morphology of North American Indian Folktales*.
5. See Jahner, "Cognitive Style in Oral Literature."
6. Herrnstein Smith, "Narrative Versions, Narrative Theories," pp. 220–29.
7. For example, Labov, *Language in the Inner City* and *Locating Language in Time and Space*; Pratt, *Towards a Speech Act Theory*, p. xiii.
8. Herrnstein Smith, "Narrative Versions, Narrative Theories," p. 229.
9. Prince, "Commentary," p. 233.
10. Herman, "Story Logic," pp. 130–31.
11. See Chatman, *Story and Discourse*.
12. Labov and Waletsky, "Narrative Analysis." See the special issue of *Journal of Narrative and Life History* 7, nos. 1–4 (1997), edited by Michael G. W. Bamberg, for essays that demonstrate and evaluate the impact of the 1967 paper by Labov and Waletsky. Their goal was to provide formal and functional guidelines for deciding what constitutes a personal experience narrative, and they set up an overall structure of narrative consisting of orientation, complication, evaluation, resolution, and coda.
13. Muriel Saville-Troike is clearly referring to event as an occasion when she writes, "Some early steps in description and analysis of patterns of communication include identifying recurrent events, recognizing their salient components, and discovering the relationship among components and between the event and other aspects of society." *Ethnography of Communication*, p. 107.
14. Hymes, "In Vain I Tried to Tell You."
15. Ricoeur writes: "Confronted with the notion of event, we chose to separate the epistemological criteria of the event from its ontological ones, so as to remain within the boundaries of an investigation devoted to the relation between historical explanation and configuration by emplotment. It is these ontological criteria that return to the front rank with the concept of a 'real' past." *Time and Narrative*, vol. 3, p. 100.
16. Mink, *Historical Understanding*, p. 186.
17. Ricoeur, "Structure, Word, Event," pp. 85, 86, 92, 95.

18. Ricoeur, *Time and Narrative*, 3 vols.
19. See, for example, George Sword's presentation of the Stone Boy story in James R. Walker, *Lakota Myth*, pp. 89–100.
20. See, for instance, Jahner, "Act of Attention." For a much more detailed study of event structure in a single tale, see Jahner, "Traditional Narrative."
21. Stalnaker, "Pragmatics," 79–80, 82.
22. Jonnes, *Matrix of Narrative*. See in particular chapters 2 and 14.
23. Prince, "Narratology and Narratological Analysis," p. 43.
24. Fludernik, *Towards a "Natural" Narratology*, pp. 12, 13.
25. Fludernik, *Towards a 'Natural' Narratology*, pp. 45, 57.
26. Tedlock says: "The teller is not merely repeating memorized words, nor is he or she merely giving a dramatic 'oral interpretation' or 'concert reading' of a fixed script. We are in the presence of a *performing art*, all right, but we are getting the *criticism* at the same time and from the same person. The interpreter does not merely play the parts, but is the narrator and commentator as well. What we are hearing is a *hermeneutics* of the text of Kyaklo." "Spoken Word," pp. 47–48.
27. Mink, *Historical Understanding*.
28. Van Dijk, *Macrostructures*, pp. 200, 175–76, 177.
29. Mathiot, *Approach to the Cognitive Study*, p. 55.
30. Mathiot, *Approach to the Cognitive Study*, pp. 5, 197.
31. Whorf, *Language, Thought, and Reality*.
32. In "The Role of Language in Cognition," Lehman, Newell, Polk, and Lewis write: "So the weak hypothesis holds pervasively. Yet surely there is much more to the role of language in cognition. Surely there must be strong effects if only we knew where to look for them. Surely there are other ways to ask the question" (p. 490).
33. Mathiot, *Approach to the Cognitive Study*, p. 2.
34. Mathiot, *Approach to the Cognitive Study*, p. 198.
35. Stock, *Listening for the Text*, p. 100.
36. Rappaport, *Politics of Memory*, p. 202.
37. Gupta and Ferguson, "Beyond 'Culture,'" p. 50.
38. Lovell, ed., *Locality and Belonging*, p. 11.
39. Downs and Shea, *Maps in Minds*, p. 6.
40. Silko, *Ceremony*, p. 2.
41. Jameson, *Signatures of the Visible*, p. 54.
42. Jameson, *Postmodernism*, pp. 417–18.
43. I published an earlier article that begins the linguistic analysis of this text, concentrating on the verbs but ignoring the crucial role of the nominal constructions. The chapter published here represents a significant advance at all levels from that initial analysis. See Jahner, "Language Change and Cultural Dynamics."
44. Ella C. Deloria, unpublished manuscript.
45. Ceremonies such as the Hunka and the Women's Puberty Ceremony all incorporate ritual elements relating to gaining the consent of one of the active participants. This consent element allows us to understand the centrality of the volitional theme as a redundantly enacted cultural preoccupation. For detailed descriptions of these ceremonies, see James R. Walker, *Lakota Belief and Ritual*.
46. Dell Hymes ("*In Vain I Tried to Tell You*," pp. 132–33) stresses "the distinction between knowledge what and knowledge how, or, more fully, between assumption of responsi-

bility for knowledge of tradition and assumption of responsibility for performance.... It has been clear, I would hope, that knowledge and performance of tradition are interdependent, in the sense that the nature of the performance affects what is known, for the persons in a community as well as for the outside inquirer into tradition."
47. See Boas and Deloria, "Dakota Grammar," p. 41.
48. Wissler, "Decorative Art of the Sioux Indians," p. 247.
49. See the Bushotter text, included in Dorsey, *Study of Siouan Cults*.
50. Robert Lowie recorded an example. Comparative study shows that the choice is an intertribal motif. In one common form, a grandmother figure presents the choice. "Men also might have visions of the Two-Women. Sometimes a man would come to a tent and see them singing there. A cousin of Whale's had a dream in which he came to a tent and entered. There were butterflies on one side, and eagle feathers on the other, and a path on each side. After some deliberation the dreamer decided to take the right-hand path, where the eagle feathers were. Then the Two Women told him that if he had chosen the other path he would have become a berdache." Lowie, "Dance Associations of the Eastern Dakota," p. 118.
51. Wallis, "Canadian Dakota."
52. Walker, *Lakota Belief and Ritual*, pp. 165–66.
53. Walker, *Lakota Belief and Ritual*, p. 109.
54. James R. Walker, *Lakota Society*, p. 107.
55. Hassrick, *Sioux*, p. 227.
56. Jahner, "Woman Remembering."
57. See Ella C. Deloria, *Speaking of Indians*, p. 49.
58. Ricoeur, "Narrative Time," p. 169.
59. See Fletcher, "Five Indian Ceremonies," p. 276.
60. Boas and Deloria, "Dakota Grammar," pp. 92–93.
61. Boas and Deloria, "Dakota Grammar," p. 94.
62. Boland, "Oral Tradition," p. 162.
63. Berry, "Cognitive Values and Cognitive Competence," p. 9. Berry's essay provides the basic methodological frames and definitions for cross-cultural studies.
64. Berry, "Cognitive Values and Cognitive Competence," p. 9.

2. The Narrating Community

1. De Certeau, *Practice of Everyday Life*, p. 23. Both at the level of theory and at that of a style of scholarly practice, de Certeau's work is more fundamental to this study than any individual notes can indicate.
2. For an exceptionally fine study of community narration, see Rappaport, *Politics of Memory*.
3. Elwyn B. Robinson, *History of North Dakota*, p. 13.
4. See also Anderson, "Historic Oahe Sites" and "Investigation of the Early Bands"; Denig, "Indian Tribes of the Upper Missouri"; Hassrick, *Sioux*; Nurge, ed., *Modern Sioux*; Doan Robinson, "History of the Dakota"; Scudder, "Human Ecology of Big Projects," pp. 48–53; Utley, *Last Days of the Sioux Nation*.
5. Anderson, "Report of Harry H. Anderson."
6. Anderson, "Report of Harry H. Anderson," p. 3.
7. Keating, comp., *Narrative of an Expedition*.
8. Anderson, "Report of Harry H. Anderson," p. 8.

9. Anderson, "Report of Harry H. Anderson."
10. Lawson, *Dammed Indians*, pp. 194, 159.
11. De Certeau, *Practice of Everyday Life*, p. 18.
12. For a groundbreaking analysis of the potential legal force of cognitive analysis of narrative, see the issue of *Michigan Law Review* titled "Legal Storytelling" (vol. 87, no. 8). All the articles have some relevance to issues presented in this chapter, but the one by Steven L. Winter is of particularly central importance to the kinds of arguments presented here. Winters, speaking from the legal perspective, notes, "Thus, the category *narrative* can be understood as a *radical category* consisting of a central idealized model that both permits nondeterminate instantiations and supports numerous conventionalized extensions." In this chapter, I am assuming that Harry Fast Horse's idealized models derive from prereservation models and that his narratives are conventionalized extensions that are sometimes determinate and often nondeterminate instantiations attesting more to the continuities of the models than to semantic determinations. Idealized models account for perceptions of appropriateness and, as such, they have generative, explanatory force. Winter adds the potential of transformative legal force. He mentions *Brown v. Board of Education*: "In this process, the advocates slowly expose the courts to ever greater accretions of experience that do not fit the reigning legal paradigm until, ultimately, the courts are led to reformulate the available models to fit the experiences they had previously ignored. Here we have crossed the divide from the persuasive to the transformative" (2275–76).
13. Written for the North Dakota Historical Society, August 7, 1919. This document is available through the North Dakota Historical Society archives in Bismarck.
14. See Ella C. Deloria, *Dakota Texts*; and Beckwith, "Mythology of the Oglala Dakota."
15. See Densmore, "Teton Sioux Music," p. 387 and following, for descriptions of how men used drawings in relation to autobiographical narrative and related songs.
16. Wissler, "Some Protective Designs," p. 52.
17. See Densmore, "Teton Sioux Music."
18. See Hymes, *"In Vain I Tried to Tell You,"* p. 82, where he presents elaborations on the notion of performance that are of central importance in considering the Fast Horse repertoire.
19. See Elwyn B. Robinson, *History of North Dakota*, p. 179.
20. See Fletcher, "Five Indian Ceremonies," p. 295.
21. The Beede family papers are in the Chester Fritz Library, University of North Dakota, Grand Forks. Other Beede papers, including parts of his diary and his correspondence with Melvin R. Gilmore, are in the North Dakota State Historical Society Library in Bismarck.
22. See Jahner, "Woman Remembering."
23. Wissler, "Societies and Ceremonial Associations," pp. 92–93.
24. Deloria, *Dakota Texts*, p. 163.
25. Lincoln, "Historical Slippage," p. 168.
26. See relevant entry in Waldman, ed., *Who Was Who in Native American History*.
27. See Hancock, "'Me All Face' Story." See also Dorson, "Comic Indian Anecdotes," p. 119n29.
28. Rosenberg writes, "What has interested most writers on the battle of the Little Bighorn is the fate of Custer and the 212 men with him in their last minutes; what will interest us here is that, despite the fact that all we know of what happened to Custer and his battalion

on the afternoon of 25 June 1876 is that they all perished, the stories about him—the popular legends—as they emerge in biographies, dime novels, movies, painting, TV serials, popular poems, jokes and antiwar posters bear a striking resemblance to the other heroic legends we have just mentioned. It does not matter that there was no such knight as Sir Gawain, that we do not know at what point in the battle the Persians killed Leonidas or the Vikings slew Byrhnoth, that we do not know who died last when the Alamo was captured by the Mexicans; even though there really was a Custer and he made a 'Last Stand' of sorts, and we know enough about him and that 'Stand' to know that many of the legends are not true, what is important here is that his story has been made over in a traditional and recognizable heroic pattern." Rosenberg, *Custer and the Epic of Defeat*, p. 3.

29. For biographical accounts of Sitting Bull, see Vestal, *Sitting Bull*; and Utley, *Lance and the Shield*.
30. Lawson, *Dammed Indians*, p. 159.

3. Narrative in Transit

1. For background on the history of German-Russians on Standing Rock Sioux Reservation, see Kloberdanz, "In the Land of Inyan Woslata."
2. For a general history of the Black Sea colonies in Russia, see Height, *Paradise on the Steppe*.
3. Long, *From Privileged to Dispossessed*, pp. 120–21.
4. See Height, *Paradise on the Steppe*, for descriptions of Black Sea land-use policies.
5. Fred Koch (*Volga Germans*, p. 221) addresses this issue: "These are not hyphenated Americans, and don't want to be because they prefer to be Americans all the way.... The inflammatory slur 'those damn Rooshians' has been silenced and most of those who uttered it never really knew who these people were. Even Reich Germans mistakenly applied 'Rooshians' to the equally German immigrants from the Volga, the Black Sea region, and Volhynia—intending an insult as ugly as any applied to any immigrant."
6. Aberle, *From the Steppes to the Prairies*, p. 113.
7. Gregory, "Lacan and Geography," p. 220.
8. Lefebvre, *Production of Space*, p. 163.
9. Interview part of Jahner family documents, in possession of the author's estate.
10. Keller, *German Colonies in South Russia*, vol. 1, p. 51.
11. Keller, *German Colonies in South Russia*, vol. 1, p. 51.
12. Height, *Paradise on the Steppe*.
13. Jahner family documents, in possession of the author's estate.
14. See Hosking, *Russia: People and Empire*, pp. 367, 375.
15. Elwyn B. Robinson, *History of North Dakota*, p. 352.
16. Robinson, *History of North Dakota*, p. 329.
17. Robinson, *History of North Dakota*, pp. 332, 334.
18. Robinson, *History of North Dakota*, p. 346.
19. Jahner family documents, in possession of the author's estate.
20. Interview part of Jahner family documents, in possession of the author's estate.
21. Robinson, *History of North Dakota*, p. 287.
22. Members of my own family knew about the practice of brauchen. Father Stanley Sticka, a German-Russian priest who was also a well-known mystic, privately endorsed the

practice, saying that healing could never be a bad thing. He was, however, an exceptional man.
23. The people among whom I did the most interviewing all came from Roman Catholic colonies with Rastadt and Landau as the main Russian colonial locations. The single most important historical event affecting colonial responses to the Roman Catholic Church was the 1820 expulsion of Jesuits from Russia.
24. The principles that allow for analytic movement between questions of religious symbolism, historical process, and the positional psychology of individuals within the colonial setting are set forth in Julia Kristeva's analysis of the symbolic economy of Christianity as it structures the dynamics of individuation (*Black Sun*, p. 132). Her theoretical positionings assume an individual dependence on historical determinations that articulate an entire economy (not just the individual instance) of representations through interactionally conditioned structures. "The break, brief as it might have been, in the bond linking Christ to his Father and to life introduces into the mythical representation of the Subject a fundamental and psychically necessary discontinuity. Such a caesura, which some have called a 'hiatus,' provides an image, at the same time as a narrative, for many separations that build up the psychic life of individuals. It provides image and narrative for some psychic cataclysms that more or less frequently threaten the assumed balance of individuals. Thus psychoanalysis identifies and relates as indispensable condition for autonomy a series of splittings. . . . Real, imaginary, or symbolic, those processes necessarily structure our individuation. . . . Because Christianity set that rupture at the very heart of the absolute subject—Christ; because it represented it as a Passion that was the solidary lining of his Resurrection, his glory, and his eternity, it brought to consciousness the essential dramas that are internal to the becoming of each and every subject. It thus endows itself with tremendous cathartic power."

In the colonial setting, the representational force of religious symbolism consolidated a full range of functions that would have been divided among multiple cultural fields in more institutionally diverse societies with higher levels of general education. But beyond the impact of highly focused symbolic influences, there are also the psychological effects of the congruence between the historical narrative of separation from homelands and the psychic dynamics of separation that are part of every individual's development. The historical experience and its communal narration can take on allegorical significance in relation to individual experiences of severance and discontinuity, thereby investing the historical narrative with affect bound to the fundamental economy of religious symbolism and bringing the full force of that binding to bear on individual experience. Communal and individual history are co-implicated in a developmental process—its narration, its valuation, and its interpretation. Mysticism finds its place in the emotional economy of colonial existence.

4. Narrative Redirected

1. See Jahner, "Intermediate Forms," p. 67, where I list several characteristics of intermediate forms: "The mental attitudes that characterize the work . . . are directly related to a specific tribal tradition as it lives today. Often the piece itself (the song or the story or the belief) is a personal performance of a traditional form. The artist writes a traditional piece in such a way that we know how he or she experiences the piece. The writer has known the piece in its totality but cannot bring the audience into a shared performance context; hence the written mode."

2. In regard to Momaday's experiments, I have written ("Critical Approach," p. 218), "Because of its generic history, the novel automatically suggests contrasts between the tribal way of life with its accompanying aesthetic modes and the non-Indian way which is so deeply linked with European tradition. Individual American Indian authors have accepted the challenge that the novel presents. By working with the tensions between two essentially different aesthetic modes, they have fashioned structures that relate as intimately to the life of the modern American Indian community as the oral forms have related to the continuing life of the community. Each new novel by an American Indian who is consciously concerned with the principles of continuity that lie at the heart of tribal life is another step in developing a new type of American novel, one that relates directly to the oldest aesthetic traditions of the Western Hemisphere." For my work on event structure in Leslie Silko's *Ceremony*, see Jahner, "Act of Attention."
3. See Rainwater, *Dreams of Fiery Stars*, p. 9.
4. Fludernik, *Towards a "Natural" Narratology*, p. 372.
5. Fludernik, *Towards a "Natural" Narratology*, pp. 373, 57–77.
6. Vine Deloria Jr., "Out of Chaos."
7. See Ewers, *Blackfeet*, p. 294: "There is no adequate record of the number of Piegan deaths from starvation during those nightmarish years 1883–84. The agents' annual report for the year preceding July 1, 1884, listed only 247 deaths from all causes. But the Indian Rights Association, which investigated the disaster, found that 'upward of four hundred were starved to death.' Almost-a-Dog, a Piegan Indian, is said to have kept a record of each death as it occurred by cutting a notch in a willow stick, and the number of the marks is said to have reached 555. Between one-fourth and one-sixth of the Piegans in Montana must have perished from starvation in the years 1883–84. So many of the victims were buried on the hill south of Badger Creek during that period that the Indians came to refer to it as 'Ghost Ridge.'"
8. See Wissler and Duvall, *Mythology of the Blackfoot Indians*, pp. 58–61. See also Wissler, "Sun Dance." As he notes (p. 232), the Medicine Lodge Ceremony was pledged by a qualified woman who was responding to some definite communal need. He is quite clear about the responsibility such a woman assumes: "As indicated above, the prayers are not always granted. In such cases, the promises are not only not binding, but to proceed with the sun dance, or to take a secondary part in it, would be to the detriment of all concerned. The fault is said to lie in the woman's life and that only the wrath of the sun would be invoked by her participation in the ceremonies."
9. Morrison, *Jazz*, p. 228.
10. The interview is recorded in the film *James Welch*, which is one of the four-part series *Native American Novelists*, sold by *Films for the Humanities and Sciences*, Princeton, New Jersey.
11. Lévi-Strauss's *The Origin of Table Manners* uses the Star Husband complex as the reference myth. The clinging wife theme that furnishes Lévi-Strauss with his primary comparative motif does not occur in Blackfeet versions. Lévi-Strauss does allude to connections between this configuration of myths and the origins of women's art. For Harjo, see the title poem in *Woman Who Fell*, p. 5.
12. The most comprehensive mapping of the tale is Reichard's "Literary Types."
13. See Wissler and Duvall, *Mythology of the Blackfoot Indians*.
14. In the story, Crane Woman addresses the woman who went to the sky as "daughter" when she gives her the digging stick. Clark Wissler notes, "In all ceremonial gifts or

transfers, the giver is spoken of as a father or mother, according to the sex; hence the thought is that this digging stick is not an ordinary gift, but carried with it ceremonial obligations" (Wissler and Duvall, *Mythology of the Blackfoot Indians*, p. 59).
15. See Mathiot, *Approach to the Cognitive Study*, pp. 136–39.
16. Frantz, *Blackfoot Grammar*, p. 44.
17. Wissler, "Sun Dance," p. 240.

5. The Stranger's Language

1. Welch, Introduction to *Winter Wheat*, p. xii.
2. Poirier, *Poetry and Pragmatism*, pp. 32–33.
3. Lovell, ed., *Locality and Belonging*, p. 9.
4. Watson, *Montana 1948*, p. ix.
5. Kowalewski, ed., *Reading the West*, p. 48.
6. Gregory, "Lacan and Geography," p. 220.
7. In this respect, Walker's novel supports the thesis Dennis Jonnes develops in *Matrix of Narrative*.
8. See Poirier, *Poetry and Pragmatism*, p. 102. Also relevant to this chapter is Poirier's discussion (pp. 86–88) of "the transfiguration of work" in a manner that shows how we can extend his arguments beyond his immediate purposes into a plea for revitalized regionalism: "Common to the Emersonian pragmatist is this acceptance of the fact that literary references are inherent in and ineradicable from daily speech." Extending these pragmatic positions into arguments for a corresponding psycholinguistic analysis is a matter of switching from the social to the subjective, or from myth as an inherited symbolic frame to interiorized mythic meaning as evidence of a negotiated subjective position. Poirier (p. 100) refers to William James's notions of truth: "The truth of an idea is not a stagnant property inherent in it. Truth happens to an idea. It becomes true, is made true by events. Its verity is in fact an event, a process: the process namely of its verifying itself, its verification. Its validity is the process of its validation."
9. Welch, *Winter in the Blood*, p. 4.
10. Welch, "Snow Country Weavers."
11. Worthman, "Cupid and Psyche," pp. 164–65.

Conclusion

1. Butler, Laclau, and Zizek, eds, *Contingency, Hegemony, Universality*.
2. Van Dijk, *Macrostructures*, p. 201.
3. The concept of textual community as used in this book and in other of my writing is coincident with and influenced by Brian Stock's notions of textual community. For all its apparent simplicity, Stock's notion of textual communities involves well-articulated slight shifts in the positions of several of the century's leading thinkers while remaining quickly recognizable in terms of what we are already doing. A textual community is "a group in which there is both a script and a spoken enactment and in which social cohesion and meaning result from the interaction of the two" (Stock, *Listening for the Text*, p. 100). The "script," I propose, can exist as a body of orally transmitted narratives with varying degrees of stability, a proposition in line with Stock's revisions of Paul Ricoeur's bias toward written texts. But what makes this general approach so useful is the emphasis on social cohesion and meaning as a continuing interactional dynamic.

4. Van Dijk, *Macrostructures*, p. 201.
5. Lovell, ed., *Locality and Belonging*, p. 10.
6. Powers, *Galatea 2.2*, p. 318.
7. Powers, *Galatea 2.2*, p. 320.

Works Cited

Aberle, George P. *From the Steppes to the Prairies.* Bismarck ND: Bismarck Tribune, 1964.
Anderson, Harry H. "Historic Oahe Sites." *South Dakota Historical Collections* 27 (1954): pp. 10–159.
———. "An Investigation of the Early Bands of the Saone Group of Teton Sioux." *Journal of the Washington Academy of Sciences* 46, no. 3 (1956): pp. 87–94.
———. "Report of Harry H. Anderson, before the Indian Claims Commission; Docket No. 74, Sioux Nation et al. v. United States of America." Washington DC: Indian Claims Commission, 1960.

Beckwith, Martha Warren. "Mythology of the Oglala Dakota." *Journal of American Folklore* 43, no. 170 (1930): pp. 339–42.
Berry, J. W. "Cognitive Values and Cognitive Competence among the Bricoleurs." In *Indigenous Cognition: Functioning in Cultural Context*, edited by E. B. Hunt, J. Berry, and Sidney H. Irvine, pp. 2–9. Dordrecht, Holland: Martinus Nijhoff Publishers, 1988.
Bhabha, Homi K., ed. *Nation and Narration.* London and New York: Routledge, 1990.
Boas, Franz, and Ella C. Deloria. "Dakota Grammar." *Memoirs of the National Academy of Sciences* 23, part 2. Washington DC: U.S. Government Printing Office, 1941.
Boland, Eavan. "The Oral Tradition." In *An Origin Like Water: Collected Poems, 1957–1987.* New York: W. W. Norton and Company, 1996.
Butler, Judith, Ernesto Laclau, and Slovaz Zizek, eds. *Contingency, Hegemony, Universality: Contemporary Dialogues on the Left.* New York: Verso, 2000.

Chatman, Seymour. *Story and Discourse: Narrative Structure in Fiction and Film.* Ithaca: Cornell University Press, 1978.
———. "What Novels Can Do That Films Can't (and Vice Versa)." In *On Narrative*, edited by W. T. Mitchell, pp. 117–36. Chicago: University of Chicago Press, 1981.
Cook-Lynne, Elizabeth. *From the River's Edge.* New York: Arcade, 1991.

De Certeau, Michel. *The Practice of Everyday Life.* Berkeley: University of California Press, 1984.
Deloria, Ella C. "Dakota Texts." *Publications of the American Ethnological Society* 14. New York: Stechert, 1932.
———. *Speaking of Indians.* Reprint, Lincoln: University of Nebraska Press, 1998.
———. Unpublished manuscript. Franz Boas Collection, American Philosophical Society, Philadelphia.
Deloria, Vine, Jr. "Out of Chaos." *Parabola* 10, no. 2 (1985): pp. 14–22.
Denig, E. T. "Indian Tribes of the Upper Missouri." *Bureau of American Ethnology Forty-sixth Annual Report* (1930): pp. 375–628. Washington DC, Government Printing Office.
Densmore, Frances. "Teton Sioux Music." *Bureau of American Ethnology Bulletin* 61 (1918). Washington DC: U.S. Government Printing Office.

WORKS CITED

Doig, Ivan. *Heart Earth*. New York: Atheneum, 1993.

Dorsey, James Owen. "A Study of Siouan Cults: Dakota and Assiniboine." *Smithsonian Institution, Bureau of American Ethnology Annual Report* 11 (1894): pp. 351–544.

Dorson, Richard M. "Comic Indian Anecdotes." *Southern Folklore Quarterly* 10 (1946).

Downs, Roger M., and David Shea. *Maps in Minds: Reflections on Cognitive Mapping*. New York: Harper and Row, 1977.

Dundes, Alan. *Morphology of North American Indian Folktales*. Helsinki: Suomalainen Tiedeakatemia, 1964.

Ewers, John C. *The Blackfeet: Raiders on the Northwestern Plains*. Norman: University of Oklahoma Press, 1958.

Fletcher, Alice. "Five Indian Ceremonies." *Sixteenth Annual Report of the Peabody Museum of American Archeology and Ethnology* 3 (1884): pp. 260–333. Salem MA.

Fludernik, Monika. *Towards a "Natural" Narratology*. New York and London: Routledge, 1996.

Frantz, Donald G. *Blackfoot Grammar*. Toronto: University of Toronto Press, 1991.

Godzich, Wlad. "After the Storyteller." In *The Culture of Literacy*. Cambridge: Harvard University Press, 1994.

Gregory, Derek. "Lacan and Geography: The Production of Space Revisited." In *Space and Social Theory*, edited by Georges Benko and Ulf Strohmayer, pp. 203–33. London: Blackwell, 1997.

Gupta, Akhil, and James Ferguson. "Beyond 'Culture': Space, Identity, and the Politics of Difference." In *Culture, Power, Place: Explorations in Critical Anthropology*, edited by James Ferguson and Akhil Gupta, pp. 33–51. Durham NC: Duke University Press, 1997.

Hancock, Cecily. "The 'Me All Face' Story: European Literary Background of an American Comic Indian Anecdote." *Journal of American Folklore* 76, no. 302 (1963): pp. 340–42.

Harjo, Joy. "We Must Call a Meeting." In *The Heath Anthology of American Literature*, 4th ed, edited by Paul Lauter et al. New York: Houghton Mifflin, 2002.

———. *The Woman Who Fell from the Sky: Poems*. New York: Norton, 1996.

Hassrick, Royal B. *The Sioux: Life and Customs of Warrior Society*. Norman: University of Oklahoma Press, 1964.

Height, Joseph S. *Paradise on the Steppe: A Cultural History of the Kutschurgan, Beresan, and Liebental Colonists, 1804–1944*. Bismarck: North Dakota Historical Society of Germans from Russia, 1972.

Herman, David, ed. *Narratologies: New Perspectives on Narrative*. Columbus: Ohio State University Press, 1999.

———. "Story Logic in Conversational and Literary Narratives." *Narrative* 9, no. 2 (2001): pp. 130–37.

Herrnstein Smith, Barbara. "Narrative Versions, Narrative Theories." In *On Narrative*, edited by W. T. Mitchell, pp. 209–32. Chicago: University of Chicago Press, 1981.

Hosking, Geoffrey. *Russia: People and Empire*. Cambridge: Harvard University Press, 1997.

Hymes, Dell. *"In Vain I Tried to Tell You": Essays in Native American Ethnopoetics*. Philadelphia: University of Pennsylvania Press, 1981.

———. "On Typology of Cognitive Styles in Language (with Examples from Chinookan)." *Anthropological Linguistics* 35 (1993): pp. 440–75. Originally published in *Anthropological Linguistics* 3, no. 1 (1961): pp. 22–54.

WORKS CITED

Jahner, Elaine. "An Act of Attention: Event Structure in *Ceremony*." *American Indian Quarterly* 5, no. 1 (1979): pp. 37–46.

———. "Cognitive Style in Oral Literature." *Language and Style* 16, no. 1 (1982): pp. 32–51.

———. "A Critical Approach to American Indian Literature." In *Studies in American Indian Literature: Critical Essays and Course Designs*, edited by Paul Gunn Allen. New York: The Modern Language Association, 1983.

———. "Intermediate Forms between Oral and Written Literature." In *Studies in American Indian Literature: Critical Essays and Course Designs*, edited by Paul Gunn Allen, pp. 66–74. New York: The Modern Language Association, 1983.

———. "Language Change and Cultural Dynamics: A Study of Lakota Verbs of Movement." In *Languages in Conflict: Linguistic Acculturation on the Great Plains*, edited by Paul Schach. Lincoln: University of Nebraska Press, 1980.

———. "Traditional Narrative: Contemporary Uses, Historical Perspectives." *Studies in American Indian Literatures* 11, no. 2 (1999): pp. 1–28.

———. "Woman Remembering: Life History as Exemplary Pattern." In *Women's Folklore, Women's Culture*, edited by Rosan Jordan and Susan Kalcik, pp. 214–33. Philadelphia: University of Pennsylvania Press, 1984.

Jameson, Frederic. *Postmodernism; or, The Cultural Logic of Late Capitalism*. Durham NC: Duke University Press, 1991.

———. *Signatures of the Visible*. London and New York: Routledge, 1990.

Johnson, Randal. Introduction to *The Field of Cultural Production*. New York: Columbia University Press, 1993.

Jonnes, Dennis. *The Matrix of Narrative: Family Systems and the Semiotics of Story*. Berlin and New York: Mouton de Gruyter, 1990.

Keating, William H., comp. *Narrative of an Expedition to the Source of St. Peter's River, Lake Winnepeck, Lake of the Woods, &c. &c." Performed in the Year 1823, by Order of the Hon. J. C. Calhoun, Secretary of War, under the Command of Stephen H. Long, Major U.S.T.E.* 2 vols. Philadelphia: H. C. Carey and I. Lea, 1824.

Keller, Konrad. *The German Colonies in South Russia*. Vols. 1 and 2. Translated by A. Becker. Saskatoon, Saskatchewan: Mercury Printers, 1973.

Kloberdanz, Tomothy. "In the Land of Inyan Woslata: Plains Indian Influences on Reservation Whites." *Great Plains Quarterly* 7, no. 2 (1987): pp. 69–82.

Koch, Fred C. *The Volga Germans: In Russia and the Americas, from 1763 to the Present*. University Park: Pennsylvania State University Press, 1977.

Kowalewski, Michael. "Writing in Place: The New American Regionalism." *American Literary History* (Spring 1994): pp. 171–83.

———, ed. *Reading the West: New Essays on the Literature of the American West*. Cambridge: Cambridge University Press, 1996.

Kristeva, Julia. *Black Sun: Depression and Melancholia*. New York: Columbia University Press, 1989.

Labov, William. *Language in the Inner City: Studies in the Black Elkish Vernacular*. Philadelphia: University of Pennsylvania Press, 1972.

———. *Locating Language in Time and Space*. New York: Academic Press, 1980.

Labov, William, and Joshua Waletsky. "Narrative Analysis: Oral Versions of Personal Experience." In *The American Ethnological Society Essays on the Verbal and Visual Arts*, edited by J. Helm, pp. 12–44. Seattle: University of Washington Press, 1967.

WORKS CITED

Lawson, Michael L. *Dammed Indians: The Pick-Sloan Plan and the Missouri Sioux, 1944–1980.* Norman: University of Oklahoma Press, 1982.
Lefebvre, Henri. *The Production of Space.* London: Blackwell, 1991.
Lehman, Jill Fain, et al. "The Role of Language In Cognition: A Computational Inquiry." In *Readings in Language and Mind: An Interdisciplinary Reader,* edited by Heimir Geirsson and Michael Losonsky, pp. 489–506. Cambridge MA: Blackwell, 1996.
Lévi-Strauss, Claude. *The Origin of Table Manners.* Vol. 3 of *Mythologiques.* New York: Harper and Row, 1978.
Lincoln, Kenneth. "Historical Slippage and Indian Humor Today." *Storia Nord Americana* 5, no. 1 (1988).
Long, James W. *From Privileged to Dispossessed: The Volga Germans, 1860–1917.* Lincoln: University of Nebraska Press, 1988.
Lovell, Nadia, ed. *Locality and Belonging.* London: Routledge, 1998.
Lowie, Robert H. "Dance Associations of the Eastern Dakota" (Part 2). *Anthropological Papers of the American Museum of Natural History* 11 (1913): pp. 101–42.

Mathiot, Madeleine. *An Approach to the Cognitive Study of Language.* The Hague: Mouton, 1968.
McGuane, Thomas. *Nobody's Angel.* New York: Random House, 1981.
Mink, Louis. *Historical Understanding,* edited by Brian Fay, Eugene O. Golob, and Richard T. Vann. Ithaca: Cornell University Press, 1987.
Moore-Gilbert, Bart, ed. *Postcolonial Theory: Contexts, Practices, Politics.* New York: Verso, 1996.
Morrison, Toni. *Jazz.* New York: Knopf, 1992.

Nichols, Bill. "Form Wars: The Political Unconscious of Formalist Theory." *South Atlantic Quarterly* 88, no. 2 (1989): pp. 487–515.
Nurge, Ethel, ed. *The Modern Sioux: Social Systems and Reservation Culture.* Lincoln: University of Nebraska Press, 1970.

Poirier, Richard. *Poetry and Pragmatism.* Cambridge: Harvard University Press, 1992.
Powers, Richard. *Galatea 2.2: A Novel.* New York: Farrar, Straus and Giroux, 1995.
Pratt, Mary Louise. *Towards a Speech Act Theory of Literary Discourse.* Bloomington: Indiana University Press, 1977.
Prince, Gerald. "A Commentary: Constants and Variables of Narratology." *Narrative* 9, no. 2 (2001): pp. 230–33.
———. "Narratology and Narratological Analysis." *Journal of Narrative and Life History* 7 (1997): pp. 39–44.
Propp, Vladmnir. *Morphology of the Folktale.* Edited by Svatava Pirkova-Jakobson and translated by Laurence Scott. Philadelphia: American Folklore Society, 1958.

Rainwater, Catherine. *Dreams of Fiery Stars: The Transformations of Native American Fiction.* Philadelphia: University of Pennsylvania Press, 1999.
Rappaport, Joanne. *The Politics of Memory: Native Historical Interpretation in the Colombian Andes.* Cambridge: Cambridge University Press, 1990.
Reichard, Gladys A. "Literary Types and Dissemination of Myths." *Journal of American Folklore* 34, no. 133 (1921): pp. 269–307.
Ricoeur, Paul. "Narrative Time." In *On Narrative,* edited by W. T. Mitchell, pp. 165–86. Chicago: University of Chicago Press, 1981.

———. "Structure, Word, Event." In *The Conflict of Interpretations*. Evanston IL: Northwestern University Press, 1974.
———. *Time and Narrative*. 3 vols. Translated by Kathleen McLaughlin and David Pellauer. Chicago: University of Chicago Press, 1984–88.
Robinson, Doan. "A History of the Dakota or Sioux Indians." *South Dakota Historical collections* 2, no. 2 (1904).
Robinson, Elwyn B. *History of North Dakota*. Lincoln: University of Nebraska Press, 1966.
Rosenberg, Bruce A. *Custer and the Epic of Defeat*. University Park: Pennsylvania State University Press, 1974.

Saville-Troike, Muriel. *The Ethnography of Communication: An Introduction*. Cambridge MA: Blackwell, 1982.
Scudder, Thayer. "The Human Ecology of Big Projects: River Basin Development and Resettlement." *Annual Review of Anthropology* 4 (1973): pp. 45–55.
Silko, Leslie Marmon. *Ceremony*. New York: Viking, 1977.
Stalnaker, Robert C. "Pragmatics." In *Readings in Language and Mind: An Interdisciplinary Reader*, edited by Heimir Geirsson and Michael Losonsky, pp. 77–87. Cambridge MA: Blackwell, 1996.
Stock, Brian. *Listening for the Text: On the Uses of the Past*. Baltimore: Johns Hopkins University Press, 1990.

Tedlock, Dennis. "The Spoken Word and the Work of Interpretation in American Indian Religion." In *Traditional Literatures of the American Indian: Texts and Interpretations*, edited by Karl Kroeber. Lincoln: University of Nebraska Press, 1981.

Utley, Robert. *The Lance and the Shield: The Life and Times of Sitting Bull*. New York: Henry Holt, 1993.
———. *The Last Days of the Sioux Nation*. New Haven: Yale University Press, 1963.

Van Dijk, Teun. *Macrostructures: An Interdisciplinary Study of Global Structures in Discourse, Interaction, and Cognition*. Hillsdale NJ: Lawrence Erlbaum Associates, 1980.
Vestal, Stanley. *Sitting Bull: Champion of the Sioux*. Norman: University of Oklahoma Press, 1932.

Waldman, Carl, ed. *Who Was Who in Native American History: Indians and Non-Indians from Early Contacts through 1900*. Rev. ed. New York: Facts on File, 2001.
Walker, James R. *Lakota Belief and Ritual*. Edited by Raymond J. DeMallie and Elaine A. Jahner. Lincoln: University of Nebraska Press, 1980.
———. *Lakota Myth*. Edited by Elaine A. Jahner. Lincoln: University of Nebraska Press, 1983.
———. *Lakota Society*. Edited by Raymond J. DeMallie. Lincoln: University of Nebraska Press, 1982.
Walker, Mildred. *Winter Wheat*. New York: Harcourt Brace, 1944; Lincoln: University of Nebraska Press, 1992.
Wallis, Wilson D. "The Canadian Dakota" (Part 1). *Anthropological Papers of the American Museum of Natural History* 41 (1947).
Watson, Larry. *Montana 1948*. New York: Pocket Books, 1995.
Welch, James. *The Death of Jim Loney*. New York: Harper and Row, 1979.
———. *Fools Crow*. New York: Viking, 1986.

———. *The Indian Lawyer*. New York: Norton, 1990.
———. Introduction to *Winter Wheat*. Lincoln: University of Nebraska Press, 1992.
———. "Snow Country Weavers." Reprinted in *Nothing but the Truth: An Anthology of Native American Literature*, edited by John L. Purdy and James Ruppert. New York: Prentice Hall, 2001.
———. *Winter in the Blood*. New York: Harper and Row, 1974.
Whorf, Benjamin L. *Language, Thought, and Reality: Selected Writings of Benjamin Lee Whorf*, edited by John B. Carroll. Cambridge: MIT Press, 1956.
Winter, Steven L. "The Cognitive Dimension of the *Agon* between Legal Power and Narrative Meaning." *Michigan Law Review* 87, no. 8 (1989): pp. 2225–79.
Wissler, Clark. "Decorative Art of the Sioux Indians." *Bulletin of the American Museum of Natural History* 18, no. 3 (1904): pp. 231–77.
———. "Societies and Ceremonial Associations in the Oglala Division of the Teton-Dakota." *American Museum of Natural History Anthropological Papers* 11, no. 1 (1912): pp. 1–99.
———. "Some Protective Designs of the Dakota." *Anthropological Papers of the American Museum of Natural History Anthropological Papers* 1, no. 2 (1907): pp. 19–53.
———. "The Sun Dance of the Blackfoot Indians." *American Museum of Natural History Anthropological Papers* 16, no. 3 (1918): pp. 223–70.
Wissler, Clark, and D. C. Duvall. "Mythology of the Blackfoot Indians" (Part 1). *American Museum of Natural History Anthropological Papers* 2 (1908): pp. 1–163.
Worthman, Carol M. "Cupid and Psyche: Investigative Syncretism in Biological and Psychosocial Anthropology." In *New Directions in Psychological Anthropology*, edited by Theodore Schwartz, Geoffrey M. White, and Catherine A. Lutz, pp. 150–79. Cambridge: Cambridge University Press, 1992.

Index

Alexander II, Czar, 97
Almost-a-Dog (Piegan Indian), 176n7
American Federation of Labor, 100
American Literary History, xv
Anderson, Harry H., 44–47, 49
An Approach to the Cognitive Study of Language (Mathiot), 16–19, 127–28

Barthes, Roland, 4
Beckett, Samuel, 118
Beckwith, Martha Warren, 4, 50
Beede, Aaron McGaffey, 49, 69
Bellow, Saul, 118
Benjamin, Walter, 169n3
Berry, John W., 38
Bhaba, Homi, 20
Blackfeet Sioux: Medicine Lodge Ceremony of, 117, 119, 121, 125–27, 129–30, 176n8; mythology of, 121–37, 176n11, 176n14; resettlement of, 45–46, 61, 116–18, 176n7; in Welch's novels, 115, 116–37, 145
Black Hoop, Thomas (Yanktonai Sioux), 44, 45
Black Sun (Kristeva), 175n24
Boas, Franz: "Dakota Grammar," 32–33, 35
Boland, Eavan, 37
Booth, Wayne, 5
Bordwell, David: *Narration in the Fiction Film*, 169n1
Bourdieu, Pierre, 169n2
Brown v. Board of Education, 173n12
Brule Sioux, 46
Butler, Judith, 157–58

Cannon Ball ND, 40–81; author's experiences in, 23–26, 40–44, 49–52, 67, 80–81; history of, 40–52; narrative traditions of, 40–42, 50–81, 160. *See also* Upper Yanktonai Sioux

Ceremony (Silko), 114
Chatman, Seymour, 4
Chinookan languages, 3
cognitive style, ix–xviii, 1–39, 157–67; critical approaches to, 3–8, 13–17, 169n1; definition of, xvi–xvii, 1–3; geographical basis of, xii, 2–3, 21–22, 39, 50–52, 116–18, 136–37, 138–43, 149–55, 164–65; in German-Russian community, 84–97, 102–4, 109; linguistic basis of, xii–xiii, xvi–xvii, 1–3, 16–19, 23–39, 40, 56–58, 90–92, 138–39, 161–64, 171n32; in oral narrative, xi–xiv, 23–39, 41, 48, 52, 54–55, 62–64, 78–81; pragmatic significance of, xii–xiii, 1–2, 13–17, 48, 50–52, 88–89, 94–96, 121–22, 163–64, 173n12; psychological theories of, 38–39, 155; spatial dynamic of, x–xi, 21–23, 25–36, 86–92, 149–55, 161, 167; in written narrative, xiv–xv, 113–15, 117–22, 126–31, 133, 139–40, 143–44, 149, 153–55. *See also* narrative theory
—(associated concepts): cognitive maps, x–xi, 21–23, 25–37, 167; cognitive sets, 2, 26, 37, 85, 126–29, 153, 158–66; cognitive themes, xvii, 2, 20, 26, 31–33, 35–36, 54–55, 80–81, 84–85, 127–30, 133–34; indigenous cognition, 38; macroprocessing, 160, 162–63; macrostructures, 9–10, 13, 16, 26, 36; motivation, 5–7, 19, 55, 128; performance, xii, xvii, 10, 12, 38, 54–55, 88, 113, 159–60, 171n26, 171n46; textual community, xvi, 19–21, 23–24, 162–64, 177n3; volition, 24–25, 31–32, 37, 127–28, 171nn45–46
Cook-Lynn, Elizabeth: *From the River's Edge*, 49–50
crane woman (Blackfeet mythology), 129–30, 176n14
"A Critical Approach to American Indian Literature" (Jahner), 176n2

INDEX

Custer, Gen. George Armstrong, 77–80, 173n28

Dakota. *See* Sioux: language
"Dakota Grammar" (Boas and Deloria), 32–33, 35
Dakota Texts (Ella Deloria), 72
Damned Indians (Lawson), 47, 80
The Death of Jim Loney (Welch), 120
Debs, Eugene V., 99
De Certeau, Michel, 40, 47–48, 159, 172n1
deer woman (Sioux mythology), 72–73
Deloria, Ella, 4, 24, 29–30, 50; *Dakota Grammar*, 32–33, 35; *Dakota Texts*, 72
Deloria, Vine, 116
Densmore, Frances, 173n15
Doig, Ivan, xi
Double Women (Sioux mythology), 28–29, 69–72, 123, 172n50
Downs, Roger M., 21
Dundes, Alan: *Morphology of North American Indian Folktales*, 4, 62

Eagle Boy, Ambrose (Yanktonai Sioux), 44
Eichenbaum, Boris, 4
elk man (Sioux mythology), 72–74
Emerson, Ralph Waldo, 138–39, 177n8
event structure: in Sioux narrative, 26–27, 30–31, 33–37, 52–53, 62–63; theory of, 8–12, 170n13, 170n15
Ewers, John C., 176n7

Fast Horse, Harry (Upper Yanktonai Sioux), 49–67, 72–81; community status of, 41–42, 80–81; historical experiences of, 45, 49–51, 165–66; performance style of, 71; traditional narrative forms of, 50–56, 62–64, 72–73, 80–81, 173n12
—(specific narratives): betraying letter, 58–60; buffalo hunting, 63–66; Custer, 77–80; elk man, 72–74; ghosts and spirits, 72–76; Indian name, 66–67; Rain-in-the-Face, 76–78; school, 55–58; vigilante killing, 60–62
Fast Horse, Lillian (Upper Yanktonai Sioux), 24–37, 67–72; community status of, 41–42, 80–81; historical experiences of, 45, 49–51,
165–66; performance style of, 51–52, 67, 71–72; volitional themes of, 24–25, 28–29, 31–37; women's themes of, 25–30, 67–72
—(specific narratives): Double Women, 28–29, 69–72; "The ghosts pushed us," 24–36, 161–62; Medicine man, 67–69
Fast Horse, Paul (Upper Yanktonai Sioux), 51
Feather Woman (Blackfeet mythology), 122–26, 132–37
Ferguson, James, 20
Fetterman Battle, 46
Fletcher, Alice, 31–32, 64
Fludernik, Monika, 14–15, 114–15
Fools Crow (Welch), 118, 120–30
formalism: new approach to, xviii, 37, 157–61, 166–67; traditional approach to, 4–5, 8, 62, 169n3
Forster, E. M., xviii, 4
Fort Abraham Lincoln ND, 78
Fort Yates ND, 35, 55, 56, 61, 82
Frantz, Donald, 129
French Structuralism, 4–5, 62, 169n2
From the River's Edge (Cook-Lynn), 49–50

Galatea 2.2 (Powers), 158, 165, 166–67
Genette, Gerald, 4
German-Russian community (ND), 82–112; cognitive style of, 84–97, 102–4, 109; double emigration of, 20, 82–87, 95–97; Edenic narratives of, 86–91; ethnic identity of, 82–84, 85–87, 90–91, 94–96, 102, 166, 174n5; family histories of, 84–85, 87, 90–109; political identity of, 96–97, 99–104; public and private spaces of, 89–90, 93, 95–97, 103–12; religious identity of, 110–12, 174n22, 175nn23–24; and Upper Yanktonai Sioux, ix–x, xiii–xiv, xvi, 20, 82, 91–92, 112
Godzich, Wlad, 169n3
Gregory, Derek, 88–89, 109, 143, 161
Greimas, Algirdas, 4, 37, 159, 170n3
Gupta, Akhil, 20

habitational conditionality, 25, 31–32, 37, 54–55, 56, 128
Hancock, Cecily, 77
Harjo, Joy, 126; "We Must Call a Meeting," 40

186

Hassrick, Royal B., 29
Height, Joseph, 95
Helena MO, 131, 136
Herman, David, 7–8; *Narratologies*, 5
Herrnstein Smith, Barbara: *On Narrative*, 5, 7
House Made of Dawn (Momaday), 114, 176n2
Huddle, David, 140
Hunka Ceremony, 171n45
Hymes, Dell, 3, 9, 12; "*In Vain I Tried to Tell You*," 54, 171n46, 173n18

Iktomi (American Indian Trickster), 76–78
immigrant narrative, 82–112, 138–56; cognitive issues in, xvi, 22, 84–97, 102–4, 109, 115–16, 139–40, 149, 155; false promises in, 82–83, 92–94; gaps and secrets in, 94, 105, 108, 141–43, 145, 148, 151–52; language issues in, 13, 82, 90, 138–39, 144, 147–48; spatial dynamic of, 86–92, 95, 107–9, 139–40, 143–44, 146–51, 153–56; women's voices in, 87, 93–94, 105–9, 142–43, 148–53
implicit narrative: definition of, xvii; theory of, 2, 7–8, 13–17, 19, 88–89, 159–60, 163–64, 165, 166; in Walker's *Winter Wheat*, 115–16, 144; in Yanktonai Sioux stories, 26, 35–38
Independent Voters Association (IVA), 100–101, 103
Indian Claims Commission, 44–45
The Indian Lawyer (Welch), 131–37
Indian Rights Association, 176n7
indigenous cognition, 38
"Intermediate Forms between Oral and Written Literature" (Jahner), 175n1
"*In Vain I Tried to Tell You*" (Hymes), 54, 171n46, 173n18

Jacobson, Roman, 4
Jahner, Elaine A.: "A Critical Approach to American Indian Literature," 176n2; "Intermediate Forms between Oral and Written Literature," 175n1; *Lakota Myth*, 12; "Language Change and Cultural Dynamics," 171n43
James, Henry, 4
James, William, 177n8
Jameson, Frederic: *Postmodernism*, 22
Johnson, Randal, 169n2

Jonnes, Dennis: *Matrix of Narrative*, 14, 177n7
Journal of Narrative and Life History, 14, 170n12

Kant, Immanuel, 169n2
Keating, William H., 46
Keller, Konrad, 94
Kellner, Hans, 10
Koch, Fred, 174n5
Kowalewski, Michael, xv, 140
Kristeva, Julia: *Black Sun*, 175n24

Labov, William, 5; "Narrative Analysis," 9, 14, 36, 170n12
Lacan, Jacques, 88–89, 109, 161
Laclau, Ernesto, 157–58
La Flesche, Francis, 31
Lakota. *See* Sioux: language
Lakota Myth (Walker and Jahner), 12
Landau (Ukraine), 175n23
Langer, William, 101
"Language Change and Cultural Dynamics" (Jahner), 171n43
Lawson, Michael: *Damned Indians*, 47, 80
Lefebvre, Henri, 88–89, 109, 161
Lehman, Jill Fain: "The Role of Language in Cognition," 171n32
Lévi-Strauss, Claude, 4, 62, 126, 159; *The Origin of Table Manners*, 176n11
Lincoln, Kenneth, 76
Listening for the Text (Stock), 20, 177n3
Little Big Horn, Battle of the, 77–80, 173n28
Locality and Belonging (Lovell), 21, 139, 164
Long, James W., 82–83
Long, Stephen H., 46
Lovell, Nadia: *Locality and Belonging*, 21, 139, 164
Lowie, Robert, 172n50
Lubbock, Percy, 4

Macrostructures (van Dijk), 16, 159, 162–64
Mathiot, Madeline: *An Approach to the Cognitive Study of Language*, 16–19, 127–28
Matrix of Narrative (Jonnes), 14, 177n7
McGuane, Thomas: *Nobody's Angel*, 136
Medicine Lodge Ceremony, 117, 119, 121, 125–27, 129–30, 176n8

INDEX

Michigan Law Review, 173n12
Miniconjou Sioux, 46
Mink, Louis O., 10, 169n2
Missouri River, 46–47, 51, 61, 82. *See also* Oahe Dam
Momaday, N. Scott: *House Made of Dawn*, 114, 176n2
Montana: in Walker's *Winter Wheat*, xvi, 115–16, 138–56; in Welch's novels, xiv–xv, 119, 136–37
Montana 1948 (Watson), 140, 151
Morphology of North American Indian Folktales (Dundes), 4, 62
Morphology of the Folktale (Propp), 4
Morrison, Toni, 118
myths and folktales, 24–37, 50–81, 117–37; cognitive power of, 6, 24–25, 31–33, 37, 62–63, 80–81, 117–31, 136–37; female agency in, 27–30, 69–73, 117–19, 122–27, 129–37, 172n50, 176n8, 176n11, 176n14; movement and travel in, 24–27, 31–32, 62–63, 125–30, 136; psychological power of, 125–26, 131–33, 177n8; transference of, to fiction, 115, 117–37, 145, 154; transference of, to history, xi–xiii, 48–58, 62–64, 72–73, 92, 109, 116–18, 125–26; volitional themes in, 24–25, 28–29, 31–37, 53–54, 56, 76, 119, 127–30, 172n50. *See also* Sioux narrative
—(specific narratives): crane woman, 129–30, 176n14; deer woman, 72–73; Double Women, 28–29, 69–72, 123, 172n50; elk man, 72–74; Feather Woman, 122–26, 132–37; ghosts and spirits, 24–36, 74–76; Star Husband, 121–37, 176n8, 176n11; trickster, 76–78; White Buffalo Cow Woman, 29

Narration in the Fiction Film (Bordwell), 169n1
Narrative, 7
narrative: family history, 51–52, 63–69, 84–87, 90–109, 118–20, 141–54; idealized, 44, 47–48, 86–91, 173n12; personal experience, 6, 9, 14, 51–63, 71, 73, 169n3, 170n12; regional, xv–xvi, 20–21, 138–40, 153–56, 177n8; religious, 110–12, 175n24; traditional function of, 50–55, 58, 62–63, 116–19, 153–54. *See also* immigrant narrative; myths and folktales; narrative theory; novels; oral narrative; Sioux narrative
"Narrative Analysis" (Labov and Waletsky), 9, 14, 36, 170n12
narrative theory, ix–xviii, 1–39, 157–67; cognitive approach to, xii–xiii, 1–3, 7–8, 13–19, 35–39, 169n1; cultural approach to, 40–41, 169n2; experiential approach to, 14–15, 114–15; formalist approach to, xviii, 4–5, 8, 37, 62, 157–61, 166–67, 169n3; narrative approach to, xiii–xiv, 157–59, 166–67; oral and written forms in, xiv–xv, xi–xii, 4, 12, 20, 113–15, 176n2. *See also* cognitive style
—(associated concepts): event structure, 8–12, 26–27, 30–31, 33–37, 52–53, 62–63, 170n13, 170n15; implicit narrative, xvii, 2, 7–8, 13–17, 19, 35–38, 88–89, 159–60, 163–64, 165, 166; intermediate forms, 18–19, 62–63, 113–15, 175n1; narrating community, ix–xii, 40–41, 47–48, 169n2
Narratologies (Herman), 5
Nichols, Bill, ix, 169n1
Nobody's Angel (McGuane), 136
Nonpartisan League (NPL), 99–101, 103
North Dakota: author's ties to, xv, xvi, 23, 104, 161. *See also* Cannon Ball ND; German-Russian community; Upper Yanktonai Sioux
novels, 113–56; cognitive style in, xiv–xvi, 115–16, 121–23, 126–29, 153, 166–67; cultural discontinuity in, 115–22, 131–32, 143–49, 153–54, 166; intermediate forms in, 113–15, 175n1, 176n2; maternal transgression in, 118–21, 123–25, 127, 129–30, 132–36, 141–46, 148–49, 151–54, 156; myths and folktales in, 115, 118–19, 121–37, 154; regional themes in, 20–21, 138–40, 153–56; spatial themes in, 125–28, 131–34, 136–37, 143–44, 146–47, 149–51, 165

Oahe Dam: buried village at, 42, 51–53, 60–61; floodwaters from, xii, 43, 45, 47; Sioux narratives about, 49–50, 51, 79–80
Odessa (Ukraine), 82, 87, 109
Oglala Sioux, 46, 70–71
Omaha Sioux, 31
On Narrative (Herrnstein Smith), 5, 7

oral narrative, 23–81, 82–112; cognitive features of, xi–xiv, 23–37, 41, 52–55, 61–63, 78–81; history in, xi, 42–63, 84–105, 165–66; intermediate forms of, xi–xii, 4, 12, 20, 62–63, 113–15, 175n1, 176n2. *See also* myths and folktales

The Origin of Table Manners (Levi-Strauss), 176n11

Papago creation myth, 127–29
Papago language, 16–19
performance: cognitive importance of, xvii, 38, 54–55, 88, 113, 159–60, 171n26, 171n46; cultural importance of, xii–xiii, 58, 62–67, 158, 163; and event structure, 10, 12; and gender, 67–69, 71; and kinship, 30; religion as, 110–11, 139; theory as, x
Pick-Sloan Plan, 49
Poirier, Richard, 138–39, 147, 177n8
Postmodernism (Jameson), 22
Powers, Richard: *Galatea 2.2*, 158, 165, 166–67
Pratt, Mary Louise, 5
Prince, Gerald, 7, 14
Propp, Vladimir: *Morphology of the Folktale*, 4

Rain-in-the-Face (Sioux leader), 76–78
Rainwater, Catherine, 114
Rappaport, Joanne, 20
Rastadt (Ukraine), 95, 175n23
regional narrative, xv–xvi, 20–21, 138–40, 153–56, 177n8
Ricoeur, Paul, 9–11, 31, 159, 177n3; "Structure, Word, Event," 10–11, 139; *Time and Narrative*, 11, 170n15
Robinson, Elwyn, 43, 99–100
"The Role of Language in Cognition" (Lehman), 171n32
Rosenberg, Bruce, 78, 173n28
Russia. *See* German-Russian community; Ukraine
Russian formalists, 4, 114

Sans Arc Sioux, 46
Sapir, Edward. *See* Sapir-Whorf hypothesis
Sapir-Whorf hypothesis, xii, 17–19, 162
Saville-Troike, Muriel, 170n13

Schlovsky, Victor, 4
Seelinger, Gregor, 95–99, 101
Shanley, John (bishop of North Dakota), 110
Shell Track, Charles (Yanktonai Sioux leader), 46, 47, 48
Silko, Leslie Marmon, 22; *Ceremony*, 114
Sioux: art and design, 27–30, 53–54, 173n15; language, xii, 12, 17–19, 23–39, 57–58, 161–62, 171n43. *See also* myths and folktales; Sioux narrative
—(Bands): Brule, 46; Miniconjou, 46; Oglala, 46, 70–71; Omaha, 31; Sans Arc, 46; Teton, 46; Two Kettle, 46. *See also* Blackfeet Sioux; Upper Yanktonai Sioux
Sioux narrative, 23–39, 40–81, 116–37; Battle of the Little Big Horn in, 78–80; formalist analysis of, 4–5, 37, 62; gender roles in, 28–30, 53–54, 67–73, 117, 123; habitational conditionality in; humor in, 76–78; naming in, 48, 63–67, 69; spatial themes in, xii, 11, 24–27, 30–37, 50–53, 56, 60–61, 62–63, 79–80, 125–37; traditional elements in, xi–xiii, 12, 50–51, 54–58, 165–66; volitional themes in, 24–25, 28–29, 31–37, 53–54, 56, 76, 117, 129–30, 172n50. *See also* Fast Horse, Harry; Fast Horse, Lillian; myths and folktales
Sitting Bull (Sioux leader), 50, 78–79
Social Welfare Committee, 94
Solen ND, 23, 25–27, 33–35
space: cognitive, xii–xiv, 8, 21–23, 25–37, 86–92, 162, 167; displacement from, 20–21, 42–48, 50–51, 61, 82–87, 95–97, 116–18; geographical, xii, 2–3, 21–22, 39, 50–52, 116–18, 136–37, 138–43, 149–55, 164–65; home, 20, 33–34, 37, 40, 105–7, 116, 141, 144, 165; in immigrant narrative, 86–95, 106–9, 139–40, 144–55, 161; legal, 44–47, 48, 79–80, 173n12; male, 30, 52–53; maternal, 120–27, 129–30, 132–37, 141–46, 148–50, 156; mythic, 6, 24–32, 62–63, 118–19, 125–30, 132, 164; narrative, 2–3, 9–10, 19–21, 23–24, 157, 161–65, 169n3, 177n3; public and private, 89–90, 93, 95–97, 103–12; in regional writing, xv–xvi, 20–21, 138, 139–40, 153, 155, 177n8; in Sioux narrative, xii, 11,

space (*continued*)
24–27, 30–37, 50–53, 56, 60–61, 62–63, 79–80, 125–37; subjective experience of, x–xi, 52, 88–91, 107–8, 109, 131–32, 141–44, 154–55; technological, xvii–xviii, 167. *See also* habitational conditionality

Stalnaker, Robert C., 13–14

Standing Rock Indian Reservation ND: Catholic church at, 82; establishment of, 46–47. *See also* Cannon Ball ND; Oahe Dam; Upper Yanktonai Sioux

Star Husband (Blackfeet mythology), 121–37, 176n8, 176n11

Sticka, Ignatz, 101–4

Sticka, Leo, 101–4; "The Venture of Ignatz Sticka into the Political Life of North Dakota, 1870–1939," 102–4

Sticka, Ralph, 101–2

Sticka, Father Stanley, 174n22

Sticka, Theresia, 101

Stock, Brian: *Listening for the Text*, 20, 177n3

Structuralism, 4–5, 62, 169n2

"Structure, Word, Event" (Ricoeur), 10–11, 139

Tedlock, Dennis, 15–16, 171n26

Teton Sioux, 46

textual community, xvi, 19–21, 23–24, 162–64, 177n3

Time and Narrative (Ricoeur), 11, 170n15

Todorov, Tzvetvan, 4

Townley, Arthur C., 100–101

the Trickster, 76–78

Turtle Mountain Reservation ND, 73

Twin Women. *See* Double Women

Two Bears (Yanktonai Sioux leader), 44, 46–47, 50, 51

Two Kettle Sioux, 46

Two Women. *See* Double Women

Ukraine: German-Russian colonies in, 20, 82–84, 175n23; in German-Russian narrative, 84–99, 109–12, 161

Upper Yanktonai Sioux, 23–37, 40–81; German-Russian neighbors of, ix–x, xiii–xiv, xvi, 20, 82, 91–92, 112; history of, 20, 40–50, 61. *See also* Cannon Ball ND; Fast Horse, Harry; Fast Horse, Lillian; Oahe Dam; Sioux: language; Sioux narrative

van Dijk, Teun: *Macrostructures*, 16, 159, 162–64

"The Venture of Ignatz Sticka into the Political Life of North Dakota, 1870–1939" (Leo Sticka), 102–4

Vetter, Joseph, 90–94

volition: cognitive importance of, 24–25, 31–32, 37, 127–28, 171nn45–46; in Papago creation myth, 127–29; in Sioux narrative, 24–25, 28–29, 31–37, 53–54, 56, 76, 117, 129–30, 172n50; in Welch's fiction, 119, 130–34

Walburga (German-Russian immigrant), 105–9

Waletsky, Joshua: "Narrative Analysis," 9, 14, 36, 170n12

Walker, James R., 29, 171n45; *Lakota Myth*, 12

Walker, Mildred: compared with James Welch, xvi, 115–16, 138, 141–42, 145, 153–54. *See also Winter Wheat*

Watson, Larry: *Montana 1948*, 140, 151

Wehrle, Vincent, 110

Welch, James, 115–37; cognitive style of, xiv–xvi, 115, 118, 119, 121, 122, 126–29, 160; female figures of, 118–19, 120, 121, 123–25, 132–37; spatial themes of, 115, 116–17, 120, 125–37, 154; use of Blackfeet history, 115, 116–20, 121–22, 130–32; use of Blackfeet mythology, 117, 121–32, 135–37, 145

—Works: *The Death of Jim Loney*, 120; *Fools Crow*, 118, 120–30; *The Indian Lawyer*, 131–37; *Winter in the Blood*, xv, 117, 118–19, 138, 141–42, 145, 153

"We Must Call a Meeting" (Harjo), 40

White, Hayden, 10

White Buffalo Cow Woman (Sioux mythology), 29

Whitman, Walt, 147–48

Whorf, Benjamin. *See* Sapir-Whorf hypothesis

Winter in the Blood (Welch), xv, 117, 118–19, 138, 141–42, 145, 153

Winter Wheat (Walker), 138–56; cognitive

style of, 138–40, 149, 153–56, 160; familial matrix of, 141–45, 147–48, 151–52, 154–55, 177n7; as immigrant narrative, xvi, 115–16, 139, 140, 145–46, 148–49, 152; reading and writing in, 140–41, 144–48, 152–53; as regional narrative, xv–xvi, 138–40, 153–56; style of, 139–40

Wissler, Clark, 28, 53–54, 70–71, 129, 176n8, 176n14
Women's Puberty Ceremony, 171n45. *See also* Medicine Lodge Ceremony
Worthman, Carol, 155

Zizek, Slovaz, 157–58

IN THE FRONTIERS OF NARRATIVE SERIES:

Story Logic: Problems and Possibilities of Narrative
by David Herman

Spaces of the Mind: Narrative and Community in the American West
by Elaine A. Jahner

Talk Fiction: Literature and the Talk Explosion
by Irene Kacandes

Fictional Minds
by Alan Palmer

Narrative across Media: The Languages of Storytelling
edited by Marie-Laure Ryan

www.ingramcontent.com/pod-product-compliance
Lightning Source LLC
Chambersburg PA
CBHW030343240426
43661CB00052B/1729